ARTHUR ANDERSEN

Answers the 101 Toughest Questions About Family Business

BARBARA B. BUCHHOLZ, MARGARET CRANE AND ROSS W. NAGER, EXECUTIVE DIRECTOR OF THE ARTHUR ANDERSEN CENTER FOR FAMILY BUSINESS

Library of Congress Cataloging-in-Publication Data

Buchholz, Barbara Ballinger.
Arthur Andersen answers the 101 toughest questions about family business / by Barbara B. Buchholz, Margaret Crane, and Ross Nager.
p. cm.
ISBN 0-7352-0038-6 (case) ISBN 0-7352-0177-3 (pbk.)
1. Family-owned business enterprises—Management. 2. Family corporations—Management. 3. Small business—Management. 4. Family-owned business enterprises—United States—Management. 5. Family corporations—United States—Management. I. Crane, Margaret. II. Nager, Ross. III. Arthur Andersen Center for Family Business. IV. Title.
HD62.25.B833 2000
658'.045—dc21 00-34102
CIP

Acquisitions Editor: *Tom Power*
Production Editor: *Jacqueline Roulette*
Formatting/Interior Design: *Robyn Beckerman*

Note: The material in this book does not constitute specific accounting, tax, investment, or legal advice. You should review your specific situation with professional advisors.

Printed in the United States of America

10 9 8 7 6 5 4 3 2 *10 9 8 7 6 5 4 3 2 1*

ISBN 0-7352-0038-6 (c) ISBN 0-7352-0177-3 (pbk)

Previously published as *The Family Business Answer Book.*

Paramus, NJ 07652

http://www.phdirect.com

To the members of family businesses everywhere who work incredibly hard to turn their dreams into reality so that future generations of owners and members may follow in their footsteps.

BBB
MC
RWN

ACKNOWLEDGMENTS

This book was years in the making. Eleven years ago Barbara B. Buchholz and Margaret Crane co-authored individual profiles of 14 family businesses across the country, and why they succeeded or failed, in a book titled *Corporate Bloodlines: The Future of the Family Firm* (Carol Publishing, 1988). The tales incorporated both business and psychological reasons for the states of the companies. In the years that followed, Barbara and Margaret found that many family business players enjoyed hearing about others' businesses and learned valuable lessons. But an equal number said they didn't have the time to read the long scenarios. Their message was heeded: they wanted help, but it had to be practical and succinct, and it had to come from a trusted advisor.

When Barbara and Margaret developed the idea for this book, they turned to Ross Nager, executive director of the Arthur Andersen Center for Family Business, managing director of Arthur Andersen's Family Wealth Planning practice, and an advisor to many family businesses. Their hope was to unite their experiences as professional writers about family business and Margaret's as a member of a family business, with the experience and knowledge of Arthur Andersen's family business advisors, who focus on the subject day in and day out. This book is very much a collaborative effort.

We wish to thank the following Arthur Andersen partners, who have spent a significant portion of their careers advising family businesses, for their assistance with this book. Their first-hand experience in advising family businesses was invaluable in crafting the responses to our 101 questions. Many thanks to:

David M. Bradt of the Washington D.C. office;

Michael T. Henderson of the Charlotte, office;

Kathy L. Iversen of the Columbus, office;

William B. Pace of the Los Angeles office;

Nancy C. Pechloff of the St. Louis office and managing partner of Arthur Andersen's Enterprise Group;

Kenneth A. Thelen of the Cincinnati office;

Steven A. Thorne of the Chicago office;

Joseph P. Toce of the New York City office;

and Mark L. Vorsatz of the San Francisco office.

We also want to thank the dozens of family business owners and their family members from all over the country who agreed to be interviewed for the book and often for multiple questions. Some preferred to remain anonymous, however. Still, other scenarios represent hypothetical situations based on true stories we've heard through the years. To each of the families interviewed we offer our deep appreciation for their help, insight and willingness to share their families' experiences. Finally, we would be remiss if we did not thank the following professionals, whom we regularly called for their input: Dr. Léon A. Danco, the "father of family business consulting," whose experience in the field is unparalleled; Craig E. Aronoff, Ph.D., Dinos Chair, Kennesaw State University, and John L. Ward, Ph.D., Ralph Marotta Professor of Private Enterprise, Loyola University of Chicago, both authors, family business advisors and senior editors of the *Family Business Advisor* newsletter; Judy Barber in Napa, Ca., whose newsletter is always invaluable; and John Davis who runs the Owner Managed Business Institute in Santa Barbara, Ca., and teaches at Harvard University.

We must also thank our own families, who now know almost as much as we do about family business, except for Margaret's husband Nolan, who now knows probably more than anybody, having worked in more than one family business (as well as two public companies). Someday Margaret and Nolan's own children may work in a family business or with either of their parents, though one of the collective brood once commented, "By then you'll be too old."

Last, we are extremely grateful to Patricia M. Brown of Arthur Andersen, who helped with editing and the many production aspects, tirelessly coordinated the authors' efforts and made sure the book finally materialized and in the exact format we wanted; to Frank L. Buttitta, also of Arthur Andersen, for his assistance in the early stages of the book's development; and to Tom Power of Prentice Hall for his unrelenting patience and helpful suggestions.

CONTENTS

FOREWORD

After some 35 years working with family business owners and their families, I know that their time is precious, very precious.

There are just not enough hours in the day to work on all the dreams and plans that take shape in their minds, let alone read another book. Yet overworked as you may be: TAKE THE TIME.

I can honestly tell you that I consider this *Arthur Andersen Answers the 101 Toughest Questions About Family Business* to be the most empathetic, yet no-nonsense, practical and "tell-it-like-it-is" resource you will have ever found. I only wish I had written it myself!! It's filled with pragmatic information and ideas you can use. It's nice to have real people talking to you in this book, whose commitment, compassion, credibility, competence and personal experiences are on the line for all to see.

Business owners, their families and key managers can have here an ideal opportunity to learn from others who have faced similar dilemmas and thus see how acceptable solutions can be created for them through cooperation, discussion and trust.

Sharing information and experiences does not come easily to family business owners. As somebody once said to me, "It's great to be independent, but why must it be so @!&%!* lonely." As an advisor over too many years to thousands of family businesses, I know that "openness" is not one of their inherent characteristics. Too many family businesses have been destroyed by the distrust that this secretiveness breeds and the lack of reliable information that follows.

I am overjoyed, therefore, to find in this book these men and women—founders, successors, managers, husbands, wives, brothers, sisters, cousins—who have told their stories so that others might learn and benefit from their experiences, and I applaud them. I see such candor as a positive shift in the psyche of some family business owners. I regret that there are so few, and that it has taken so long.

In "the old days" business owners knew of very few people who even understood their problems, much less who knew what to DO about them. Today, everybody is an "expert" and the question is now, "Who can be trusted?"

Today, the family business has been discovered as a "market." Everyday, it seems we find more "experts" dedicated to family business issues, more books, magazine articles, websites, university programs, research organizations and professional associations. While this proliferation of resources provides family businesses more options than ever before, it also demands that business owners exercise more care than ever in finding relevant information and getting the best advice. You will find both in this book.

I want to repeat some words I said earlier about family businesses, because I believe in these words even more strongly today than I did 25 years ago . . . when I wrote them in my own book, *Beyond Survival,* first published in 1975:

> "One of the major qualities of business owners is their courage. They work best when the chips are down, when the tide is rising, and the alligators swarm around their ankles. It is affluence that causes them trouble, for they don't know what they are supposed to do with it. Business owners are fighters. Give them a good scrap and they will come out ahead. They have the flexibility to change and adapt, if change and adaptation are the ingredients of survival. They can remain lean and hungry and still not starve. They can ride out a storm until better times arrive. They have the confidence of battles fought and won. They may not like to relive some of the hard times, but they know that they can do it and survive. This time around, they need not be alone. They need to recognize that their heirs, and their successors, their junior officers, must learn to share in their struggle, and must, themselves, in due time take over command. Though many may face the radical changes of the future with fear, business owners can face them with hope. They have the ability and the guts to win. And, by their example, to lead."

Léon A. Danco, Ph.D.
Cleveland, Ohio

PREFACE

LEARNING FROM THE EXPERIENCE OF EXPERIENCE

We've known and worked with Ross Nager for nearly a decade. We have produced with him a monthly newsletter, *The Family Business Advisor*. We have taught seminars with him for business-owning families. We have done significant research together. We have spent scores of hours talking "family business" with him. We know of his special talents as an advisor to family firms, and we admire his eagerness to learn from family firms all over the world.

Ross genuinely cares for families that own businesses. He deeply believes that family firms bring indispensable strength to our economy and our society. He believes that the family's goals precede all advice and counsel. He's sensitive to each member of the family business system. He's a model of collaboration with other professionals.

Ross is also a witty and crystal clear writer. Rare is the professional who can combine the insights of massive experience with the skill to communicate succinctly and easily.

We've also known for many years Barbara B. Buchholz and Margaret Crane, Ross' writing partners on this book. Barbara and Meg have long chronicled the world of family business with sensitivity and skill through numerous articles and in their prior book on family business, *Corporate Bloodlines: The Future of the Family Firm*. Nager, Buchholz and Crane make a great team of authors.

The issues facing family firms are endless and varied. Different questions come up almost every day, and readers will find answers to at least 101 of the most common and crucial ones. Families in business will find *Arthur Andersen Answers the 101 Toughest Questions About Family Business* a valuable resource full of insights and guidance on a wide range of issues.

In fact, that's one of the special contributions of the book. As readers scan the table of contents they will be both comforted by the realization that business-owning families share so much in common and also reassured that there are lessons to be learned from seasoned professionals and the family businesses themselves.

Regardless of one's role in the family business, each reader will benefit from the book. The authors address issues faced by owners, their spouses and children, extended family members, employees, managers and shareholders, who may not be employed by the business but deeply care for its destiny.

The authors well understand from their tremendous experience that families who meet together regularly, discuss key common issues, and develop their own policies and expectations for each issue are the most proactive and successful. With *Arthur Andersen Answers the 101 Toughest Questions About Family Business,* they have provided family businesses an agenda to stimulate discussion and communication. Indeed, the book and its questions serve as a great resource for identifying topics for family meetings. The book's chapters also provide great background reading before family meeting discussions.

Consider using this book to assess the "best practices" for your family and to plan its long-term success.

CRAIG E. ARONOFF, PH.D.
Dinos Chair
Kennesaw State University
Marietta, Georgia

JOHN L. WARD, PH.D.
Ralph Marotta Professor of Private Enterprise
Loyola University Chicago
Chicago, Illinois

INTRODUCTION

Earlier this year, the founder of a chain of hardware stores faced a dilemma. After 30 years, he had grown tired of the rat race of owning and running a business and wanted to step down as chairman and CEO. He worried, however, about retiring comfortably and having enough income to do so. He also faced another, all-too-common problem. He wasn't sure whether he should appoint any of his three grown children as his successor. The only one qualified was not interested in joining the business. Nor were the other two, qualifications aside. The entrepreneur debated his other options. He could join forces with a competitor and eventually sell. He could sell immediately and have a nest egg to retire on or reinvest in another business that one of his children might be tempted to join. He could sell to his most senior employees in a leveraged buyout, appoint a nonfamily CEO, or continue to run the business alone, hoping that one of his children would have a change of mind some day. He could even elect to go public, but dreaded the exposure, all the red tape and the long, drawn-out process.

Each time he contemplated one of the choices, he felt a twinge of sadness. He knew that no matter how much money he walked away with, he would miss the company that he had founded, built and nurtured and which had brought him friendships and status in his community. Furthermore, he had never had time to pursue hobbies; the business was the all-too-familiar baby.

At the urging of his accountant and lawyer, he consulted a family business advisor, who sat down with all three to weigh the financial and emotional pros and cons of each option. They recommended the owner sell and take advantage of the strong economy. Moreover, the owner realized it would be foolhardy to expect his children to have a change of heart. So he sold.

In terms of how this entrepreneur handled the situation, he may be the exception. However, he is far from alone in his quandary of not knowing how to deal with the future of his company, yet resistant to walking away because he loved running a family business. (Many businesses are owned by women, but for the sake of simplicity, we use the male pronoun throughout the book.)

Once your business is sold or goes public, nothing is the same, says a young successor in a former family business. There are the subtle and not-so-subtle changes. This particular young man's father elected to sell the business he built to a larger competitor, which offered the son an employment contract. The son found out the hard way that this was no longer his family's business. One day he needed a new fax machine at home and put the cost on his expense report. The new employer questioned the expense. In turn, the son asked his new employer whether he had a fax at home. The new owner replied, "Sure I do, but this isn't your family business anymore. It's my family's business." The young man realized for the first time that he was indeed just another hired hand and had to spend the $135 for the fax.

Many family businesses appear in our book, who have had to navigate the challenges of family ownership. Family businesses, regardless of size, industry and location, share many common issues: Who to tap for succession? How to avoid and circumvent sibling rivalries? Whether to distribute ownership to those children not entering the company? When to start estate planning? When to sell or shut down? How to raise capital to continue? Decisions on these and a myriad of other issues are critical to the business' future and family members' relationships.

How successfully families manage these challenges is rarely determined by their business know-how or how much money they have in the bank. Rather, the key ingredient is open and honest communications. Ironically, to those who can build successful businesses from virtually nothing, this is tough terrain.

No matter how much most family business owners want to succeed financially, many find it difficult to do anything that might jeopardize family harmony. As a result, they become secretive or avoid disrupting the status quo. Despite the increased knowledge about what it takes to make and keep a business successful, many family business leaders fail to demand that their successors have the appropriate qualifications, education and experience; that they build their careers at the appropriate pace with reasonable compensation; and that they be judged by the same standards used for nonfamily employees. Many owners also are wary about sharing ownership with their inactive children or spouses, and are terrified of sharing too much or any information, out of fear it will backfire.

On the flip side, potential successors and nonfamily managers, too, are often guilty of not communicating. They fear they will be perceived as too pushy, critical or antagonistic. At the same time, they are frustrated when the owner doesn't share vital company statistics, introduce them to important clients and suppliers, and delegate responsibilities, even as retirement approaches.

Even when these "play it close to the vest" types of business leaders pass the baton, often because of a serious illness or other crisis, they may come back to sabotage decisions by bringing in their old-time colleagues or talking to customers behind the backs of their new successors. Unwittingly, they may undermine their own ventures and their successors' success.

The first decade of the 21st century, with its more competitive domestic and global pressures, will demand even smarter business dealings and family harmony. Fail in the first, and you won't have the second. As one savvy business head explained, "My father taught us that a family business must first operate as a business, then as a family operation." Many believe that; too few put it into action. It is very hard to do, but it's possible and it's essential if the business is to remain in family hands.

This book was written for founders and owners, as well as for their relatives both in and outside the business, for nonfamily employees and entrepreneurs who some day may run family businesses. Business-owning families have little time to read. Therefore, the book is structured in a question-and-answer format so that you can start at the beginning, at the end or somewhere in between, depending on the nature of your dilemma. While there is no limit on the number of challenges family businesses must manage, the 101 questions contained here represent some of the more common questions the authors have heard scores of family businesses ask over the years.

The book offers more than answers. It includes real-life stories that show how various generations and family members can view situations very differently. Many of these situations will ring familiar. Be assured that you are not alone; other families have been there before you. There are solutions. In most cases no single person is right or wrong in dealing with any issue. There are almost always multiple options to consider and that is the lasting value of this book: to offer choices and raise your level of consciousness. Families that can recognize, face, and openly and honestly discuss their major issues stand the best chance of successfully resolving them. We hope you will share appropriate portions of this book with those involved in your issues as a way to generate this discussion.

There is a rapidly growing body of family business knowledge and resources. Not so long ago, there was virtually none. There were only a few sources of information and support, a handful of people who called themselves family business advisors, and a single guru dominating the field: Dr. Léon A. Danco. A consultant and prolific author, Dr. Danco broke ground for the field of family business consulting, having established the Center for Family Business several decades ago. With the assistance of his wife Katy, also an author, Dr. Danco helped spawn the profession of family business consulting and an entire academic field focused exclusively on that topic.

The business of studying and helping family businesses has exploded in recent years. There is a much larger pool of advisors and sources of information and help, including Dr. Danco's successor, the Arthur Andersen Center for Family Business. The Center, led by co-author Ross Nager as executive director, builds on the philosophies of Dr. Danco, supports research on family business issues and provides extensive assistance in family business consulting and family wealth planning. As part of Arthur Andersen's Private Client Services group, the Center also makes available investment advisory services, personal financial planning services and others to help family businesses achieve their wealth management goals. It is ever more important for family businesses to take a holistic approach to planning for their family's and business' financial affairs. To be effective, all planning should be integrated and done throughout the family's lifetime and business life cycle to reflect changing circumstances and needs.

We list many resources in the book—books, websites, programs, and newsletters to name a few, and hope family business readers take advantage of them. They will need them, especially over the next decade, as family businesses face unprecedented changes. For example, the leadership of some 43 percent of family-owned businesses will change hands by the year 2002, according to the *Arthur Andersen/MassMutual American Family Business Survey '97*. Relatively few family businesses have strategic plans in place to get them through the often tough transition.

Meanwhile, women are expected to play a larger role in family-owned businesses in the years ahead. Indeed, slightly more than one-quarter of the survey respondents indicated the next CEO may be a woman—five times more than the number of survey respondents whose businesses were headed by a female CEO. In addition, more are considering co-leadership for the next generation.

In the first decade of the new millennium, other new challenges will arise—and faster. As author, professor and family business consultant John L. Ward of Loyola University, Chicago, says, change will come in many forms. "Internationalization will become a hot issue, and family businesses will need to determine what role they will want to play in a global economy; consolidation in various industries will cause family firms to feel threatened; publicity versus privacy will be challenged as families are forced to run their firms more like public companies; family freedom will mean more family members might take jobs outside the firm and family businesses will have to entice them to come in; and blended families will be the rule where the head of a company will be forced to decide a number of issues based on this new type of 'family.'"

Entrepreneurship drives the American and global economy, and the businesses of many entrepreneurs eventually become family businesses held for generations. This book will enhance the communication among family members, employees and others whose lives and careers are dependent upon the success of family businesses around the world. It will aid their understanding of how to tackle the challenges that lie ahead.

CHAPTER I

CRITICAL ISSUES FACING FAMILIES IN BUSINESS TODAY

1. How well is your business doing in your industry and in the context of the current economy?

There's one constant in business that makes owners nervous: all industries have a disconcerting habit of changing from time to time. Sometimes companies are caught off guard. Those firms willing to change will find it can pay off, however. One family that can attest to this is the Schulmans of Chicago. Their second-generation cheesecake business, Eli's Cheesecake Company, has kept up with changes in its industry and changes in people's tastebuds. As a result, this family business has survived and thrived in spite of competitors who are bigger and more diversified, some who are smaller and others who are consolidating. Through it all, they've stuck to their basic philosophy of taking pride in the quality of their cakes as a branded rather than private-label manufacturer.

The late Eli Schulman, who passed away in 1988, perfected a cheesecake recipe in his restaurant's kitchen. When he put it on the menu of Eli's, The Place for Steak, a venerable Chicago institution, people's mouths watered. By 1980 the cheesecake was so popular that Eli, who was then 70 years old, wanted to sell it outside the restaurant. It was offered on a limited basis at a local summer food fair. Just four years later, when Eli Schulman's only son Marc, now 44, a corporate attorney who had been in private practice since 1979, came into the firm, the product took off like a 777. Marc says his father had a dream. "He respected Hershey and Wrigley and wanted a special food product to bear his name that would be sold to the public." Marc set up a company separate from the restaurant, expanded the line beyond its plain and chocolate chip flavors and sales and business boomed, making Eli's Cheesecakes a major player in the entire dessert category.

In the beginning, the company whipped up 100 cheesecakes a day from a bakery on Chicago's Northwest Side. Currently, over 15,000 roll off conveyor belts daily. To accommodate growth, in 1996 the company moved to a state-of-the-art bakery on the city's West Side, a 60,000-square-foot facility called Eli's Cheesecake World which today has become a tourist attraction.

Marc has given resonance and glamour to the company's cheesecake in the same way that coffee brewers have given designer status to their blends. There are more than 50 flavors of cheesecake, including the most popular Original Plain, and such mouth-watering varieties as Key Lime, Apple Streusel, Eggnog, Turtle, Mud Pie and White Chocolate Raspberry, which are sold all over the world at the retail level in supermarkets, gourmet shops and restaurants, through the mail and over the Internet.

One ingredient has not changed, however. Making cheesecakes is a labor-intensive labor of love: all cakes are still made by hand from fine ingredients and flavorings including premium cream cheese, sour cream and bourbon vanilla. The company is involved in research and development, experimenting with new sizes and flavors and ferreting out new sources such as Michigan apples for flavoring.

Since its inception, Eli's Cheesecake has become a Chicago icon. "We made a 1,500-pound cake for Chicago's 150th birthday, inaugural cheesecakes for both Mayor Richard M. Daley and President Clinton's first- and second-term inaugural festivities. The first for President Clinton was a 2,000-pound Terminator-size inaugural Eli's 'Red, White and Bill' cheesecake with a combination of Raspberry, Blueberry and Eli's Original Plain, plus 160 pounds of sugar and 170 pounds of sour cream. For Hillary's 50th birthday, bakers concocted a gigantic cheesecake of Original Plain, Chocolate Chip and Mocha Latte, says Marc."

Marc says he's a cheesecake zealot who would love to get the word out more about his superior product through cheesecake tastings. He is determined to beat the competition which comes in all sizes. "It's anyone with a pan," says Marc. "We have competition from Sara Lee and Kraft down to local bakers. We're the largest specialty company making cheesecake and we're a significant player especially on the branded side. We're not a contract packer. Our philosophy is 'let's take pride in our cakes as a branded manufacturer.'"

With such a stance, sales hit more than $20 million last year. What's helped the firm to keep growing and survive downturns in the economy is the desire of management to listen to its customers. In addition to new items on its menu such as tortes, cakes and tiramisu, representing about 10 percent of the business, the company has just expanded its single-serve offerings for the home takeout market. "People want to indulge and diversify their tastes and we have the ability to tap into these trends. We are sticklers for quality and the fundamentals of good business: good service, innovation and reinvesting in the business. And there's a real commitment to our brand and to our culture. We come from a service culture; after all, the restaurant business is the ultimate service business. We are committed to what we make, not just what we market," Marc says.

Trends in the industry will include more consolidation of customers and distributors, which will shrink the firm's distribution network, says Marc. There's too much emphasis in all businesses on company size, with financial investors buying up three or more small players. "Ours is not a high-tech industry. We don't want to be a mass-market private label supplier and lose our quality. We're neither a buyer nor a seller. We may expand to other parts of the country, but we're not going to take on a venture capital partner who has different goals than we do. The fear is that we'll lose our uniqueness as a family business," says Marc. His is a family firm that intends to be around for the next generation. Any or all of his three young daughters might be the next scions.

For those with an entrepreneurial spirit, starting your own firm is one of the most compelling prospects in the world of business. Like a golf game, you start out to learn the shots and the moves, and you work hard to hone your skills as you progress. Just when you think you've mastered the game, you find your success can turn on a dime if you don't stay on top.

As a family business owner, you care deeply about your firm, but you have a plethora of important decisions to make on a day-to-day, week-by-week and long-term basis. Before you make any critical ones such as when to step down, who to appoint to head your company in the next generation or whether to sell, merge or close, you need to understand how well your business is faring in order to structure a game plan.

But how do you begin? Start by looking at the historic trends of your business and reasonably foreseeable changes in the future. You'll need to analyze your strengths and weaknesses and what you need to do to improve. Know up front that there are few right or wrong strategies. Make a list and note the following:

- Have sales been trending up or down over the last five years?
- Are you making more or less of a mark-up on your core products or services?
- What has happened to administrative expenses supporting the business?

- Are there significant changes in sales and distribution costs?
- How healthy is your income statement and does it take more or fewer assets to conduct your business today?
- Is inventory going up faster than sales or not?
- What are the level and condition of your receivables balances, relative to prior years?
- How has your capital structure changed in recent years? Are you thinly capitalized or overcapitalized? Does your cash flow readily cover debt service?
- What changes can you foresee in your industry, as well as in the businesses of your customers and suppliers?
- Can you envision new competitors entering your market, perhaps from new and different fields?
- What roles might technology play in changing the way your industry functions?

You will begin to get a snapshot of where your business has been, where it's headed, and exactly how healthy or weak it is. Your job isn't over yet, however.

Analyze your management team and consider your place in it. Do they have the skills, drive and experience to take your business to the next level? Think about what your role in the business is today and how it has possibly changed over the last few years. Ask yourself if the organization is less or more dependent on you and what your role should be, given your age, health and interests. Ask yourself if you can honestly envision a time when your business can continue without you or, if something horrific happened to you, who would lead the management team. In short, your goal should be to consider whether your entire management team is strong enough with a sufficient number of qualified people. If it isn't, decide how to rectify it. Possibly you have qualified people, but they may be young and a bit unseasoned. You'll need to do some quick training. Or, if you feel your talent pool lacks certain strengths, it's time to find the right people and develop future leaders of the company. If you've never developed any type of formal leadership program, it's time to do some education or mentoring.

Simultaneously, you could use a board of independent directors to turn to for another point of view from non-self-interested, successful people. If you haven't set one up, it may be time to do so.

Hard numbers are not the only issues to consider as you wrestle with the state of your business. You also need to look at the softer people side, since no business runs itself without significant human capital. Peruse your employment rosters and determine your employee retention level. Analyze the demographics. You want to have longtime employees as well as fresh talent. Walk the halls, talk to employees, check their morale. Many company heads rarely think about these issues and leave it to their executives, middle management and human resource personnel, but you should pay attention, too.

To be an effective family business leader, learn from your mistakes, work to position and stabilize your ship, and your family company should have a bright and healthy future.

Now, look beyond your company and study your customer base. Consider whether it is increasing or stagnant. What business issues face your customers that will indirectly impact your financial health? Also, understand what their businesses need to do to improve service, product and finances. You want to be sure you're dealing with healthy customers.

Reality Check: You can't make tough daily or long-term business decisions unless you truly understand the state of your business. You need to consider trends in hard numbers over a reasonable time frame for sales, profits, capitalization and the like. You need to look at your management team and judge whether you have sufficient talent and depth. You also need to ask yourself whether you have sufficient objective advice and input, perhaps in the form of a board of independent directors. Finally, you need to take the pulse of your staff. They are in the trenches and must be behind your business strategy and objectives. Only when you think deeply about the answers you're gathering can you gain an honest, accurate picture of the state of your firm. With that information, you can go forward and plan for a successful future.

2. What is the best way to develop a long-term strategy, including developing a framework to continue the business over the long haul?

Freedman Seating in Chicago has overcome the odds of family business succession and moved into its fourth generation. One of its secrets for success has been its ability to shift gears as the market demanded, says Craig Freedman, chief operating officer, a member of the fourth generation, and son of head Gerald "Jerry" Freedman. The company began by outfitting buggies, when Craig's great-grandfather started the company in the late 19th century and showcased his products at the Columbia Exposition in 1893. It switched to manufacturing seats today for mid-size buses, delivery trucks and shuttle buses such as the ones that scurry about airports.

In recent years, the family has made another change for the long term. It knew it needed to bring in nonfamily managers to fill key positions in the 250-employee firm to continue growth and adequately service customers. "Sometimes we find ourselves so busy that we react to customers rather than perform proactively," says Craig, who joined the company six years ago after working as an investment banker and earning an MBA from Harvard University's Graduate School of Business. He, his father and several other family members expanded management from four to 15 and included different disciplines. They have also started to develop a strategic plan that addresses the planning process. "We don't want to put together a document that sits on a shelf, but have a hands-on plan for the medium if not long term, and one which we can alter annually," Craig says. The management team meets once a year and addresses strategy over a time frame of three to five years out. "We meet bi-weekly to monitor progress and address other important issues," he adds. Already, the company has seen its revenue and profits improve.

Having a long-term strategy sounds wise, and it is, but be prepared that there's no easy way to develop one. It requires getting in touch with your customers and your customers' customers, so you truly understand the trends that drive everyone's businesses.

How do you gain that information in the first place? Here, too, you need a multistep plan. Become an ace reporter and secure background information from the Internet, business publications and experts in various fields. Second, start talking to your sales force rather than only depending on the reports they turn in after they've made a call. Third, gather your sales force and run an internal focus group at least every six months to generate a deeper understanding of the market conditions they face. Fourth, and perhaps most important, get out of your office and talk directly to your largest customers and suppliers, preferably to the CEO, who will give the broadest perspective. Ask specific questions:

- What keeps you up at night worrying?
- What's really driving your business these days?
- Why is business turning up (or down)?

- What are you most worried about in your market? What are your customers' greatest concerns?
- How are your customers reacting to your products or services?
- Where is your competition coming from?
- Are there specific technological or other changes in your industry that are causing the cost and price structures to change?

Because situations change, make these kinds of inquiries every six months. Don't think you'll be viewed as a pest. Most customers and clients love this type of personal interaction and interest, particularly because it shows you want to keep revising your strategy to provide better service to them. Tell your customers explicitly that your inquiries are intended to help them. Be sure you or someone else in senior management does the asking.

As you gather information, you will gain a sense of what will happen in your industry and your markets in the future. Based upon that information, you can draft a longer-term strategy to deal with the trends that you can foresee. The main point of a strategic plan is to anticipate market conditions, so you have time to make changes cost effectively.

Once you have a strategic plan in place, you're not yet home free. You now need to decide what you're willing to do to make it become a reality. "It's the difference between having a vision and having a reality," says one Arthur Andersen family business advisor. Make those decisions, write them down and then tell the world—or at least your employees. You'll want to communicate your ideas in writing and in meetings. You'll need to get input from your people and gain their active involvement and acceptance. Besides disseminating information, your goal is to put into place performance measures that enable long-term strategy and also keep you apprised of progress in achieving it. For example:

- Share the financial outcome measures of your company such as net income, revenue and shareholder value. Carefully analyze what contributed to those results, e.g., merely cost cutting or adding new products.
- Analyze which operational activities, if performed well, can be predicted to produce the desired financial outcome. This requires consideration from many different angles. For example, a contractor's

number of sales and revenue gains may be a function of advertising in the local market, sales calls or a combination. You need a clear understanding of the sales and cost drivers so that you can better target your activities and measure people's operational efforts.

- Reward employees' smart work by linking operational measures to compensation. Some staff may be able to achieve results without advertising, which holds down costs. They should be rewarded.
- Develop timely management information reporting systems for these operational measures. People respond to specific evaluation measurements and typically will modify behavior when it directly affects their compensation and advancement, and they know about their progress and its impact in time to take actions.
- Invest in any necessary training and communications to enable employees to understand the operational measures and their roles in producing the desired results and financial outcomes. Be sure to train employees on how to analyze important management reports. The goal is to keep everyone informed rather than in the dark, which will aid in accomplishing your long-term plans.

How do you get your company's leader to focus on strategic planning? Bring up the idea and suggest a process to develop the plan. Most company leaders understand how quickly markets are changing today compared to the past. Strategic management professor John L. Ward of Loyola University puts it this way: "Fifty years ago a company's market changed once every 30 years. Twenty-five years ago it changed once every seven to 10 years. A decade ago it changed once every three years. Now it's changing every 18 months." A wise leader recognizes the need to plan, but may not be enthusiastic about such lofty notions as "mission" and "vision." These leaders prefer to focus on more concrete planning techniques that lead more quickly to action. You may need to modify your process and promise reasonably quick progress to generate enthusiasm. If you can gain support and demonstrate that the management team has become enthusiastic about strategic planning, you should be able to get the leader to agree to allow the process to occur.

Reality Check: You want to produce results in the short term, but if you don't have a long-term strategy, you may create only band-aid solutions. Think for the long haul; this is a luxury that a privately held firm can afford. Find out what's happening in your sector among your customers and suppliers, and discover what's happening in the broader market. Then plan accordingly. Write down goals, communicate them and get everyone on the same page. Results will materialize. Most important, you'll be prepared for challenges by being able to act proactively rather than reactively.

3. How do you generate the capital needed to satisfy all the demands placed upon your business?

Phil Camp, 58, heads Spokane, Wa.-based Camp Automotive Inc., the car dealership his grandfather founded, which now has four franchises—Chevrolet, Subaru, BMW and Volvo. He was in a bind. He managed the dealership in a manner similar to the way his father did. Any profit generated was plowed back into the company, but a few years ago profit margins began to slip as overhead climbed. Concurrently, privately held competitors and public firms started knocking at his door trying to buy the dealership. In fact, it was happening to independent dealers all around the area. One large automotive group had sold to a public company and had come out with flying colors. Now the same public conglomerate was dangling big bucks and even bigger dreams before Phil's eyes.

Because Phil held all voting shares of stock in the firm, whether to sell was his call. However, equity in the firm was split equally among Phil, two brothers also in the firm, one older and one younger, and a sister, who is not an employee. The offers were tempting at first, especially when Phil's three siblings intensified their grumbling over a dearth of dividends. They wanted their share of the spoils. There were other family predicaments that might have made selling an easy solution.

Phil had a lot to mull over. Another consideration was that one of his two sons, Travis, 26, who had graduated from the University of Arizona almost four years ago and had come into the firm, managed the body shop. To make the decision whether to sell even tougher, Phil's mother pushed for him to keep the company in family hands for sentimental reasons.

A meeting of the family didn't help Phil reach closure, except that he agreed to distribute bigger dividends from the profits to his siblings. In the meantime, he's still courted by one public company. Says Travis, "Personally, I'd love to see the business remain a family firm. Thus far, my father has opted to retain the business because he loves it, wants to see it continue to grow and, if I am the person to run the business some day, so be it. Whether to sell or not is a thorn in his side every day."

With business and society changing so rapidly, it has become relatively common for management to face major dilemmas in the business. New or increased competition, major technological change and insufficient capital required for expansion can create a major turning point in the life of a company. Businesses that cope can survive and prosper, while businesses that cling to the past may wither and die.

Family-owned businesses face these challenges, plus unique pressures resulting from the passage of time, which inevitably means changes in family members' needs, objectives, abilities and demands. These issues often are evidenced by increased capital demands on the business and questions concerning the family's ability and willingness to manage properly the succession process. Compound the external market pressures and the family challenges with an innate desire to keep the business private, and the family business can become stagnant and resist considering actions necessary for its survival.

Any major change in your family business is an emotionally charged life event on the scale of leaving your child off on the first day of kindergarten or giving your daughter away at her wedding. You and possibly other family members probably have been totally wrapped up financially and personally in your business. However, a change at some point is inevitable because, as a business matures along with the owner, the question of what to do with your business comes more clearly into play and demands an answer.

In the family business world, the need for change often is stymied by insufficient capital. Money is needed to finance normal business operations and expansion, fund the buyout of unwilling or uncooperative inheritors, sustain the lifestyle of the senior generation, pay inheritance taxes, and finance the lifestyles and objectives of an ever-expanding number of family members. You may continue your business and pass it on to the next generation, but will there be enough capital? What alternatives should you consider? Drastic action may be needed, and you may need to consider taking on significant new debt or selling all or part of the business.

Whatever tactic, the first step is to communicate with all family members and top nonfamily management. You must face the various issues and discuss them openly with those who have a stake in the outcome. Understand their views and try to reconcile their perspectives, which may be quite different from your own.

Many families claim they want to keep the business in their hands. Yet, in some cases, they end up doing the opposite. Often, the family comes to a different decision once the patriarch or matriarch leaves the scene. If a sale is to be the ultimate outcome, it typically is best for the sale to occur while the senior generation is alive and active. After all, who knows the business better and can best enunciate its value to a potential buyer? The heirs-apparent may not have the business savvy or understanding to maximize value and resulting sales proceeds.

The starting point is to carefully analyze your business and its capital needs. Can the business be competitive given the changing marketplace? Is a major change in product mix, geographic coverage or some other action required? A strategy must be developed that considers these issues. Perhaps most important, do your key employees and family members have the leadership and management skills to guide the company through the changes necessary to be effective in the marketplace? What capital is needed for the expected changes as well as for family objectives? A formal analysis with financial projections is a must. Your managers and advisors can help. Only the strength of your plan to respond to the necessary changes, combined with your family's and managers' commitment to the plan, will determine your potential for success.

If your decision is to cash out some, but not all, family members, you must take a close, hard look at your business' ability to generate the capital to buy out shareholders who want to exit. It may be possible to do that simply with a note payable over a number of years from expected operating earnings. Outside capital sources to buy out shareholders include:

- Borrowing from a lending institution.
- A sale of a part of the business that is not critical to its strategic objectives.
- A sale of part of the stock to employees.
- A joint venture for an existing or future market opportunity, thereby freeing up capital that otherwise would be needed to operate your business.
- An equity partner who purchases part of the stock, or an initial public offering (IPO). An IPO rarely can cash out the entire family because the public market, as a rule, does not absorb all the stock. What it may do, however, is generate enough capital to "take out" the shareholders who want to leave as well as provide an infusion of fresh capital for the business.

Reality Check: There are many ways to raise capital. Which way should you proceed? If you don't want to or can't continue a family business, you have numerous options: a sale to employees or other strategic buyers, a partial sale that may lead to a later disposition of the entire business, a private placement of stock or debt, or a public offering. Be sure to consider the long-term consequences of the alternatives and carefully project their cash flow impact. Take your time, seek out the best advice and debate all the pros and cons of each alternative before you decide.

4. How does a family firm finance growth and what are the risks?

The late Leonard Levine grew up in the furniture business and was passionate about it when he founded his Baltimore, Md., retail store in 1954, named Garon's after his two sons, Gary, now 45, and Ron, 48. Just six years later, Levine became one of the first independent retailers in the country to carry the Ethan Allen furniture line exclusively. He kept the corporate name Garon's, but renamed the store Ethan Allen Interiors. He soon added one more store. After his two sons came into the business, the triumvirate added two more stores. Business was brisk.

However, the family was thrown a curve. In 1982, Leonard died suddenly at age 60, leaving a very young president, Ron, then 31, and vice president, Gary, then 28, in charge. "We felt invincible and never worried that we'd crash on our system of making money and growing. But," says Gary, "we had also had the wisdom and guidance of our father. This was no longer the case." By the late 80s and early 90s, the recession kicked in. The boys never figured business would go as far south as it did. They could have bailed out and sold the company, but their father had left them the legacy of a business they cared too much about to give up.

"We were at the breaking point. Two of our stores were really struggling," says Gary, adding that they were leveraged up to their eyeballs. "In order to stay in business and to grow, we mortgaged our homes and dumped all the money back into the business," he said. When this was insufficient, in 1991 the brothers closed one store and one year later they sold the other back to Ethan Allen. In 1994, they remodeled the first of their two remaining stores, and in 1995 they remodeled the other. "That shrinking process was painful, but it paid off," says Gary. Today, the two remaining stores are more than 15 percent ahead of last year and growing with sales of some $12 million a year.

A common scenario: You need money to fuel your company's growth and you're experiencing a cash-flow catastrophe in an industry where margins are tight and accounts receivables are delinquent. You've already proved that you can outperform the industry norm and have discovered that there are two ways to boost your company's growth, either through regional expansion or major product-line additions.

Yet, any method you use to expand the firm will be capital intensive. With insufficient capital within the company to fund growth, you consider borrowing from your bank. You think to yourself: If piling up debt to finance growth were a sport like tennis, you'd probably be a Wimbledon champ. But if you hanker to play like a pro in business, you must learn there are ways to finance growth in your firm that show similar professionalism.

First, there is no free lunch. If you're looking for an easy answer to fund growth with minimal risk, don't. Raising capital from outside sources comes in two variations: debt and equity financing. Both involve risks. In addition, before you begin your quest for funds, you need to ask yourself some important questions:

- What is your tolerance for risk? Can you sleep at night with debt hanging over your head?
- Do you need more funds to grow your business, hopefully generating future cash flow, or do you need them to finance generational transfers and taxes that won't create a financial return on investment?
- Do you have valuable assets or reasonably certain revenue streams that can be pledged to support repayment?
- Would it make sense to consider a strategic joint venture with an investor, a competitor, a foreign concern, or a private or institutional placement to share risk?

DEBT FINANCING

Debt financing, where you borrow money and pay it back with interest, is by far your most attractive method from the standpoint of cost. It's a relatively cheap way to fund growth or improvement, or to provide funds to retiring family members. There are two types of debt financing known as recourse and nonrecourse. The borrower can be the business or the owner or both.

RECOURSE DEBT. Most borrowing is recourse debt, meaning that the borrower is liable to repay from all its assets, not just the asset purchased with the loan. If your business is set up as a corporation, the corporation would be fully liable on its recourse debt and all its assets would be at risk. Sometimes, your lending institution requires you to personally guarantee repayment. This means that if your company cannot repay the lender, you must find other personal sources of funds. With a personal guarantee, you risk not only the proverbial farm, but also your home and other personal assets. So try to avoid personal guarantees if possible.

NONRECOURSE DEBT. Since nonrecourse debt is payable strictly from the asset that secures it, it is by far the safest and most preferable way to borrow. If you buy a building using this method, only the rent and the building or the proceeds from selling that building are subject to the debt. If the rent and value of the building are insufficient, the lender loses the difference. Unfortunately, lenders typically are willing to lend less when their repayment rights are limited to specific assets, plus they may charge a higher interest rate.

Fortunately, you as a borrower are in the driver's seat today, especially if you contemplate substantial borrowing. The cost of money has come down and capital is plentiful. Also, when looking for sources, don't confine your options to your bank just because it has offered funds in the past. Check out the benefits other banks offer. If your business is growing, you may reach a point where your local bank can't meet all your needs. Send out an informational packet to larger banks across the country describing your company's performance and evolving needs. Include projections and actual numbers.

The head of a telecommunications firm did just that. He used an outside accountant to perform regular audits on his company. He verified the accuracy of inventory and accounts receivables. This not only kept him on his toes, but when he needed debt financing, he piqued the interest of 10 banks that were practically beating down his door to lend him money. Moreover, the bankers were impressed by the owner's decision to upgrade financial reports without prodding. His diligent reporting and recordkeeping helped the owner expand the firm's credit line as necessary.

EQUITY FINANCING

Equity financing is another way to raise capital, though the idea of selling stock may give you palpitations. Essentially, equity financing means you're changing your mindset and philosophy, going from a company that's family owned to one that is, perhaps, family controlled. The outsider investor typically buys a minority stake, although some insist on acquiring control.

Investors put capital into your firm and typically let the family run the business. Sometimes an equity partner may be involved in the day-to-day operations, serve on your board of directors or simply choose to be a silent partner. Investors feel entitled to look over your shoulder to keep tabs on their stake. Most expect their investment to reap benefits within five to seven years and will want an exit strategy for themselves.

If you take on an equity partner, it's important not to sell short. One paint store retailer undervalued his company. In hindsight, he wishes he had consulted professionals for the valuation. If he had structured his equity sale to include a buy-back feature, that would have let him reacquire stock at some fixed future date or growth stage if his firm reached certain sales and profitability targets.

JOINT VENTURE. Another capital-raising alternative is a joint venture, which usually involves a pooling of talent, resources and money. This approach typically requires you to share control, management and profits relating to a specific activity, rather than your entire company. It often is used when an activity is important to both companies' strategies. It is a way for you to avoid incurring the entire capital cost of an investment, although the obvious trade-off is that you must share the profits.

LOSS OF CONTROL. A joint venture doesn't mean you've given up control, but it means your share has been diluted. However, if you sell the firm to raise capital outright or go public to raise capital, you risk losing virtually all control. Once a company is sold, and you stay on, you become another hired hand, your benefits and perks may diminish, decisions are no longer made just by you, and your daily schedule will be less flexible. Along with a loss of control, comes a possible change in values, history and prominence of your family firm in your community.

INITIAL PUBLIC OFFERING. If the company goes public, you may still head it, but you will experience a loss of privacy and the edge you had before when you didn't have to show your hand. You will be required to issue public disclosure documents. There's also the added worry of a potential takeover. However, it usually is possible to retain actual or effective control by having the family keep somewhat less than 50 percent of the stock.

Reality Check: There is no such thing as minimal risk when it comes to raising capital. Debt financing is the safest, easiest, and least expensive tack that allows you to maintain full control of your business. Equity financing right now is a hot enterprise with money readily available for private placements, but it means taking on a minority partner or considering a joint venture. A straight sale means giving up control of all or some of your business in exchange for equity. In an initial public offering (IPO), you may still run the business, but everybody will know your business goings-on. Take your pick, but carefully heed all pros and cons.

5. How do you decide if you should pass on the business?

George S. Grostern, 61, is an accountant by training in Montreal, who went into a family photo vending business and also now works with his son. He says you have to ask yourself some realistic business questions when it comes to making succession decisions: How is the company functioning? Who's available to take over? Is the business likely to continue functioning with this person? What is the best time to pass on the company?

At the same time that you pose these business questions, he says, you have to ask yourself some equally tough personal questions. Are you willing and able to step aside or share ownership and management?

George's father Samuel still comes to work daily at age 91. "The business offers him a place to come," he says. George himself has no plans to retire but does plan to turn over greater ownership of the company to his son Jeffrey, 35. "I've thought about retiring and don't plan to do it. I will take more and longer holidays but not become a snowbird. My son and I work well together. We do similar but different things at work. I do more of the accounting functions; he's more into marketing since many of the contacts in that area are closer to him in age. That's a distinct advantage of having younger family in business. It happened with my father and me and now it's happening again," he adds.

A family business brouhaha can be the ugliest scenario. Squabbling siblings, dysfunctional relationships with Dad or Mom and other nasty family conflicts can undermine the business. When it's time to decide whether you want to retire and pass on the company, you may find it best to abandon ship and sell when there's out-of-control family conflict. Otherwise, your family firm may sink faster than the Titanic.

At probably no other time in American history have so many owners of family businesses had to consider retiring and decide what to do with firms. These companies, many of which were founded shortly after World War II, have owners who are now in their 70s and 80s. Based on commonly accepted statistics, of the estimated 8 million to 12 million family firms in this country, only a third will survive into the next generation.

Decisions to pass on your business must be weighed as objectively as other business decisions, such as entering a new market or offering a new product. You must examine the various alternatives from both a family and business point of view. Your planning must start years before retirement, before a crisis such as major illness or death forces your hand or someone else's and ends up costing your family hefty estate taxes and possibly the business itself. A well-orchestrated succession takes a minimum of five years, but you should ideally start it the instant your potential successor enters the family firm.

Many family business owners want to pass on a business when there's a motivated understudy who's been waiting in the wings to take center stage and contribute. But as in any good play, you, as the director, must believe that the person is primed for the part, ready to take direction, has the proper training and education, as well as the right personality and values to be a team player with other family members, employees, customers and suppliers.

In most cases, your potential successor will be a family member, though not always. Perhaps your children are too young to take over or they're not quite ready. You may decide to bring in a nonfamily professional manager to run the show in the interim. More often than not, however, you may ignore or not realize your children's inadequacies and bring them into the firm as successors before they are ready, which eventually will do everyone a disservice and cause problems. On the other hand, you may never stop viewing your grown, competent children as rebellious teens who haven't yet settled down or aren't mature enough to assume control.

ADDITIONAL CONSIDERATIONS

Your views and the existence of a qualified successor are not the only considerations. The decision to keep a family business within the fold usually is affected by cultural dynamics that should be periodically reassessed. For an almost 200-year-old firm that manufactures and distributes food products, the business is the family members' web of connectedness, the place and time they cherish coming together. The company's economic value is secondary. However, such connectedness may become diluted in successive generations and the business' reason for being needs to be rethought as each new generation comes on board, makes its mark and takes over.

The role of the business in the community should also be considered. A family business produces status and creates pride. Your desire not to give that up may provide sufficient reason to retain control. You also have to consider the future of your employees and whether they may suffer if the company is sold to someone else who will look for ways to cut costs.

Family members' commitment to the business may wane in light of increased competition and other industry changes, looming estate taxes, the health of those in charge or other, more pressing objectives. Family members may disagree strongly over the company's direction or the dividends paid, and may not be able to resolve their conflicts. Some family members may want to enjoy their accrued wealth or put it to some unrelated use. You may be worried that the new-found cash will damage family members' work ethic and social and moral values. Can you teach them to properly manage the money that comes from a sale of the company? Perhaps you view the business as the glue that keeps your family together. And what will you do with your time if you no longer have the business?

In addition to considering the family and personal half of the equation, you need to examine your company's and industry's financial health. Pressing questions come to mind:

- Can the company afford to continue? Can it generate the profits necessary to continue to grow despite current and future capital needs?
- Is the company in a strong enough market position to remain competitive or does it require a major overhaul of its products?

- Can current managers and personnel be sufficiently creative, energetic and resourceful to maintain and grow the company's market position?
- Will the family's demands for their support needs prevent the company from taking advantage of new market opportunities?
- What is the state of the industry in which the business operates? A shrinking or consolidating industry can bode ill for the business and its long-term prospects.

There are no easy answers to these questions. Finding them requires soul searching, open discussion and some hard work. Try a simple two-column listing, with one column enumerating the reasons to keep the business and the other describing the reasons for sale. Discuss these pros and cons with your family and selected others who are critical to the decision. This is a classic case in which a board of independent directors can play a pivotal role in helping to make this crucial decision.

If all signs to pass on the firm point to "yes," start the process by doing the following:

- Decide on a successor, then groom that person, demanding commitment and gradually expanding responsibilities. Ensure that your successor develops necessary skills, experience and confidence to lead the company.
- Clearly designate your heir-apparent to the rest of the family, as well as to employees and outside suppliers, clients, bankers and others. Actively work to gain their support for your decision.
- Mentor your successor and consider someone else in the company as an additional or sole mentor.
- Set a timetable for retirement or a deadline to shift power, put it into writing and stick to it.
- Develop an estate plan for assets to be divided and transfer ownership to the next generation appropriately.
- Let your heir-apparent begin making decisions without sabotaging those decisions. You must give your successor the latitude to make some mistakes.
- Find a new role for yourself in the firm and simultaneously develop interests outside your business.

Families whose squabbles hit the papers never expected or planned for egregious disputes. But this can be what you or your family may experience. You must act affirmatively to assess your family and business and their potential to succeed together. Perhaps your best decision is not to keep the business in the family. Weigh the pros and cons. If the pros win out, you must take extensive and thoughtful action over a significant period of time to ensure the future success of your business and harmony within your family.

Reality Check: Don't assume that you should automatically pass on your business. Assess whether there's a competent cooperative successor who's interested for the right reasons, who will be able to survive the inevitable tough times faced in business, and whether your business has reasonable prospects for its ongoing success.

6. When is the best time to sell a family business?

The late Leroy Bednar founded Fashion Floors in Austin, Tx., a firm that refurbishes residential flooring and sells carpet, sheet vinyl, laminate and wood flooring and area rugs. He thought he was doing the right thing when he brought his four children into the business. However, when he turned 73 and was in ill health, he wanted to step down and turned to his four children to select a successor. None was prepared to take over or was even interested in the offer. Leroy didn't want to see the firm he built from scratch sold or liquidated. He desperately wanted to hand the reins to someone who would continue to run the company by his same standards.

In August 1997, he called colleague Mike O'Krent, 40, whom he had met years before when Mike was managing his own family's San Antonio-based carpet-flooring business. Leroy asked Mike if he wanted to buy his firm. Mike jumped at the opportunity. He had left his family's firm in 1991 and had gone into business with a long-time friend. "When I worked for my family, I begged my father and grandfather to attend some seminars and to do succession planning. They wouldn't listen," says Mike. So he left. Mike's grandfather and father subsequently passed away and his brother was given sole ownership.

Mike agreed to buy Leroy's business, keep Leroy on as a consultant as well as his daughter and one son, although there are no formal employment contracts.

You're tired and ready to retire from the business you founded 45 years ago and pursue another challenge. The marketplace is intensely competitive. You need to cut costs, boost quality and pay endless attention to customer service. The more you do, the more you need to do. Year after year, the only reliable edge you have is continually leapfrogging the competition and jumping into new niches. But you're sick of the responsibility, the debt, costs and administrative headaches. Unfortunately, you have no one interested in taking over. So after consulting with your family and advisors, you decide to sell and enjoy the spoils of your hard work.

After sprucing up the business, you receive an offer and you decide to grab it. It may never materialize again. Of course, you cannot discount the security that money from a sale will provide your family.

How do you know if it's the best time? If you're the first in the industry to sell, you might get shortchanged. Easy sales will go out in the first round of purchases. Wait too long, and you might grovel for another chance or never get one.

Success in selling a business is about timing. Trying to figure out whether your firm's value is about to rise or fall can be akin to the short-term trader who tries to time the market. Here are some ways you can come out on top:

- Examine your industry closely before you make a move. Decide if it is in a sell cycle and why. (Geography also influences cycles.) Keep tabs on what's happening with sales of similar companies. Are they selling above or below what you perceive to be market value?
- Look at your competitors and see if there's a trend toward doing roll ups, which are conglomerates that acquire small businesses in the same and/or related industries and consolidate them under one big umbrella. Some of these consolidations have been enlarged through IPOs. When this is the case, selling later rather than sooner might be advantageous. IPOs tend to decline in value initially. Typically, in an IPO consolidation, the deal promoters get as much as 15 percent ownership, the public receives 30 percent, and the owners of the rolled-up businesses get about 55 percent. In other words, the value of the rolled-up businesses may be diluted in the public offering, resulting in a later price decline.

- Note whether your industry has changed and matured. Has your business kept up with the changes? Companies that are the most successful at changing and build themselves around constant learning and innovation will make it. Or decide if your business is becoming obsolete and whether it will be too difficult to alter internal workings. If you don't, your business may not be around in five years for a possible sale.

The gaming business is an example of an industry that has matured. Many of the major companies with deeper pockets and more market share are gobbling up the mid-tier family firms. However, if owners of independent companies wait too long to sell, the increased competition may decrease their value. Furthermore, the owners may have trouble finding buyers in the future if the largest players have already met their expansion objectives.

On the other hand, a real estate developer did a great job timing the sale of his property and the business he owned. He studied real estate trends and what was happening to the cost of property in his area. Three years ago, when he first entertained the thought of selling, he opted instead to do a joint venture with an insurance company to raise capital to expand and position himself to get the most he could when he finally sold. He knew that he had a hot commodity and wanted to get out when he was still young enough to move on to a fresh challenge. Real estate prices at that time were just beginning to escalate as interest rates were coming down. When he finally put his company on the market, he sold it for four times the property's worth at the time of the joint venture.

The real estate developer timed the sale to fit financial as well as personal goals. He knew not to expect fast results. He was right. It can take more than six months to pursue a private-equity deal, IPO or sale. There's a lot of going back and forth. If you're a 58-year-old company head and you want to work until age 64 or 65, consider the time factor. Don't wait until your 65th birthday to make your move because some buyers may want you to continue in the firm for a couple of years or may sense your urgency to retire and offer a lower price. This alone makes it more crucial that you evaluate suitors on the same basis that you'd judge a joint venture partner. There should be chemistry and a meeting of minds. Find out what the buyer plans to do with your business. Does he want to keep your company name, consolidate under his company's name, or restructure your firm from the bottom up? Determine if the buyer plans to retain your management team. If so, your team must be willing to bend and blend into the new corporate culture. Some may stay; others may leave.

If you sell, be prepared to acknowledge your sense of loss while remembering your successes. That happy medium will spur you to another challenge, whether in a different business or hobby.

Reality Check: If you sell or go public, timing is crucial to get the best price and terms. Look at your industry, note trends and cycles. Look at your business. If you plan to stay on after the sale, make sure you're simpatico with the new owner and that you're still at an age where you're interested in working, particularly for someone else. Be prepared for some sense of loss. Even if you feel relief after all is said and done and you've deposited a big check, you are likely to experience some loss of power, authority and involvement. You may need to find another challenge—fast—to fill the void.

CHAPTER II
BRINGING YOUR SUCCESSOR ON BOARD

7. Should an heir go into a family business and under what conditions?

Steven Lefton Sharp always knew that he wanted to go into the giftware and decorative accessories business founded in 1941 by his late grandfather George Zoltan Lefton. After graduating from American University in Washington, D.C., in 1991, he stepped into the family firm, based in Chicago.

When Steven first came on board, he started, as he believes most heirs should, at the bottom, literally sweeping floors. Then he rotated through the company's many departments and gradually moved up from office manager, to vice president of operations, and then to vice president of finance.

In 1996, when Steven's grandfather died suddenly, the business went into a trust managed by outsiders, but was run on a daily basis by his grandfather's second wife Magda. She died a year ago, and Steven and his mother Margo Lefton, who had also worked in the business, bought the company from the trust.

Their first decision: to quickly restructure the company so it would be more efficiently operated. Steven, 30, and a native of Chicago, was named CEO and president in March 1999. Says Steven, "You think you understand a business, but not until you are really in charge do you fully understand all the implications that brings. You have to be able to explain all your decisions: to your other partner, your employees, bank and/or financial institutions."

Another decision Steven made was to set about learning everything he could about the designing, importing and selling of the 3,000 items the company imports. "It was essential for me to know more about product development, marketing, sales and the customs areas as well as the various legal and financial relationships a business has. I'm learning on the job and quickly! I've brought in a lot of nonfamily talent, including a CFO. These additions helped increase sales 20 percent for the first quarter of this year and with administrative expenses reduced considerably, we hope to be more profitable than in the past."

In retrospect, Steven would advise other scions who are thinking of going into the family business,"Just because you're family doesn't mean you deserve employment in the family business. First I would suggest working for a period of time in a complementary type of business. Then, when you do enter your family's company, start out in an entry-level position and prove yourself before moving up."

Since his company's merchandise is sold retail, including at some Hallmark stores, he says he might have been wise to work at such a retail store. "I could have seen first hand what kind of merchandise people were buying. This presents an opportunity to talk with your customers one-on-one, to ask them what they like about the product and why."

Last, he also would suggest the guidance of a nonfamily member to be a mentor as well as someone who would offer honest critiques. He has no qualms about his current position and the kudos he thinks he deserves."I've brought in personnel who are the best in their field which, in turn, led to a great first quarter this year. I'm excited. We've got a great future, and I enjoy working with my mother."

You want to change careers. The corporate life is too much of a rat race and you ask yourself:"Why make money for someone else?" Anyhow, your father has been asking you for more than a year to join the family firm. He needs you if the business is to remain in family hands. For you this is where the road first forks. If your family business is to stay in the family, you have to make a choice about your life and career. Before you do, however, look long and hard at the advantages and disadvantages.

As with any new career move, going into a family business isn't a ticket to a lifetime of personal and professional happiness. However, the odds can be greatly stacked in your favor if you have made the decision for the right reasons, have the right skill set to contribute, and have thoroughly checked that the dynamics within the business and among family members are healthy. It's also important that the business have a positive outlook for both the short and long term, or, if not, that changes can realistically be made. The business also must have room for another family member. But let's look at each of these factors individually and from the heir-apparent's perspective.

GOOD REASONS, BAD REASONS

Looking at the prospect of joining a family business is like evaluating a balance sheet: there's some good news and some bad news. As the successor, you need to be genuinely interested in your business and the products or services it offers. If your business manufactures something as unsexy as widgets and you have absolutely no interest in building or marketing them, there's little chance you'll attain great personal and business satisfaction in dealing with them day in and day out. You're not likely to put in the necessary hours or make any valuable contribution. The most successful family businesses are run by owners who work not just hard but extraordinarily long hours. They don't punch a time clock; they work around the clock if necessary. They know they occasionally need to put their family relationships on the line for the business' sake. They do it because they love the business.

Why is such all-consuming dedication critical? Because you need to do your own job and be sure others do theirs. You need to set a positive example for your employees and family. You also need to know what's happening in your industry and in the economy at large so that you can add your imprint and be ready to make changes when necessary. Finally, you need to feel that working in the business will improve rather than hurt familial relationships.

Here's a litmus test of how you decide:

- First, test your passion quotient: How much do you really care about manufacturing, selling and thinking about widgets or whatever the business produces or sells? Think about getting up each morning and going to work selling and marketing widgets. Will you have the energy and enthusiasm to do so? Or is another profession tugging at your heartstrings?
- Second, analyze your familial relationships. If you've always fought with a sister who's been working in the business and attained some degree of authority, you might be wise to go elsewhere. Or you could consider working in a different part of the business if boundaries are discussed and agreed upon in advance, possibly in writing.
- Third, make sure this isn't the only place you can get a job that offers you the amenities you feel you're entitled to but haven't necessarily earned. Perhaps the worst reasons to join a business are because it offers you: a) power, money, perks and special

treatment you wouldn't normally obtain working for another company, b) a way to enhance a fragile ego through a connection to your parent's drive and dreams, or c) a chance to even the score with a relative you never liked.

If you follow the family path for the wrong reasons, it might be a road of no return. You're likely to be found out before too long and possibly become a prisoner of your own entrapment because of the lifestyle, paycheck, company car, country club and other perks to which you become accustomed. Even if your firm can't afford to shower you with the riches of the wealthiest family business owners such as the Tisches or Lauders, you're likely to get and expect more in working for Mom or Dad than if you worked for a comparable nonfamily firm, which probably wouldn't tolerate any slack in your work ethic or attitude.

The worst part about going into a family firm for the wrong reasons is that, by the time you wished you could forgo the throne for a place of employment that offers you true personal satisfaction, it may be too late and you won't have the skills to do something else. The only item on your résumé might be that you worked for your parents. Nothing is more detrimental to an individual's self-worth, to his family and your family business than a lack of true zeal.

- Fourth, be certain that if you go into the business, you can make a contribution. This requires the right set of skills, be they financial, managerial, engineering, retailing, technical or legal. You also need a healthy attitude and good interpersonal traits so that you can work well with others inside and outside the business.
- Fifth, you must be willing to meet and comply with appropriate entry and ongoing work standards. The smartest parents will establish in advance certain minimum entry requirements that pertain to you as well as to anybody joining the firm. You don't want anyone to think you're being favored, or resentment will build and morale will suffer. Such standards might be a high school, college or graduate degree, a specific grade point average, and certain work experiences both outside and inside the firm for a specific number of years. Most important, once you join, you should be willing to be treated and evaluated like other employees. You should report through a regular chain of command instead of just to Mom or Dad. You should have to adhere

to regular business hours, dress codes and other company policies. You should receive regular evaluations by a nonrelative. You must recognize the importance of earning each promotion, rather than receiving one due merely to your lineage.

- Sixth, your parents (and/or other involved older-generation relatives) must want you to come into the business. Sometimes they don't.
- Seventh, check out the forecast of your industry to decide if it holds promise for the business' future success and consider whether your business can surmount any problems.
- Eighth, ask yourself the following questions before you finalize your decision:
  - Is this the position I'd put at the top of my wish list or is there something else I'd rather do professionally?
  - Do I feel a tug to enter just to please my parents, grandparents or because of family tradition?
  - Is this the only place that will hire me and offer me so many entitlements?
  - Am I equipped to join or do I need some more work experience or another degree?
  - Do I like and respect all the relatives working in the firm?
  - Will I like being with my family so much?
  - Will I be able to get along with relatives whether active or inactive in the business, or are old rivalries likely to resurface and even intensify?
  - Do I respect the nonfamily members in management, and am I prepared to work underneath or alongside them and possibly be critiqued by them?
  - Do I want to run the business some day? Am I equipped to do so?

Edsel B. Ford II, who joined the four-generation automobile manufacturing business and left after many years of employment to pursue personal interests, may have said it best: ". . . the one thing I do know is that my father's, my grandfather's, and great-grandfather's achievements are not mine—that no matter how tall they were, I still have to do my own growing. And that is the challenge, and the opportunity of a family business."

From the leader's vantage point, it's now your turn to ask some tough questions before you allow your potential scion to join. You'll both be much happier in the end:

- Is he joining for the right reasons or is it a job of last resort and the easy way out? Is it a way to support him and keep him dependent on me? Is he the only person around to whom I can pass on the business?
- Has he earned the right credentials, both in terms of education and work habits, or have I given too much leeway?
- Is he qualified or would I turn him down were he not a family member?
- Do I believe he has a contribution to make? Does he seem passionate about our company's product or service?
- Will his joining hurt or help our relationship and that with other family members?
- Will I and others be able to critique him honestly and respect his contributions?
- Does he have the right temperament to work with other family members, nonfamily managers and employees, suppliers and vendors?
- Do I want him running the firm someday?
- Can he run the firm someday?

Reality Check: Successors can make an intelligent decision about whether to join only if they examine and understand their motivations, assess their potential contribution, and consider the company's and industry's financial stability and growth prospects. The senior generation should go through a similar soul-searching about potential successors. The more thought that goes into the decision, the better for the business as well as for the family.

8. What is the most propitious time for a successor or other family member to come on board?

Sometimes it seems as though sales and sales alone should be the focus of your family firm. In the early years when you're building your business, that makes sense. But that focus must shift and expand along with the business. The firm grows and needs to professionalize. At some point you may need to step back and hand your business over to someone younger and perhaps a little wiser to take the firm to the next level. The best way to do this is to plan a succession of your choice that you can oversee. Unfortunately, this was not the case for Daniel Driscoll, 57, now president of Beitler McKee Optical Co., a Pittsburgh, Pa.-based firm founded in 1922 that was purchased by his father William Earl in the mid-40s. Dan was thrown head first into his family's wholesale eyeglasses, contact lenses and examination equipment company in a crisis when his father died suddenly in 1978. Fortuitously, his father's will stipulated that Dan was to take over the firm, but it was a mandate his siblings resented.

Dan was determined this would not happen with his successors. He wanted to make sure there would be a smooth and well-planned transition without acrimony. His son Bill, 29, and son-in-law Richard Hughes, 28, already work in the business. Bill and his wife as well as his three siblings and their spouses are addressing succession and using professional advice.

The family consensus is that Bill will become president in three to five years as his father steps down. "When I went to college in 1987, I didn't want anything to do with the family business. It was an ulcer factory that was bottom-line oriented. There was a lack of vision for the future," Bill says. All that changed in 1988 when his father experienced a spiritual renewal. He became aware that he did not need to keep his Christian faith separate from his work; he could live out his Christian faith in the workplace. Fellowship of Companies for Christ International, an organization of CEOs trying to run their businesses according to Biblical principles, played an instrumental role in his paradigm shift.

After Bill received his degree in secondary education from the College of William and Mary in 1991, he went to work for the family business on a temporary basis while looking for a teaching post. He saw firsthand how the company had changed. "My father was much more humble, more sensitive to the needs of employees and to different situations. We were focused on more than the bottom line." Bill was interviewed by the sales manager, unbeknownst to his father, and was hired to do outside sales. Since then, he's worked his way through most of the other divisions, currently oversees marketing and customer service, and is becoming more involved in the day-to-day management.

The family has also been doing succession planning. Dan has given his wife half his shares in the firm and each child has been given seven percent of the voting shares. Although Bill is prepared to take over the presidency, the Driscolls have decided that if a rift occurs among siblings and their spouses in the transition of control, family relationships are more important than the business.

If your family's business is thriving, it's easy to look at it and think you, too, can have that magic touch. What a great place it would be to work. You could really add a lot to make it grow more. But, wait a minute, the time may not be right to bring you on board. Inside the business, operations may not look or be so rosy. Resources might be stretched. Once-exciting opportunities might be morphing into problems, and employee morale might be at its lowest ebb. Not exactly the best time to come into the firm, you think. On the other hand, if you have the right skills and experience, you may be needed more than ever.

While many successors join the business straight from high school or college, many experts say gaining outside experience is a must before coming into the family firm. Generally, outside experience can offer a scion numerous long-term advantages. It makes you more attractive as a potential employee and gives you some bargaining room. In working elsewhere, you'll expose yourself to another company or industry, then consciously decide to enter the family business because you prefer it and believe you can add value from what you've learned. Perhaps prior experience can give you the knowledge to suggest a different way to market a product, a new way of connecting with customers, or an alternative to your firm's manufacturing process. By working elsewhere, you've also been judged by nonfamily members. Your ego may have been bruised in the process, but in the long term you will have greater self-confidence and be able to deal better with others, particularly when you're in a leadership position. You'll be much more sensitive and you'll probably listen better. Perhaps most important, nonfamily employees within your family's firm will know that you've earned your way into the business because of your training and successes elsewhere, rather than because of your birthright.

How long you work elsewhere should depend on what you're learning and doing, but typically three to five years represent a good timetable. You want to have earned at least one promotion and developed new and practical skills that can be useful to your family firm. You will probably have experienced at least one or two significant failures, which offer good learning experiences and prove to you the validity of risk taking.

While you're working in another company, keep abreast of your family business' goings-on. Check in regularly with Dad or Mom or Uncle Ted on how the business is changing, who's doing what, what its long-term strategy is. You're not meddling but rather helping to mind the store from afar and not losing contact with something you care about and which could one day be your legacy.

In addition to gaining experience elsewhere, you need to come into the firm when there's an appropriate opening, not because you feel ready and want Dad or Mom to create a position for you. Strolling into the business when you wish and as you wish sends a terrible message to family already in the business and to other employees. It also sets you up for a situation that is destined to fail. You'll probably have little to do, be bored, lose self-confidence and risk losing others' respect. When a proper job materializes, be sure you don't report immediately to Dad or any other family member, but to someone who can mentor and critique you objectively.

Joining should also be done when three factors that involve the family network are in alignment, somewhat like when the moon and the sun are positioned precisely in a row to produce an eclipse. What's critical are: good communication among family members, a mechanism to resolve the inevitable conflicts that arise when multiple family members work together, and the need for additional management talent beyond what currently exists in the business.

Reality Check: If you decide you're ready to join the family firm, do so only if the time is propitious. As with a nonfamily business, you shouldn't be entitled to a position if there's no opening. Wait until you have the right professional and interpersonal skills; wait until the company is at the right stage of development so you can contribute. Patience is a virtue in family business as well as in life.

9. Should a rocky relationship with a child, parent or sibling while growing up be a deterrent to entering the business? Is it possible to repair these relationships?

Tumultuous relationships between siblings don't necessarily dissipate when you're older and in business together. In fact, differences may be exacerbated. Even when brothers have a good relationship, some just know that they could never work side by side. Two brothers who had such an epiphany early on are Jim Abraham, 26, owner of Pittsburgh, Pa.-based Bee Control Inc., a pest control company, and Matt, 24, his brother, owner of Bee Pro, a similar company and friendly competitor.

The brothers made a conscious decision not to work together in the family firm, Bee Control, founded by their father Kevin in the 1980s. After Jim finished Allegheny College where he majored in economics with a minor in biology and chemistry, he came into the firm to run it for his father. However, in 1994, Jim asked to take a hiatus from the business to travel out West.

Matt, who attended Pennsylvania State University, was asked to come in and run the business in his brother's absence. However, when Jim returned in 1995, he stepped back into his former position, and one year later purchased the firm. But what about Matt?

"Our father," says Jim, "discouraged partnerships. Partnerships in general can be a bad idea unless the two are extremely compatible, and partnerships between brothers can be troublesome because there may be fighting over duties, liabilities and resources." The brothers found they bugged each other so Matt picked up and started a competitive business in 1997. "The split was friendly but spirited," says Jim.

The two admit this was the best arrangement to maintain their sanity and relationship. "We're alike because we have similar values and ethics," says Jim. "But," Matt adds, "our management styles are completely opposite. Jim is more detailed. He thinks things through by steps. I'm more impulsive. I jump in and sort things out after the fact. Jim and I are both strong willed. I like my way and he likes his way. It's a lot easier going into business separately."

Initially, Jim was upset that his brother started a competing firm, but in time realized it wouldn't affect his business. "I was happy to see him doing something he enjoyed and it was beneficial for him." That doesn't mean their paths don't cross. Often the two may bid against one another for the same job. This is when they know they must consciously separate business from personal life.

In an interesting twist, Matt recently became engaged, and the couple plans to move to Cincinnati. Before they leave Pittsburgh, however, Matt will sell his business to Jim. Says Jim, "I won't miss him as a competitor, but I'll sure miss him as my brother."

Many children have a rocky relationship with their parents and each other at some point during their growing-up years, particularly the teenage ones. Yet even if differences have been extreme, it may be possible to rectify the relationship. There's a big caveat, however. Unresolved anger may not dissipate when your son or daughter comes to work with you. In fact, that anger may become detrimental to your firm. The same is true of siblings with poor relationships.

What's critical in the healing process is for both sides to be aware of their differences, difficulties and ensuing problems. This requires honesty rather than secrecy, open communication about different expectations, and an ability to remain flexible, grow and change. Each person needs to acknowledge his strengths (write them down if it helps), build on positive attributes, and downplay and even eliminate weaknesses (you can write these down as well). This requires hard work, time and a good dose of humor, which too often is tossed aside during family squabbles.

Often the best way to resolve considerable differences is to bring in an objective outsider who can listen to each side, help you see the importance of agreeing to disagree, and resolve pressing issues openly rather than by sabotaging each other's efforts or forcing other family members and nonfamily employees to choose sides.

Sometimes, there are red flags that indicate a rocky relationship can't be repaired and that working together is untenable. These include significant conflict over differences of opinion, lack of respect for the person and his accomplishments, or any substance abuse problems, says psychologist Lawrence Kogan."It's not as important to look at the past, however. The key to whether the relationship can work today is whether things are improving in the present. Are the father and son relating to each other differently and making substantial and healthy changes?"

Following are 10 steps to repair a rocky relationship:

1. Communicate by phone daily or weekly and put in writing what takes place so you have a record (like a journal).
2. Meet regularly, either weekly, semi-monthly or monthly and keep each other apprised of what you're doing.
3. Begin statements with "I" rather than with "you" to avoid heightening hostilities.
4. Ask questions to show you're interested in what your parent/child/sibling has to say and what he does.
5. Invite each other's participation in and understanding of what you do.
6. Encourage risk-taking, since it's the only way the company will grow and change. Then resist pointing fingers when things occasionally go wrong.
7. Inspire individuality since differences will also make your company stronger rather than weaker.
8. Agree to disagree, respectfully.

9. Treat each other with dignity. Remember, you are colleagues and business partners. Be polite and use good manners as you would when dealing with someone outside the family.
10. Avoid what family business expert Dr. Murray Bowen describes as triangulation, or bringing a third person into a two-person relationship to defuse tension. Adding a third wheel usually prevents the original twosome from resolving their conflict.

Reality Check: As long as you care about your family members and opt for open communication, it's possible to change old unhealthy patterns in a relationship. But you must be able to listen to one another, remain flexible to each other's opinions and way of conducting business, meet regularly despite disagreements, be honest but not hurtful, and treat each other as you would treat a nonfamily colleague.

10. How does a successor prove that he is capable and got the job based on ability rather than genes?

Donald Trump initially worked for his father Fred, who first built houses, then added apartments. Few remember that. Instead, they equate a now fabulously successful real estate and gaming empire only with the younger, flashy New Yorker. How did that happen? Part of the reason is Donald Trump's zealous ambition to prove himself and expand the family business in Manhattan. While his over-optimism may have contributed to the business' plummet into bankruptcy, his abundance of confidence spurred him to bring it back to a new higher level, all of which he chronicles in his autobiographies, *The Art of the Deal* (Random House, 1997) and *Trump: Surviving at the Top* (Random House, 1990). His father turned over the company's major development decisions to his second-born son, according to Jerome Tuccille's book, *Trump: The Saga of America's Most Powerful Real Estate Baron* (D.I. Fine, 1985). For both his successes and failures, Donald Trump had no one else to credit or blame.

Suddenly the founder of a large wholesale furniture firm dies with no succession plan in place. The torch passes to his only living successor, a member of the next generation: his 29-year-old daughter who has a degree in business from a major university and who worked for a bank in the East for two years. The buzz around town is that she got the job because of who she is. Everyone thought the senior vice president of the firm was slated to take charge. Now everyone is worried: Who is this person? Is the daughter tough, is she tenacious, is she persistent, or is the strikingly attractive brunette just a major shareholder who will depend on the professionals in the firm to tell her what to do? Worse yet, will she make decisions on her own without proper information or guidance?

And so it goes. This is the albatross any successor who enters a family firm must carry, whether through a well-planned succession or a spur-of-the-moment entry. Many people will never be convinced that a successor got a job based on ability rather than on the right gene pool, regardless of the facts, an impressive curriculum vitae and laudable work experience. In many cases, if you're the parent trying to do the convincing or the successor trying to make your case, you may as well not try. You're wasting valuable time.

Nevertheless, you should be concerned about the opinions of key employees with whom you may have to work, customers, suppliers, vendors and other professionals you would consider colleagues.

Actions speak far louder than words. Get as good an education as possible, work outside the family business and round up some achievements. Wait for an opening in the company rather than have a position created for you. Once there, work very hard and passionately. Come in early and stay late. Prove that you love your company and know it well. A healthy work ethic is tangible and something everybody will chart. Remember that first impressions are long lasting.

Be prepared that when you start you may have to begin at the bottom (or at least not at the top immediately), unless you've been in the workforce for several years and have special expertise to share. On the job, listen raptly to everyone who has advice or questions and ask lots of questions yourself. Be compassionate rather than condescending. Mingle with employees, and don't act like a prima donna by driving a flashy car, wearing expensive designer outfits or bragging about the last vacation you took to some swank resort, or the tony country club you just joined with its tournament-level golf course.

Furthermore, don't ask for preferential treatment by tossing around your relationship: "I'm the boss' son" and referring to the boss as Dad or Mom. Don't go outside the system and don't report (or tattletale) to your parent. Keep learning as you move up through the ranks and broaden your vision by gaining a global perspective and understanding different cultures.

Go through a formal appraisal system so you get evaluated by somebody who will be objective, such as key managers or an independent board. Gradually, take on more authority, but only as you earn it. Do not allow your parents to promote you to vice president six months out of college. Learn to motivate and mentor others. This is an important mark of a good leader and successor. Eventually you'll line up your own loyal and capable team. Be prepared as well to accept responsibility for failures and successes rather than passing the proverbial buck.

By following this game plan, people will get the message that you deserve to be in the business and that you're more than just a member of the lucky sperm club. Along the way, you're likely to impress your colleagues, superiors, parents and yes, even yourself.

Reality Check: If people need to be convinced that you earned your stripes rather than had them handed to you, remain undeterred. First, it's a given that you'll make a litany of mistakes, but there are steps you can take to establish an impressive track record and to prove that you are a modern-day executive playing by modern-day rules of the game. These include getting a good education, gaining outside work experience, joining the business only when there's an opening, working hard, learning all you can, listening well to everyone from the bottom up, following the company's prescribed evaluation and promotion system, and being patient with yourself and others. Your time to run the show should come if you're willing and able to go through the paces to get and keep the lead.

11. Should a successor or in-law joining a family business have an employment contract?

"Our family business is a business-first family business," says Travis Burch, 50, president and CEO of Burch-Lowe Inc. in Atlanta, Ga. As part of that philosophy, Burch feels that successors, whether blood relatives or in-laws, should come into the firm with prior experience, start in an entry-level position, work hard and remain at the company because they're qualified and do a good job, not because they're related to the boss or enjoy having the perks and prestige.

Travis and his younger brother Gregg, a president and COO of the company's largest division, both came to work at the company more than 24 years ago and within nine months of each other. The business is in the construction equipment industry, selling, renting and servicing products such as asphalt pavers, compaction equipment, wheel loaders and hydraulic excavators. The company employs 280 and does between $75 million and $100 million in annual revenue. Each sibling had previously worked in the business during summers and college, but neither was given a contract upon entering full-time. Their sister Milbre Burch followed a different career path as a professional and nationally recognized storyteller.

There are reasons Travis feels that employment contracts usually don't accomplish what their crafters intended them to do. Too often they contain a negative connotation. "What are you really trying to accomplish?" he asks. "So much of what's put in the contract deals with these issues—expectations each party has for the relationship, compensation and performance, how the parties will handle conditions for the termination of the agreement, non-compete clauses." Is it appropriate to start a relationship by negotiating issues that contemplate failure? While contracts can define issues in clinical business terms, are they an acceptable substitute for trust? Do they ensure that good business decisions will be made and good business practices will be followed just because they exist?

There are exceptions in which his company has used employment contracts, Travis says, but for very specific situations. Two of those are:

- To attract employees with bonuses and other performance incentives who might otherwise not come to work and to tie them to the company for a set period. "We did that with an acquisition we made," Burch explains. "We wanted to hire the president of a company we acquired that was a competitor. The contract made him feel secure, and five years later he's still with us. The initial contract was for two years and it became self-renewing. We didn't want him to think we'd drain his brain and toss him out on the street. It no longer defines the terms of our relationship because we've had time to develop a trusting relationship."
- To keep a senior team when a company division is sold so that the members stay during the transition.

Would Travis ever want a contract for himself? "Yes, if we ever sell the business," he says.

Family firms can be a hotbed of family problems. If relationships are rocky or a successor is unsure whether he wants to come into the firm but feels compelled to do so, he may want an employment contract. Some experts contend that a contract is the first step to sitting down, structuring and communicating the parameters of involvement in the business. Others say it may cause ill feelings and start things off on the wrong foot.

Most family business consultants do not advocate having a family member sign an employment contract for an entry-level position because few employees, family or nonfamily, are held to a rigid set of rules upon joining. Typically, there should be an across-the-board all or nothing policy on contracts for family and nonfamily employees. Coming in at a higher level or being an in-law in the family business may warrant a contract, however, but usually only if comparable nonfamily members sign such a document.

If the generations agree to sign a contract, they need to decide in advance what its purpose is and what's to be included. Ideally, each side should be represented by separate legal counsel. Points to address in the contract include starting salary, year-end bonus, commission if applicable, stock options, voting rights, perks, length of time for which the contract is valid, reasons for promotion, demotion and termination, and a noncompete clause.

The most common reasons to sign an employment contract are to protect the business' proprietary assets from competitors rather than motivate someone to work hard. Employment contracts set forth the employee's compensation and severance rights; yet pieces of paper cannot inspire diligence and hard work. Pieces of paper also cannot assure that family member relationships remain favorable. Therefore, you should focus your efforts on creating understandings that lead to long-term success in your relationships and mutual understanding of expectations and objectives.

Perhaps more important than a written contract is for the two generations to have a clear understanding about their positions in the company and its direction. Topics can include:

- Each person's role in the company.
- Each person's expectations.
- When and how evaluations are conducted, how often promotions and raises are offered, and whether bonuses are given.
- The company's mission and long-term strategy.

To make these points clearer and more effective, they should be written down, periodically reviewed and occasionally rewritten as a successor gains experience and racks up achievements, and as the business and industry in which it operates change.

There's something else besides a contract or verbal agreement that family members can draft to put each other at ease as they begin to work together. They can write their own personal and business mission statements, and then discuss and agree to them.

For example, a son who knows that his Dad always interrupts and second-guesses his actions may suggest that he be allowed to make all decisions in his department, though he must run certain critical matters by his immediate supervisor. A father who rarely takes vacations out of fear that the company may not survive without him may have to agree to take four weeks annually, stay away and avoid calling the office, unless others seek his counsel. Tough rules, but important.

Reality Check: A contract is only as valid as its contents, but in most cases it's unlikely to motivate a reluctant successor or in-law or force a meddling founder to alter his ways. Instead, the family members who are about to begin working together can test if they are able to communicate. They can do so by drafting a statement, agreeing to the different points, signing, and periodically updating it. It gives them food for thought as well as some structure to their different roles.

12. Where should a successor start in the family business and how much should he be paid? How should responsibilities be determined?

There's probably no one right way to start a business, but there are some definite steps that can be taken once that business begins to grow to keep it in family hands. An appreciation of antiques turned into a family business for husband and wife team Samuel and Sally Pennington, who started *Maine Antique Digest* in 1973 in Waldoboro, Me. But Samuel, editor, and Sally, managing editor, never dreamed they'd be working with three of their five children some day. Each child worked elsewhere first: Katherine was business manager of a theater company and later an English teacher; Samuel Clayton was a cable TV-installer who has a degree in theater, and Sarah was office manager of a printing company.

When the children came into the firm, they took different jobs: Clayton works full-time on the editorial staff and is acting editor; Sarah Pennington McCleary is the business and circulation manager and works part-time, and Katherine, also on the editorial staff, is a part-time copyeditor. While each child was in college, the senior Penningtons started giving nonvoting shares of stock to them. Sam and Sally kept all voting shares. Today, whether active or inactive in the firm (Nellie and Mary are not in the business), a total of 30 percent of nonvoting shares has been given equally to each child.

Every year each child (who owns six percent of the shares) receives six percent of the profits, if there are any. In terms of salary, Sam and Sally don't believe in paying each child in the business the same amount. "Their salaries are pegged to what they do, their hours and their length of time in the business," says Sam, who adds that he and his wife also decided a year ago that they wanted the children in the firm to assume more responsibility. "My wife and I are gradually backing out. We raised their salaries a bit and cut ours," Sam adds.

Perhaps no issue gets an owner's blood boiling more than deciding on salaries for family members. This becomes a particular bugaboo when a family member steps into a firm and expects the same standard of living as his parents or more than he's worth in the outside world. Family business owners tend to have black or white views on this matter; some pay too much, some pay too little. Both approaches can have damaging effects, but here are some suggestions for how to diffuse this delicate issue.

Each company should have a policy based on the goals and values of the family. In the long term, the best answer is that family members should be paid on the basis of what they do, hours they put in, degrees they have, experience they've had outside the firm, and special skills they possess. If, for instance, a member has a very specific computer skill, it might be worth paying more for that talent because the supply of outside professionals is limited.

In almost all cases, family members should be compensated and receive perks the same as nonfamily employees in similar positions. Be sure that the pay is competitive for your industry. You can give family members other sources of income to augment their salaries if you feel that is appropriate as a parent. Don't confuse compensation for services with gifts. You'll set a terrible example for the next generation.

Family members should learn to live within the means they can obtain elsewhere based on their abilities. If you overpay them, they become addicted to the money and may feel trapped in the firm. Inactive family members will come to believe that the actives take advantage of their employment. If you underpay them, you demoralize and demotivate them.

When you employ more than one child in the business, setting compensation can get difficult. Should you pay each of your children the same? Some business owners pay all their children identical sums, regardless of longevity with the firm, their positions or their contributions. Some do so when their children have a history of working well together and not competing. Others do so precisely because their children have had a history of competing and paying them equally diffuses rivalry.

The downside to equal compensation for disparate contributions can be tremendous discord. Paying the same for different contributions, different talents and experience can cause jealousies and rifts. Imagine how you would feel if your older sibling barely passes muster working on the loading dock while you run the firm, but you each get paid the same.

If you are unsure what to do, a board of independent directors can provide invaluable advice. If the board sets the standards, the family is less likely to squawk. Or you can form a compensation committee to set the parameters for salaries, perks, benefits and life insurance for family members. A third strategy is to hire a compensation specialist.

Where should a family member start with the firm? From an objective standpoint, it should be obvious that a successor should start in a position or job commensurate with his education, skills and abilities. However, too often a parent will put a child through a six-month whirlwind tour of all of the company's major departments and then promote him to vice president. In reality, because he is not ready, a child becomes a vice president of odd jobs, reporting to his parent. It's only natural to want your children to move up rapidly in your organization and to work directly with you. But take care not to move family members up the corporate ladder faster than their performance and experience merit. Don't give them a position until they have earned it and don't give a title simply because they are your children.

If you want to groom a family member to take over one day, you must permit that person to develop the leadership skills and gain the business savvy necessary for that role. Certainly, your potential successors should be given increasing responsibility and authority, but only as they become capable of assuming it. Consider the 25-year-old daughter of one business owner who was promoted to co-head of personnel (along with the nonfamily manager who had that role) just six months after graduating from college. Was she really capable of handling that role for a 1,000-employee business? What signal does that send to the employees? Perhaps more important, what signal does that send to the 25-year-old daughter?

Reality Check: Compensation is a sticky issue. Some owners feel it's only right to compensate all their children in the business equally. Others compensate on the basis of experience, skill set, hours put in and the type of work they do. Both systems have a downside. If all children are compensated equally, it can diffuse the conflict of one receiving more. However, one sibling who does more work than the others or who is in a position of more responsibility may resent receiving the same remuneration as everybody else. Whatever the policy, it should be decided upfront before anyone enters. The worst compensation mistake: paying family members for doing nothing. The worst starting position: one for which the family member is underqualified.

13. When and how is it appropriate for a successor to make suggestions for changes in the business?

"When they've got something important to say," is probably how Sam Walton, the late founder of Wal-Mart, would wisely respond. In his autobiography, *Sam Walton: Made in America* (Doubleday, 1992), written with John Huey, Walton says one of the hallmarks of the company's strong corporate culture is its weekly meeting where employees, known as associates, can bring up important business issues that are on their minds. "Its purpose is to let everyone know what the rest of the company is up to. If we can, we find heroes among our associates in the stores and bring them in to Bentonville, where we praise them in front of the whole meeting. But . . . I like to hear what our weaknesses are, where we aren't doing as well as we should and why. I like to see a problem come up and then hear suggestions as to how it can be corrected. The Saturday morning meeting is where we discuss and debate much of our philosophy and our management strategy: it is the focal point of all our communications efforts. It's where we share ideas we've picked up from various places."

In addition to the open forums, the author shares his 10 rules of success in the book, one of which is to listen to everyone in the company and design ways to get them to talk. "To push responsibility down in your organization, and to force good ideas to bubble up within it, you **must** listen to what your associates are trying to tell you."

Should successors in a family business be seen and not heard, at least while they are young and inexperienced? The timing of a family member becoming highly vocal with others should depend, as with nonfamily employees, on a mix of factors:

- Prior work experience outside the firm.
- The time they have spent in the business.
- Age and position in the company.

Generally, you should take a wait-and-see attitude for a while after joining the business. It's more important that you listen well and absorb all you can rather than do a lot of talking in the first year. Shooting from the hip and making quick judgments and comments can do you and the firm more harm than good.

You should get your feet wet, meet as many people as possible, see who does what, ask as many questions as you can about why and how business is conducted, learn about short- and long-term goals, and get a clear understanding of what shape your business and the industry are in from both a financial and nonfinancial view.

By following this procedure, which one advisor terms "getting smart," you will gain an understanding of your entire operation and cast of characters, hone your leadership skills and gradually gain a sense of authority.

You should also take into account what you hear and see around you and learn what to discount as gossip. How do other employees or managers make suggestions? Do they go to their immediate boss or straight to the top? Do they offer ideas verbally or put them in writing? Which people seem most eager to embrace new ways of doing business and which ones seem most reluctant?

Of course, this does not mean you should be so quiet and meek that you barely are noticeable in your first few months or year on the job. It does mean, however, that you'll make more intelligent suggestions and contributions, and more likely be viewed as a hard-working team member rather than as someone who is out for personal glory. Suggestions based on experience, responsibility, contributions and authority will be taken much more seriously.

Finally, be wise about how you make recommendations or point out deficiencies. Don't threaten or place blame. Be humble. Ask why something is done the way it is being done so that you can be sure you fully understand the situation. Make suggestions by asking whether a different way might be better rather than denigrating the current approach and demanding that a change be made. Take your time; you're in the firm for the long haul if all goes according to plan.

Reality Check: Though your enthusiasm may soar sky-high and years of outside experience may number in the double digits, you should rein in some of your suggestions and criticisms until you've had time to plant your feet firmly on the family business' soil. Roll up your sleeves, show you're willing to study the new landscape, its culture and players; work hard; and become a member of a team. Then you can open your mouth and offer constructive ideas and criticisms. Be careful and nonthreatening in the way you make suggestions for change and understand that you will not always get your way. Accept that those with the power have the right to offer a counterpoint.

14. How should a successor address his father, mother, uncle or other relative while in the office? Does it make a difference?

Four years ago 22-year-old Emily Johnson joined Taylor Johnson Associates in Chicago, a public relations, advertising and graphics firm started by her mother Deborah Taylor Johnson. She came in thinking the job represented an interim position, so she referred to her mother casually as "Mom." After a few months, she became more interested and entrenched in the job and felt there was a definite need for her talents. She remained full-time. When she did, she switched of her own volition to calling her mother by the more formal, more professional "Deborah" at work. The tactic was effective. "When I was at a meeting and there were 10 of us sitting around the table, it seemed inappropriate to be saying 'Mom.' I also didn't want others to think I would be getting preferential treatment."

Calling her mother by her first name also set a boundary. "It kept our work and personal lives apart, which was healthier for both of us." Her mother concurs. "I had never thought about the matter, but after Emily made the decision, I agreed it made a lot of sense. It helped cut the umbilical cord. The staff also told me they liked the idea," says Deborah. It just makes their relationship in business much sharper.

Before walking in that first day, before making that first sale, before performing that first service, you must establish your credibility, even if you have all the right credentials and qualifications. That credibility can be destroyed in a flash when a supplier, employee or important client hears you call the boss "Mom" or "Dad" or, worse yet, "Mommy" or "Daddy." This can be perceived as childish and make you sound like a dependent.

Many family business members try to maintain relationships at work with other family members on a businesslike level. They prefer to call a parent they work with by the first name, title or by "Mr." or "Ms."

The choice, however, may depend to a large extent on the culture of the company. What's more important to employees, suppliers or clients, however, is how the generations interact, whether they share a mutual respect, and whether they follow the chain of command within the firm's hierarchy or try to circumvent it for their advantage.

"But," you ask, "isn't it important that we capitalize on the image and fact of being a family-owned business?" Having family members address each other as "Mom," "Dad" or "Daughter" clearly evidences family involvement in the business. Absolutely, it's important that everyone know that your business is family owned. You should let everyone know that family members are involved, along with the continuity that that fact connotes. However, you should avoid giving the potential negative impressions of nepotism and favoritism. It's important to foster the appearance that you represent a successful company run by professionals, some of whom happen to be related. If that means calling your mother, father or uncle by a first name in the office, so be it. People, especially employees, will perceive you unfavorably if you invoke "Dad said . . ." or "Mom won't . . ." in your conversations. Professionalism need not be sterile or override the pluses of family involvement, but it is important in maintaining business relationships.

Reality Check: The matter may seem trivial, but how family members address you or any other relative sends a clear message to employees and outside contacts about your company's degree of professionalism. Calling your father or mother "Dad" or "Mom" implies a small Mom-and-Pop operation and suggests that family matters may take precedence over objective business decisions. It may be tough to use first names or the even more formal "Mr." or "Mrs." rather than familial names, but doing so will generate more respect for you and the business.

15. How can a successor be judged as a fellow employee and not just as a son or daughter of the founder or head?

When Debra Izenstark joined her mother Gail's direct mail marketing business in Skokie, Il., six years after it was started, she knew she'd have to work hard and pull her own weight if the other employees at Direct Mail Source were to take her seriously. She also knew she had some factors working in her favor. She had previously worked at two companies. She was working toward her MBA at night, which lent credibility, and the company was small so that there wouldn't be any slack time for taking advantage of Mom as boss. Twelve years after joining the company, she has learned other lessons—to refer to her mother as "Gail" rather than "Mom" since it sounds more professional, never to ask for favors and not to take an excessive amount of time off from work. "Don't do anything you wouldn't want another employee to do. You earn respect by your example," says Debra, now a vice president.

The surest route to win friends, influence people and gain respect remains a combination of ingredients—hard work, competence, an engaging personality and a bit of humility concerning the perception (or fact) that your genes certainly helped a little—or a lot—in gaining employment. But even with those attributes you may never totally escape being judged by reference to your parents and having your achievements belittled by comparison to your parents' prior ones. For the same reason, no matter how good a job you do, you still may not receive all the credit for your successes since some skeptics may think you received a big break or were handed an opportunity on a silver platter.

One way to get some well-deserved but not overinflated recognition is by thoughtfully developing a plan that helps the company overall rather than by just pushing yourself into the limelight. Among some specifics that are likely to impress others: if you can articulate a new or improved direction for your company, modify an existing strategy or identify information needed to help the business solve a specific problem. However, you must time your move correctly. Your plans to make your mark will backfire if you do so too soon before you're entrenched in the firm and have established credibility as a hard-working employee. You also should approach this challenge slowly and cautiously. People may react negatively to it simply because they don't like change or because you are the one suggesting it. Therefore, the plan should be a team project and others should receive credit for their involvement in its development. You should test each aspect of it and get input from key managers and family before you actually propose it.

There are many additional ways to be judged as a successful employee, not a silver-spoon successor. For example:

- Don't seek special treatment due to your birth status.
- Work harder than everyone else.

- Don't accept perks, like a company car or club membership, unless they are offered to nonfamily employees who work at a similar level.
- Don't go over your supervisor's head unless it is absolutely necessary or unless that is part of the company's culture.
- Don't claim credit for or brag about your achievements. They will be noticed and recognized without your having to toot your own horn. Give credit to others when you can.
- Don't be a namedropper as it relates to senior family members. If you want to be judged on your own merits, don't constantly invoke the names of Mom, Dad, my brother, etc.
- Volunteer to help other employees with their jobs and coach them, but with humility.
- Report to a supervisor other than a relative if at all possible and insist on receiving periodic reviews.

Reality Check: The traits that your parents said you needed to get ahead in life are also critical once you enter the business and seek approval from your colleagues and supervisors. But don't be surprised if you need to prove you're capable of even more imagination, more creativity, more success, more teamwork and more humility than nonfamily members. It's hard for many around you to think that you did it all on your own and without being on the inside track. Finally, don't even consider standing in the limelight; initially most expect you to take too many bows.

16. Should a nonfamily employee who has been with the company a long time mentor and critique the successor(s)?

Steven Good, now 42, entered his father's Chicago real estate business full time in the fall of 1981, after graduating from law school at Chicago's DePaul University. Steven's father Sheldon, now 66, and a commuter between Chicago and Palm Springs, Ca., founded the company in 1965 as a commercial brokerage firm for hard-to-sell properties. "He was enamored of the idea of selling older industrial buildings that had significant carrying costs through auctions which offered a shortened selling time and more bottom-line dollars for their owners," says Steven. When he entered the firm, it employed 20;

today it has on staff between 400 and 800 employees and a core of 100. The bulk of business is auctions of real estate. Steven credits his own success to being given numerous opportunities, and always taking advantage of each through hard work and finding a mentor. "When I was growing up there were a lot of prominent people around who told interesting stories. I learned to listen. But my first real level of mentoring occurred in college, then graduate school. I sought out people close to my Dad and to the company who could be of help to me as I was trying to find my identity and develop people skills," he says. "Sometimes my father also asked people to work with me. While I always did whatever they wanted, I questioned everything that they did."

Along the way he also recognized that while it was easy for many to serve as his mentor, as he moved up the ranks and made more money, he sometimes eclipsed them. "It's hard to watch your protege surpass you, especially when he's the boss' son," Steven says. With his ascendancy both to chairman and CEO of the auction company, Sheldon Good & Co. Auctions, and president and CEO of the parent company, Sheldon Good & Co. International, of which his Dad is chairman, Steven now finds his mentors outside the company through support groups such as the Young Presidents Organization. Even Donald Trump has served as a mentor. "I sold 88 condos for him in Palm Beach, Fl., after the auction company he first hired failed to do so. We did a terrific job for him and he helped us penetrate the New York market and be acceptable to the New York real estate club."

Through the years, Steven has turned the tables, also serving as a mentor to others and says he has never resented those who succeed. "I'm thrilled when they succeed, make lots of money and even form their own companies."

Whether it's in business or for purely social reasons, everybody can learn from an older seasoned confidant who takes a younger protege under his wing and shows him the proper ropes. When the late Princess Diana was betrothed to Prince Charles, she moved into the Queen Mother's home to learn the ins and outs of "princesshood." Unfortunately, she probably wasn't sufficiently prepared for the glare of publicity and the peering into her private life that came with her new position and at so tender an age.

The same type of guidance can be offered in a business environment with young employees or scions being taught the do's and don'ts of the business world and of their own company by an older colleague or executive. The teaching and constructive criticism that should be imparted become much more objective when offered by a nonfamily member, as long as that person truly believes he has the authority and respect to offer honest advice, which sometimes may be quite critical.

How do you choose or seek out a mentor and what should you look for? Ideally, it should be someone who is 10 to 15 years older, commands the respect of employees and senior family members, has worked at the company for years and understands how it functions, can listen well and is eager to perform this duty. You will need to meet regularly, perhaps once a month or every few weeks, at least in the beginning, to forge an understanding of where each of you is coming from and to gain the necessary trust and respect for each other. You probably will want someone of the same sex so that gender does not become an issue.

Generally, you should not seek this person's advice regarding expertise and knowledge related to your specific business function. Rather, seek input on ways to best conduct business and develop professionally—how you network inside and outside the company, what type of advancement route you can expect, how you can best take advantage of your colleagues' skills and how you need to work with your vendors and clients.

To do your part, identify your responsibilities, areas in which you feel weakest and strongest, what you want to get from the mentoring relationship in terms of personal and business growth, and decide how much honest feedback you want and can handle.

The trusted employee serving as mentor must get comfortable with his role and believe that he can be completely candid, both with the person he's mentoring and with supervisors. He should not feel that his position can be placed at risk because of the important responsibility he agrees to assume. Plus, the older generation must clearly demonstrate a willingness to carefully consider and act on recommendations that he may make.

Because today's world is so much faster paced and global, you may find it useful to have two mentors, one within the company and one from the outside. The outsider could be another business owner or acquaintance from another company, or one of your company's outside advisors. In the best cases, a true bond will develop over time, with friendship, love and success the ultimate rewards.

Reality Check: A family member, just like any nonfamily employee, can benefit greatly by developing a mentoring relationship with an older or seasoned nonfamily leader. The experienced executive imparts knowledge about the best ways to conduct business, networking, decision-making, advancement and ways to learn the ropes. A mentor helps you stay one step ahead. In case you trip up, which you probably will at various times, a mentor will be among the first to tell you what you did wrong and among the first to offer you a helping hand in getting up, brushing yourself off and moving forward.

17. How does a successor maintain a sense of privacy while working in a family business?

Few tasks are more enigmatic than maintaining a sense of privacy in a high-profile family business in a small town. Rick Hustead, one of two third-generation members of the family that owns Wall Drug Store in Wall, S.D., has been lucky. He says that it has never been that difficult to maintain a degree of privacy about himself in spite of living and working in the town of 800. He cites several reasons.

First, he grew up in the family business that his grandfather Ted, 95, started in 1931 and which now employs 235 and does about $10 million in annual sales. Everyone knew him and his family and as a result seemed to have less curiosity.

Second, he earned his stripes elsewhere and didn't start full-time at the store until 18 years ago when he was 30, which he believes gave him an important sense of credibility among employees. They respected him and his expertise, he believes, which cut down on the gossip and prying. "I approached my Dad after I had sold real estate and run a fast-food restaurant. He was also interested in me, saying the business had grown too large for him." Third, Rick and his younger brother Ted have always followed the example of their late father Bill, who lived simply and worked very hard. "My father believed in the working manager concept, which means I'm out there with employees working away and we keep our business and personal lives separate. Today, I was helping a cashier make change," says Rick, 48, who was made chairman during his father's serious illness. Rick spent two years recruiting his brother Ted from the oil fields; Ted is now president.

But Rick's ace in the hole is a conviction not to divulge too much about himself and not to listen to any chitchat. "The business is well-known and famous, but I'm not. I'm a very private person. When I went through a divorce seven years ago and got remarried, my brother asked me, 'How do you take all the talk so well?' I told him, 'I don't think about it.' And as time went on, I was out of the spotlight."

Once you enter a family business, you might find yourself living in a fishbowl of sorts. A definite lack of privacy comes with the territory. Your life comes under scrutiny from all who work in the company. It's only natural that employees, clients and suppliers are curious about your personal life—where you live, how well you live, what you earn, what your spouse and children are like, what your interests are, how capable and hardworking you really are. This can be especially true if you were "wild" as a young adult.

Current thinking among many family business experts is that you shouldn't try too hard to keep personal information under wraps since in many cases it will be wasted energy. You can try, however, to limit the most personal details revealed and gossiped about by maintaining a respectful distance. In turn, don't delve into the personal lives of your staff unless it's germane to their work.

If you're absolutely adamant about keeping something totally private, like where you go on vacation or even where you live, discuss that as a family and together set boundaries that respect each other's wishes. Keep family and business-related disputes out of earshot of nonfamily members and resolve them away from the office. It's important to present a united front, which will eliminate any chance of giving others anything to chew on.

Probably the easiest way to dispel interest in personal matters is to give colleagues more business-related issues to address. Talk about sales, incentives, marketing ideas. Rather than tell them, show them what a good leader you are and how hard you work. Listen to their ideas and suggestions. Work toward common goals. It's important that family and nonfamily employees play on the same team.

Most of all, if you don't want people to gossip about your personal life, don't do things that engender gossip. Getting drunk and driving around town will cause talk. Like it or not, driving flashy cars, living in palatial homes and throwing lavish parties stoke the rumor mill. Spend conservatively and people will be less interested in how you live. Act in a friendly, professional manner and people will respect you as a businessperson and honor your privacy.

Reality Check: Knowing what's going on in someone's personal and business life is tempting. If not, why would so many people be such voracious consumers of the information about the late Princess Di's unhappy marriage and her affair with Dodi Fayed, or be so eager to learn what actually occurred between President Clinton and Monica Lewinsky? Being part of the family that owns and manages a business puts your life under the microscope for eager eyes and ears. The best you can do is work hard and try to maintain a sense of decorum and high ethical standards to provide as little grist for the gossip mill as possible. When problems arise at work or home, keep your head high, your mouth closed and be gracious so there's less to gossip and grumble about.

18. How does a successor deal with employees who use him to influence the boss and owner, who may be a parent?

Ted R. (not his real name) was caught off guard as a successor in a family business. He thought he had done everything right before entering his family's firm. He had graduated from a good college with a strong academic record, earned his MBA from another prestigious university and worked for a large public company for five years before entering his family's third-generation wholesale and retail carpet business. He thought he knew much of what he needed to trim expenses, attract sales and manage employees. However, no one taught him how to deal with the steady barrage of colleagues who viewed him as a direct conduit to his father, the president and CEO. These colleagues made their requests in a host of ways. Some were subtle. "I'm having a tough time with our house payments; I can't wait until I come up for review and maybe get a raise," he was told by one employee as they stood in the office coffee line with nobody in earshot. Other laments were more overt. One employee confided that she was having problems with her boss. She said that she couldn't fathom how he had gotten his job in the first place and second, how he managed to keep it. She couldn't wait, she added, for him to make a major mistake and maybe get reprimanded, demoted or even fired.

When Ted began to realize he was being used, he decided to mention the problem to an older sister, who also worked in the firm. He confided that he was sympathetic yet annoyed since he wasn't yet in a top management position and couldn't resolve the employees' problems. Moreover, Ted's gut instincts told him that if he did say something to his father, his Dad might be so angry that it would have a backlash effect on the employees. He'd be caught in the middle. Fortunately, his sister had encountered similar requests and could counsel him on alternatives. She suggested that he tell those who complained to him to work through the company's organization structure, which had clearly delineated the appropriate steps for complaints, pay raises and other personal issues, or to hear the person out and do nothing with the information, beyond being compassionate.

The next time Ted felt cornered, he had a script in mind. He felt uncomfortable telling a white lie and saying he'd do something with the information if he weren't going to. Instead, he very politely said, "Thank you for telling me what you're going through. I greatly commiserate, but I have absolutely no power. You need to take your thoughts (complaints) to Ms. So-and-So." As Ted used this explanation more frequently, he became more comfortable doing so. One night over dinner, Ted told his father about this problem. His father chuckled and told him the same situations had occurred when he first joined the business, but that he hadn't received the same good advice. He naively had taken most of the complaints to his father, who had been unsympathetic and annoyed and had reprimanded him.

Nonfamily employees do not often try to take advantage of a successor's position. However, they may try to circumvent the usual line of command and take a shortcut through a family member.

You don't need to be rude or even avoid these situations. Instead, explain how the company deals with issues and what systems are already in place to gain the boss' ear. You want employees to take the action on their own rather than have you do it for them. It's important that they gain credit for their ideas or for raising potential issues. This will deliver the message that they are valuable and empowered to exercise some control over their work lives rather than become dependent on you or anyone else.

If they are hesitant to move ahead on their own, ask why. Help them think through the issues. They will be better respected if, instead of just presenting a complaint, they provide a reasonably thorough analysis of the issue and alternative solutions. If they can't help you understand these, perhaps you should be careful about going to the boss on their behalf. Again, they are probably not using you maliciously. But, like any employee, you risk your credibility if you are unprepared to fully discuss the issue.

Ultimately, if you are uncomfortable with the situation, simply do not be the messenger. If you think that you are being used, consider discussing the situation with your mentor, supervisor or a senior family member. If you believe the issue is important, you certainly should be sure to address it. Owners and leaders do not hide their heads in the sand. Just do not let any employee, or anyone else for that matter, override your judgment. A good book with advice is *Working Without a Net* by Morris Shechtman (Prentice Hall, 1994).

Reality Check: Caring for people, whether family, friends or co-workers, is not synonymous with taking care of them and taking on their problems. You don't want to get into a situation where you feel you're being used. People need to do their own work and pitching, whatever the issues are. If the matter is important, take the initiative to make sure that it gets addressed. You can offer advice on how to get time with the boss and how to analyze and present issues and solutions. Try to mentor employees on the proper way to do so. Don't let them use you as a conduit for matters that you neither understand nor believe warrant attention, however.

19. How does a successor get the older generation to retire and what happens if they won't let go?

Prince Charles seems to have set one model for the successor-in-waiting. As a dutiful son, he keeps himself busy with numerous charitable functions, spends more time parenting his own sons, and accepts the fact that his mother the Queen, now in her 70s, is in no rush to step aside. With good genes on her side, he may have to wait years, if not decades, to gain the top slot in the British monarchy. She is said to like her position and has no interest in stepping down. Charles' only other alternative would be to find something else to do—become a paid architecture critic or sell his organic vegetables and flowers *à la* Paul Newman. Yet, in his case, were his mother to die suddenly, he would need to step back into the royal fold on the spot.

Often, many aging owners' reluctance to step aside is due to financial uncertainties. They simply lack the energy to start all over again if war or depression takes away what they've built. They worry about their health and whether they'll have enough money for medical care and a nursing home, if needed. Others simply can't give up the power or cannot imagine what they would do with all their spare time since they never developed hobbies or other pursuits.

It's important for an older generation leader to let go. Although he has a wealth of experience, he may become out-of-date in this rapidly changing business world. He may become too conservative and unwilling to take appropriate business risks. The employees may get confusing messages about who's the boss—the outgoing, semi-retired person or "the kid." And it can be extremely disheartening to "the kid" to wait until he's 50 or 60 years old to get out from under Dad and have the opportunity to be boss.

The best way to get an aging family leader to let go is not through a gradual retirement, but by sticking to a good succession plan. You need to consider the problems from his point of view, with a heavy dose of compassion and empathy. Do so by engaging him in a discussion away from the office, without people knocking at the door and constantly ringing phones. Find out his fears and apprehensions. Talk with his spouse and seek help in developing solutions.

You, the successor, must help deal with the financial concerns. The retiring leader must feel confident in his and his spouse's financial security in retirement. That may mean the need to build wealth away from the risks of the business. Few owners will totally release power and control if their well-being is dependent upon the company's success, even though they may have great confidence in their successor's abilities.

The aging leader also must find a way to be productive in retirement. The key here is that he must retire "to" something, not "from" something. Help him come up with a way to continue to make a contribution and to be tapped for advice. He might choose to set up a foundation, mentor younger employees, advise other companies in a different industry perhaps by sitting on another firm's independent board, teach at a local community college or even start another business. It will take some experimentation, but it typically is critical to find something far more challenging and rewarding than merely playing golf a couple of extra times a week and traveling more. As people get older, it seems inevitable that they know of someone who retired and then died a few months later. Or the retiree's brain seemed to turn to mush. Most entrepreneurs treat retirement like the plague for fear it could happen to them.

Once retired, the former leader should be kept well informed about what's going on in the company through a healthy flow of communications. Seek him out for his opinions. Perhaps involve him in the board, occasional management meetings or participation in management retreats.

You may not want him helping to run the show, but he has years of experience, wisdom to contribute and a great sense of self-respect honed by building the company. You don't want to diminish that.

Instead of saying, "Don't worry," when he expresses concern, it's better to say, "I understand your concern. What can we do to deal with it?" Often it's simply a matter of better communication.

Some aging owners need additional encouragement. Your board of independent directors can be a tremendous resource to help with the retirement process. Consider hiring a consultant who specializes in succession planning. Participate in seminars and family business programs available at many universities. Read and learn about succession and retirement issues from both generations' perspectives. Try to get both generations to participate in these activities together.

Be prepared to accept that some aging family members will never retire. They plan to die in the saddle and nothing will make them change their minds. It's naive to think that these personality types will change their tune. Perhaps you can accept the situation and still maintain your self-esteem and gain satisfaction. However, in the worst case, you may decide to pursue another career elsewhere. Just as the aging leader often cannot be forced to leave, the eager successor cannot be forced to stay or wait his turn.

Reality Check: The hardest step for many owners to take is to retire. They fear losing their self-esteem; having nothing to do with the long days ahead and no place to go; being financially crippled or scaled back; or even having their pride and joy destroyed by their own protege. Be sure you protect them from all four possibilities. Engage them in other activities but of their choosing. Make them secure monetarily so they can enjoy their retirement without risk if the business performs poorly. Early on, when it is clear that you are the heir-apparent and vague promises are made, get your parent to set a timetable and try to stick to it. By doing so, both generations can celebrate together the transitioning of the business to another generation. Your elder will benefit by witnessing the change during his lifetime. It will be his ultimate legacy of success.

20. Is there room in the family business for a successor to grow personally and professionally?

Alexa Hampton, 27, always knew that she'd eventually land in her father's prestigious New York interior design firm. Encouraged by him, she worked there part-time as a teenager, then went off to Brown University to study literature and history and to take art classes at the nearby Rhode Island School of Design. After graduating, she matriculated for a Master's degree in art history at New York University's School of Fine Arts, but left in 1993 to work full-time for her father. Mark Hampton had helped refurbish Blair House in Washington, D.C., and his clientele included such notable homeowners as Barbara and George Bush, Gayfryd and Saul Steinberg and the late Pamela Harriman.

Father and daughter worked full-time side-by-side until his death a year ago. In that time, she felt she developed both personally and professionally. "My father used to joke when I was in the cradle that I would be a decorator with him and my older sister Kate would be a dancer and actor, which she is. Once at the firm, I progressed from being a shopper to an assistant decorator to one of the six decorators. Professionally, I'd show things to him or he'd start me off with advice making sure I went to see this or that for direction. Gradually, I acted as an intermediary between clients. Our personal-professional relationship also evolved. Obviously, when you have an employee-employer relationship, you have to have and show the proper respect. You can never say to a parent certain things and he could never say to a child certain things at the office. Several times we'd be in a meeting and my father would make me furious, but it was different at home where either he'd let me have it or I'd be upset with him. We had funny moments because of the back-and-forth dynamic. Although he never said anything, I know he was happy with the way we managed our two separate relationships so successfully, and I was, too. I initially called him nothing at work, and then 'Mark' since 'Daddy' seemed so infantile. I also realize the differences between us. I'm not the workaholic he was. And now that he's gone, I'll continue to change personally and professionally."

Alexa adds that she is the youngest decorator on staff. "My colleagues are not going to come to me and say, 'Is this OK?' We'll work as a team, which we also did when Mark was here. The difference is that when he was here the firm had his name, not ours, and his ideas were the guiding light. One of Mark's favorite phrases was, 'Two sets of eyes are better than one' and that will continue to guide us. Because none of us is Mark, we'll have to evolve and grow in a new way or else we'll fail. We'll uphold his standards but change. It isn't the time to try to reinvent the design wheel, but we will rejuvenate what we are doing. My mother Duane will help. She's extremely important as a figurehead and will continue to license the Mark Hampton collection." Because of the unfortunate premature death of her father, Alexa probably will find in coming months and years, however, that her growth curve and that of her colleagues is speeded up immeasurably.

As with any career, there should be opportunities in a family business for a successor to grow personally and professionally and to maintain interest. But, to a great extent, room for growth in a specific family business will depend on the size and state of that business; how many family members already participate; the leader's willingness to delegate responsibility and authority; and the industry's and overall economy's condition. All those factors affect what challenges exist for the business and the family members. A stagnant business already fully staffed by a large family probably offers little opportunity.

Most businesses, large and small, provide opportunity for personal and professional growth. Family businesses may stifle that opportunity through paternalism and by accepting family members' poor work habits. The way a family member enters the business and progresses through a career is important. Your family's business should only hire family members when there is a position available that is appropriate for the candidate's skills and interests. Creating a spot just for the sake of employing a family member likely will mean that there's nowhere to go when it's time for advancement. If your company's policy is to promote based on merit, you'll also be more likely to grow professionally than if you are quickly rotated through the business' various departments and promoted to a vice presidency after only a year with the firm.

You'd be well advised to take charge of your own career. If you're happy doing what you're doing, fine. But if you want to grow and experience new challenges, the family's business can create an opportunity for you to take the bull by the horns. Don't expect people to come to you and tell you how to develop your career. In fact, employees probably will look to you as a family member to initiate action. People in the corporate world know that they have to take responsibility for their careers. You should do the same.

What if other older or more experienced family members block the way to the top? There's no easy answer here. Just like in the public company world, family businesses offer only so many top spots. However, unlike many nonfamily businesses, your business may offer family members a joint role in decision-making, or at least more involvement in management processes. You may need to adapt your definition of "personal and professional" growth to accept the realities of how high you can go in the organization.

Some family businesses may just be too small to provide much opportunity for professional growth. However, the opportunity may be there for the taking. Small businesses are not stuck in first gear. They require someone to take the initiative, have the courage and take the risk to make them grow. Successors also need to know that personal and professional growth sometimes brings new challenges. They may need to master new skills to keep up (perhaps take management or computer classes), or they may outgrow their jobs and the company and want to move on.

Reality Check: Most people want to be able to grow personally and professionally. The same is true for a successor in a family business. Safeguards to be sure that challenges will exist are to hire only qualified family members when a legitimate slot is available. Once in the firm, family members need to set and periodically revise goals and skills. Ultimately, personal and professional growth will depend on what opportunities the family member seizes.

21. Can an heir-apparent leave his family's business without feeling a sense of betrayal?

Tom Bloch is the son of Henry, one of the two brothers who founded H&R Block, the giant tax preparation firm based in Kansas City, Mo. He decided to shift gears and left the family business in 1995 to teach math at St. Francis Xavier School in a blighted, lower-income East Side neighborhood. Then 42 years old and president and chief executive officer, Bloch said his decision to exit was not rooted in a family disagreement, but in a desire to spend more time with his wife Mary and two sons, then 9 and 12. He also wanted to make a meaningful contribution to the community where he grew up. He took a huge pay cut to do so. His annual salary as president and CEO of H&R Block had exceeded $600,000. As a first-year part-time teacher at St. Francis he earned less than $10,000. Fortunately, he had the cushion of stock dividends and sound investments.

Although he had discussed with his father the possibility of leaving, Tom said his Dad, who remains chairman but is not active in day-to-day management, was nevertheless surprised when he made his announcement. "He was initially sad, but fully understood and was supportive, as was my mother," says Tom. "Going into his office and telling him was actually one of the hardest parts of the change." Although Tom could have stayed on in the company in another capacity, he didn't want to, believing that his presence would intimidate any replacement. However, he agreed to serve on a committee to find a replacement.

Would he ever go back to H&R Block when his sons are grown and because none of his siblings or first cousins works in the business? "I don't envision that at all. I love teaching and am co-teaching education classes at Rockhurst College, in addition to the middle school work I do. I enjoy the school; the kids are wonderful. I also love not traveling and being home for dinner every night. My involvement in the community is extremely fulfilling."

Tom's advice to others thinking of making a career switch away from the family business is to consider the implications for themselves, their immediate family and the future of the company.

As a scion of a family business, you can successfully leave the company if you deeply believe that there is another career you want to pursue. The decision to leave must be your own and not an idea of your spouse's parents or someone else. Nevertheless, some successors feel tremendous guilt at the prospect of going in another direction. You may feel gut-wrenching heartache because of a sense of lost time. You may feel that you are abandoning your family when they need you the most.

Examine why you joined the business, and why you want to leave. You may have never wanted to go into the business in the first place, but it was expected. You may have been pushed aggressively by such comments as, "We sacrificed and built this business for you" or "This is the legacy we want to leave to you, your siblings and our grandchildren." Or you may have been subtly enticed aboard as your parents continually discussed how hard they worked and how difficult it was to find competent outside help in their industry. After being worn down, you felt you had no alternative.

You may be among those who joined their family businesses simply because they couldn't find a comparable job with as good or better pay and benefits. Or, in a slightly different twist, you may have worked elsewhere first, had a terrible boss and came to view the family business as a life raft. Either way, you may have eventually realized that the business and line of work did not suit or interest you. You may find working with relatives to be too constraining for any number of reasons. Or you may be simply attracted to some other calling.

Once you've begun to toy with the notion of leaving, discuss the idea with someone who knows you well, knows your parents and knows the company. This may be a trusted nonfamily manager, advisor or mentor. Or it may be a support group of fellow successors you're in contact with on a regular basis. Have any of these people or groups play devil's advocate for you. You need to sound out the pros and cons to be sure you're not acting in haste, simply leaving because you dislike your immediate supervisor, or are annoyed you didn't get a bonus you expected. You may be able to resolve those types of issues and stay.

Sometimes people also find it helpful to list on paper the advantages and disadvantages of a major decision and see how the results pan out. The answer of what to do may hit you squarely in the face.

Whatever you initially decide, take some extra time to rethink your decision; you won't regret the extra week or month you deliberated since you may have made the decision in haste and need to cool down. Craig E. Aronoff and John L. Ward, business professors and family business advisors, list 11 helpful questions in their book, *Another Kind of Hero* (Business Owner Resources, 1992), that potential successors should ask themselves before joining a business. These are the same basic questions you should ask yourself before leaving:

- What are the reasons for my decision?
- Does it offer the career I want?
- Does it fulfill my personal goals?
- Do I like what the business does?
- Do I find the work meaningful and challenging?
- Is it better than my alternatives?
- Am I working well with my family?
- Do I make a real contribution?
- What skill, talent, drive and knowledge do I bring to the business?
- Do we resolve conflicts that inevitably arise?
- Do I understand that being a good son or daughter is different from being an effective manager?

If you decide to proceed with your decision to leave, be brave about telling your parents rather than letting them hear the news from someone else. Tell them calmly and rationally why you made the decision and what you plan to do. Try not to leave in the heat of anger. Assuming that you are unhappy working in the business, explain why. Perhaps changes can be made. Explain that you can't be a good employee or successful leader if you don't like your job. If you yearn to accomplish something different or more rewarding in your life, try to help them understand. If you truly believe in your decision, you won't get railroaded by comments like,"How can you do this to us?"Stick to your guns and don't back down. But listen to their side of the argument. If you have any inkling of a doubt, you may want to leave the door a bit ajar and ask if you can discuss your decision in a year or so after you've tested your wings elsewhere.

Finally, offer to try to make your decision an opportunity for everyone to benefit and grow. Suggest that you help find and mentor a replacement. You may also want to help guide the company in a much less involved role, perhaps as a member of a family council or participant in a yearly family retreat. Depending on what you plan to do, you may, however, want to sever the umbilical cord completely.

Whether there will be lasting repercussions or ill will depends so much on the relationship and mutual trust you and your family have established through your years of growing up. If your parents still view you as a child, they may not react well. But if they've seen you mature, take responsibility, succeed elsewhere, or know you have a dream you feel compelled to pursue, they should applaud your decision. Don't be surprised, however, if they seem upset for themselves and the company's loss. You don't have to leave the family in order to leave the business. You must help your family to understand your intentions in that regard. Your parents' disappointment in your departure from the business may be aggravated by their fear that they won't see you or be able to be involved in your life any more. Be patient with them. For them, your departure is just as hard or harder than the day they dropped you off at college or sent you on your first airplane trip alone and worried until you came home safely again.

Reality Check: Others, inside and outside the family, may perceive you as ungrateful, but if you have another dream, it's best to pursue it rather than stay in the family business and be unhappy. Or if you'd rather be home with the children when the clock strikes 5 p.m. and you know you cannot put in the hours required of you in the family business, why stay and cause trouble? Think through your reasons carefully; consider listing pros and cons. Talk over your possible decision with a trusted mentor or advisor, then with your parents so that they understand your reasons clearly. If possible, test your alternative and always leave the door open in case you change your mind.

CHAPTER III

DAUGHTERS AND SONS IN A FAMILY BUSINESS

22. What role do daughters play as possible successors and is it different from that of sons or sons-in-law?

CEO Marilyn Carlson Nelson had big shoes to fill. Her late father Curtis Carlson, chairman of Carlson Cos. Inc. of Minnetonka, Mn., a travel and hotel colossus with estimated revenues of $7 billion, tapped her to be his heir-apparent in spring 1998. At the time, Mr. Carlson held 100 percent of the voting stock. Marilyn was not, however, his first choice. Her father had brought on board a string of potential male successors, starting with his youngest daughter's husband, Edwin C."Skip" Gage. Gage left after two years. Subsequently, Carlson brought in several nonfamily managers, who also didn't stay very long.

A light bulb finally went off: What about appointing his eldest daughter to run the day-to-day operations of the company, then ease her into his role of CEO? Although she was not his initial successor, Marilyn had solid attributes as a leader, team player and academic star. She had experience outside the family firm as a stock analyst for PaineWebber Inc. She had earned a bachelor's degree in international economics from Smith College. She had studied at the Sorbonne in Paris and at L'Institut des Hautes Etudes Economiques Politiques in Geneva, Switzerland. She owned and operated two rural banks in Southern Minnesota.

Internationally, she successfully orchestrated a global celebration on behalf of five Scandinavian countries, earning her medals from Sweden and Finland and honors from Denmark, Norway and Iceland. She was serving as a corporate director at Exxon Corporation, US West, Inc. and First Bank Systems, Inc. Once she was appointed, her father promised to give his daughter free rein and to focus on business matters outside the day-to-day operations. Nelson's sister heads the family's charitable foundation. Her son Curtis runs the company's hospitality unit and is slated to take over from her within a decade.

As the Bob Dylan song goes, the "Times They Are A-Changin'." More women are being tapped as successors of family businesses and not just small Mom-and-Pop operations. The numbers hardly represent a groundswell, but there are signs of an increasing number of women at the helm. A 1997 survey of more than 3,000 family businesses conducted by the Arthur Andersen Center for Family Business and MassMutual–The Blue Chip Company found that 25 percent of all family business heads (mostly male and mostly older) would consider tapping a daughter as a successor CEO.

Furthermore, the number of women starting businesses is rising faster than the number of aging founders who are anointing them as successors. There were about 8 million female-owned businesses in 1996, or 36 percent of all businesses. This is a 78 percent increase since 1987, according to the National Foundation for Women Business Owners. In fact, the number of female-owned businesses is growing at nearly twice the national average.

There's good reason for this. Many women have substantial credentials which include degrees at both the undergraduate and graduate level, years of business, financial or legal experience and well-honed leadership talent, as well as superb interpersonal skills.

No longer should women be ignored as contenders for the top slots in family firms because of their gender. Successors to the throne should be considered based on the right combination of characteristics. The changing social perspective of women is critical to family-owned businesses. Why? It means there are now twice as many potential candidates for leadership. There is no longer a reason to settle for a son who is less than qualified.

In reality, the idea of appointing women as heirs-apparent still disturbs a significant number of older male owners who started their businesses 30 to 40 years ago. Too often, they can't look equally at their sons and daughters when choosing a successor and are more concerned about helping establish sons in the business, even if the sons are disinterested or less qualified. Some owners may even prefer to bring aboard sons-in-law, sell their businesses or have nonfamily males succeed them rather than pass the business on to a daughter.

The reason? Often times it's because these fathers are traditional and believe that their daughters would be better off staying home to rear children. It's not a matter of thinking their daughters are less qualified to run the business; rather they may not want their daughters to be bothered with such business-related headaches as employee problems, demanding clients, exhaustive travel, labor unions and fluctuating economies. Sexist or not, it's reality in many cases.

Ironically, a father–daughter combination can be a terrific and sometimes the best multigenerational match. A father, who tends to compete with a son or son-in-law, whether consciously or subconsciously, actually may be more helpful and supportive of a daughter-successor. But here the daughter walks a thin line. It's up to her to set the boundaries. She must keep Dad from treating her like a helpless little girl; ensure that he prepares her for a leadership role; and convey to others, including long-time employees, clients and suppliers, that she was selected for her talents and experience. This communication is particularly important in male-dominated industries. Often critical to the success of a father–daughter team is the mother's attitude. She also may have out-of-date notions of a woman's role or may view her active daughter as a threat to her relationship with her husband.

Mothers and daughters can be a good working duo, and many more are joining forces in women-created or inherited firms. Mother–daughter teams owe part of their success to their good relationships. It's unlikely for a mother and daughter to choose to work together in a family business if they didn't like each other before and didn't have a history of getting along through the growing-up years. Or, if they did argue during the daughter's teenage years, they've long since ironed out their differences and found that working side-by-side takes their relationship to a stronger, more equal partnership than the traditional boss-versus-underling role. It's common for mothers and daughters in business to view each other as supportive colleagues. As a result, it's usually easier for a mother to bequeath the top slot to her daughter and easier for the daughter not to feel the need to force her mother out in order to establish her own identity in the business.

Another reason for the success of daughters in family firms, whether headed by Mom or Dad, is their motivation for entering the business. Women usually seek the successor's job to find fulfillment and become closer to their families. They also tend to be negotiators and exhibit a team management and nurturing style.

Men, on the other hand, often want a shot at the highest office because they think they can do a better job at running the business. Male egos also can be at work. Men can tend to be more bottom-line oriented and want a job where they can earn the best salary and the best perks. They also relish the power that is inherent in the top position. Yet, because they're sometimes more assertive in business, men may display their independence faster, which can rub Dad or Mom the wrong way. They also typically fashion a clear-cut hierarchy that places them above and in competition with others.

If a woman wants to be a serious candidate to run the family company, she must send the right signals and exhibit the necessary leadership. This means taking a stand early and letting her parents know that she's considering the business as a career. She needs to go to college and possibly graduate school, and preferably work elsewhere first to expand her knowledge of the business world and build her credibility with siblings, nonfamily employees, clients and other stakeholders.

Women who don't follow this path often end up in the family business as a doormat, tucked away in a back office as a bookkeeper or public relations manager. Although these positions are important to the business, women who are serious about running the company someday need to be sure that their objectives are known. It is unfortunate that gender stereotypes still exist, but they remain a fact of life for many people. Stereotypes can create an unfair disadvantage for women, but they often can be overcome.

Consider the case of a food distribution firm in the Midwest run by the eldest son. His younger sister, who is more capable, handles a lower-level credit manager's job. She is paid considerably less than her brother, but works longer hours. Unwittingly, this was the role for which she was groomed. It was understood from day one that her brother would inherit the CEO's position. Sadly, she never challenged this arrangement.

Reality Check: When deciding who will make the best successor, family business heads need to look at daughters and sons not according to their gender but according to their skills, training, leadership ability and experience. But daughters need to do their part and let it be known if they're interested in a top job; then they must get the right education and experience. They can expand their understanding of issues and solutions by networking with other daughters working in other family firms. Perhaps the best way for potential successors, male or female, to prove their abilities is to be successful outside their families' businesses. They may want to start a business of their own to prove to Mom and Dad that they, too, can be successful.

23. How does the female successor deal with male resentment and domination and gain the respect of family members and others associated with the business?

Terri Swain-Leaver, 36, who runs her family's fourth-generation hardware business, never accepted male resentment and domination. Swain's Hardware, a 103-year-old family firm in Cape May, a small town on the southern tip of New Jersey, needed some shoring up and Terri was the woman for the job. Not only did she have her CPA license, but she had worked for one of the international accounting firms and for Colgate–Palmolive Corp. in New York as a financial analyst. Her father Charles "Bud" Swain, 68, was doing all the firm's taxes and financials and knew the company needed a computer system as part of an effort to professionalize operations. Terri took time out of her busy schedule to set it up. When she took a leave from Colgate in 1994 to work in her sister's restaurant in Cape May, her father implored her to help him in the business with the paperwork so he could think about cutting back his hours and possibly retiring.

However, Terri's half brother, who was 10 years older and had worked in the firm since 1982, assumed he would run the show one day. According to Terri, he resented her entering the firm and even more so when she began to take over some of the duties he had been handling. Terri's father named the pair co-managers and tried to give each sibling his or her own bailiwick, but their duties kept overlapping. Bud encouraged them to work it out, but Terri's half brother seemed unwilling to share power with a woman, a younger sister no less.

Bud knew that he'd have to make a choice to put one in control and he tapped his daughter. Terri's half brother eventually resigned to pursue self-employment in a customer-service business. Today, the relationship between Terri and her half brother is cool at best. She remains confident not only about her capabilities and contribution to the business, but also about the company's strength and ability to survive in an industry teeming with chains gobbling up smaller independents.

As more women enter and progress in the workplace with top credentials and leadership skills, they are qualified to take over top positions in corporations. However, promotions for women in many publicly held companies are still scant, causing many to leave and either start their own firms or consider entering their families' businesses.

Today, the family business is a credible alternative for qualified women. More successors than ever are chosen on ability rather than on gender. According to the *Arthur Andersen/MassMutual American Family Business Survey '97*, nearly 41 percent of the more than 3,000 respondents had at least one female family member working full-time in the firm, and almost 10 percent had two full-time female family members.

Some male heirs simply don't have the necessary skills to run family firms, yet their female relatives do. Or the female simply may have stronger skills and advance beyond the males. As a result, women may find themselves dealing with male resentment and domination. Dorothy Cantor and Toni Bernay in *Women Power: The Secrets of Leadership* (Houghton Mifflin, 1992) quote a Congresswoman who addresses the issue of male–female power struggles:

> "I think men tend to be a lot more nervous about the male–female relationship in a professional or powerful body than the women do. I don't think women are as affected by the power that's around them. They're not often as awed by it. I don't think women aspire to powerful positions as eagerly as men do. Maybe it's because we don't aspire to use the power for our own purposes."

Feeling male domination and resentment because you're in a position of power need not be an insurmountable problem. You can diffuse these issues with a little sensitivity and savviness. "Women tend to have a caring kind of power," say Cantor and Bernay. "It's not self-serving; instead it's directed toward advancing an agenda."

The cornerstone of any successful business is relationships. Women, more often than men, are masters at cultivating relationships with other family members, nonfamily key managers, employees, clients and suppliers, whether male or female. Relationship nurturing takes a great deal of time and hard work; it also takes work and time to mitigate some large male egos. A few simple givens and principles can help you downplay problems:

- Expect politics, but keep them in perspective. There will be power struggles in the course of your job and you will have to learn to navigate your way through them. Don't automatically assume that the politics are gender-related. Everyone has an agenda and limitations. But you have your right to perform your role as long as you don't leave people out of important policies and decisions.
- Find a high-visibility, important role for the capable male who feels threatened. If he has been at the company a sufficient time and is capable, include him in management-level discussions so he feels part of the decision-making. He'll feel more motivated to work for the success of your firm and not undermine the business or you.
- Confide in male counterparts and key male employees. Demonstrate confidence in them and give them credit for good things that happen in their area. Make sure they are kept apprised of what's going on. Have regularly scheduled meetings to convey progress or just to publicly thank them for a job well done, if they meet a quota or go the extra mile.

  Be a good listener. You can gain respect by valuing people's opinions, asking effective questions, seeking their input and resolving differences.
- Know the facts when you make a decision. This enhances your credibility. Do your homework before making any decision. You should also communicate the thought process behind key decisions to let others understand how you arrived at a conclusion or plan.
- Look and act like a professional. If you want to be taken seriously, be poised, courteous and punctual. React professionally.
- Mentor male, as well as female, employees. All employees will take notice. Convey the message that everyone's contribution to the business counts, regardless of gender or position on the corporate ladder.
- Offer sincere appreciation. This can go a long way to distinguish you as someone with whom others want to do business. Be sure you mean it. The thanks also must fit the deed. Tell a male employee what a good job he's done and how he's valued. Make his working life better than it was before you were at the helm. Women are often good at making people feel important and part

of a team. Not only thank them for a job well done, put it in writing. That way the recipient may pass the note around the office. Others will pick up on this and try to please the boss as well.

- If possible, get to know every employee, every client and every supplier on a first-name basis. Don't be intimidated or get hung up on formalities or be so unreachable that employees can't get to you with a complaint or problem.
- Don't shirk responsibility or try to pass it off on somebody else. You'll probably have to work harder than any male to prove you deserve your slot. People will be watching to make sure you don't cut corners or hours or take more pay, vacations or benefits than you deserve.

Reality Check: More family business leaders are looking at the best-qualified family member to run their business, regardless of gender. As more women with top qualifications and skills are groomed to take over family businesses, there will be occasions on which they must deal with a male's resentment or domination. To mollify the situation, a female successor must be a team player who is confident, decisive, qualified and sensitive to the male ego as well as to other females' egos.

24. How does a woman deal with patronizing behavior, including a lower salary?

Cindi Bigelow, 38, vice president of operations of R.C. Bigelow Inc., a specialty tea company in Fairfield, Ct., never stood for patronizing behavior from anyone, but she had the credentials, work ethic, education and self-confidence to back her up. "To establish real relationships with people in business, you have to get beyond gender issues as quickly as you can. You have to be confident about your talents and what you can bring to the table. That's the hand you expose in business. Soon a client or employee will forget gender and realize that you are there to make them succeed," says Cindi. It helps too that it's part of this family company's culture to have a woman at the helm. Cindi's grandmother the late Ruth Campbell Bigelow, who was a graduate of Brown University, founded the company in 1945. Cindi joined the family enterprise in 1984, after having graduated from Boston College with a marketing degree, doing a stint as operations manager at Seagram Co. and receiving her MBA from the Kellogg School of Management at Northwestern University. "I worked elsewhere first because I wanted to. No one told me I had to, but it was an unspoken thing. I wanted to do something on my own, to see what else was available. Also, I wasn't ready after college to enter the family business," she says.

Once Cindi did come on board, her boundless energy, leadership skills and commitment to the family business gave her credibility among employees and key management to help her rise quickly through the ranks. In her current position as vice president of operations, she puts in 13-hour days overseeing a good portion of the company's 400 employees as well as three manufacturing plants, and handling quality control, purchasing, distribution and planning. Cindi works alongside her father, who is chairman of the board and president, her mother, a vice president, and her older sister Lori, vice president of blending. Today, the business does almost $80 million in annual sales.

A female successor comes into the family business with multiple talents and fabulous qualifications. Naturally, she expects an equal-opportunity salary and job, but the reality isn't always so. More often, she not only earns less than her male counterparts, but also is treated in a patronizing manner by employees, who sometimes introduce her as "the boss' daughter" or comment on her appearance rather than her work results. (If you're married and use your husband's last name or, if single, your mother's maiden name, it can help to dispel the stigma of nepotism.)

Having to constantly counter the perception that you owe your position in the company to your lineage can be wearing mentally and physically. Sure, you can quit, but why give in? Here's what you can do to help change your colleagues' and customers' thinking:

- When you initially enter the firm, develop an employment strategy with your father or mother, negotiate what you want and agree on what is expected of you.
- Draft a mission statement that reminds both you and your parent or other relative of your main goals, how you plan to help improve the organization and how you intend to contribute to the company's success.
- Stay focused and prove yourself. Focus on why you work at the business and what you plan to do. Give 110 percent to the job. Sometimes being paid less than nonfamily counterparts can unwittingly help a female and also male successor gain acceptance. The other family members and nonfamily employees will be less resentful than if you're overpaid, but don't accept

less for long. The level of pay you receive will equate to the level of expectations.

- Devote energies to the part of the business that offers you the best chance for success and uses your talents most effectively. Demonstrate your competence by doing quality work, meeting day-to-day challenges head on, and setting high standards of integrity and honesty.
- Establish a track record and assert yourself. Use facts to substantiate your contributions. Facts and low-key discussions typically are better accepted than passionate and public demands. You'll be more likely to succeed in compensation discussions if you have had formal performance reviews to know where you stand, plus objective data concerning what a nonfamily employee would earn in your position and at your performance level.
- Propose any good ideas for the company to explore that will improve the bottom line, but don't be dogmatic. Make sure your ideas are consistent with your mission statement and that they won't dilute or sabotage your current effort, operations or budget.
- Know what the business is all about before you come on board. Take courses and read books to improve your business and technical knowledge. If you are most informed about a situation or product, you will distinguish yourself. Don't allow others to think you're not smart or informed enough to run the business someday.

If the situation is untenable and you continue to be treated as a second-class citizen after you've made all the overtures and efforts, it might be time to make your way in life outside the family business or at least temporarily work elsewhere.

Reality Check: Focus on why you're in the business. Understand what the firm does and, as unfair as it may sound, work harder than anyone else to make your mark. This should be demanded of all potential successors regardless of gender. You can eliminate patronizing behavior by taking a positive approach and doing a great job rather than whining and running to Daddy or Mommy with problems. Choose the right time to ask about salary raises and promotions, once you've established a track record. Make sure that you get objective views of your performance and contribution so that you can use facts to counter improper treatment.

25. Can a female, who is seen as a good little girl, change that image, be more assertive and confident with male colleagues and be treated as an adult?

We've all heard it, the family business founder who says, "Our daughter would do the best job, but we have to offer the business to our first-born son." How about: "My daughter is my little helper." Maureen Steinwall, 44, president and owner of Steinwall Inc., a Coon Rapids, Mn.-based thermoplastic injection-molding company, remembers hearing in high school limitations placed on women. However, she says that her father never treated her like his good little girl. "On the other hand, he never said to me, 'Daughter, some day this will all be yours.'"

Maureen also didn't hesitate to speak up when she wanted to head and own the business her father founded in 1965. She had the education, experience and confidence to succeed him. It was made easier by the fact that the business was never viewed as a family heirloom. "It was merely a way for Dad to make a living. It's a business and it never defined the family or who we were as individuals."

After receiving her degree in accounting, Maureen was a self-employed tax accountant. In 1981, she sold her practice and went back to school to receive her MBA. Next, she went to work at Honeywell Inc. in marketing where she gained small and large corporate experience. In 1983 when her father Carl, who was then 55, called her up and asked for her help in selling the business so he wouldn't have to give it all to Uncle Sam, Maureen says, "My immediate reaction was, 'Hey Dad, why don't you sell it to your daughter?' Of course, he had the very typical and traditional reaction for about five minutes. He said: 'Who will raise my grandchildren?' (Maureen wasn't even married at the time.) And . . . 'What does a girl want with a manufacturing company?' My response was: 'The same as a boy.' My father then caught himself: 'Oh, you're right. This is incredible. You're a prime candidate for this business and you'd make a wonderful buyer.'"

Maureen's sister, who's a corporate attorney, wasn't interested. Her brother, who is much younger, was being trained to be a mold maker to craft a career with the family company. "But he didn't have the skills to be owner–president," says Maureen. "It took more business savvy than craft skills. There was this piece that was unspoken, that some day this would all be his. However, my Dad didn't make a commitment to this. It might have been more of a gift to my brother, but Dad needed a sale. It was his only asset to take him into retirement. There might have been some hard feelings, but my brother became an artist and he's happy."

After agreeing to an appraiser's valuation, Maureen entered the firm in 1983, became president in 1985, and bought the stock in 1987. She worked alongside her father who became her coach–mentor. On the day the sale went through, however, her father was gone and the business was hers. "Even though he sold it to me on an installment basis, and it was still really his, he was able to let me run it with the understanding that I could turn to him for advice. His letting go was at the root of my ability to succeed. If he had been there, people would have gone to him which would have undermined my credibility." Today, gross sales are at $8 million with 70 employees. "When I first took over, it was difficult for most of the male employees to deal with a woman. Many employees as well as customers left, wondering 'What's a girl know about running a manufacturing company?'" Maureen stresses that it's easy to prove yourself regardless of gender when something is your passion. "Nobody will beat you if it's something you love. If you do it for the sake of doing it, you might not succeed."

Remember the Girl Scout motto: Be prepared. This is apropos when you decide to enter your family firm. Even if your family treats you like a child or a good little girl, show that you're much more than that. Work to change your image. Otherwise, you'll be handed a job for which you may be overqualified and a salary to match it.

A "good little girl" is a woman who is not career-oriented, does not have credentials, is unfocused, and winds up in the family business because it's there and an easy job. She has low expectations of herself and is not terribly ambitious. She may be a dilettante who comes and goes as she pleases—running off to long lunches or shopping expeditions with friends. She can't handle too much responsibility, and family members and employees who knew her growing up often view her as an extension of the child she used to be.

There are developmental steps you can take to avoid being swallowed up in the syndrome of not being taken seriously. Before you step through that door to join the family enterprise, you should have the right credentials and experience outside the family business where you will mature faster, receive more objective feedback, and gain a better sense of self-worth. You will also have the guts and the credibility to back up your ambitions and ideas, because you've had to do so before outside the comfort zone of your family. This will help dispel right from the start the image that you are a lightweight. If you have distinct personal goals, express them, which adds to your professionalism. Others will take you more seriously.

Make sure there's a job available that matches your qualifications and meets your expectations. If so, polish your résumé, go in and sell yourself to your father or mother, to key managers and to other employees if necessary. Let everyone know what you have to offer and how your skills can help the company. Grab face-time with your parents and tell them what you expect.

Once you're part of the operation, convince any naysayers that you are the best one for the job. Get yourself into meetings with the top dogs and project the image of a leader. Look and act poised and professional. Be agreeable at the outset to any assignment, any extra work, extra hours and work that others may not want. Once you've worked in the trenches for a few years and been successful, be prepared to stand your ground. Let it be known loud and clear that you want your share of the responsibility. Your parents can't just turn the business over to your brother; you're a force to be reckoned with, too.

According to Dorothy W. Cantor and Toni Bernay, authors of *Women Power: The Secrets of Leadership* (Houghton Mifflin, 1992), parents are usually the ones who empower their daughters to think like capable adults. On the flip side, it's also parents who keep their children, particularly daughters, dependent on them for self-esteem, money and authority.

Here are some common threads the authors found among successful powerful women:

- When young, their parents told them they expected them to succeed, that they were capable and responsible, and treated them accordingly and equally to males in the family.
- Their parents encouraged them to take risks, make mistakes, to think for themselves and be independent. In fact, many successful career women say their parents treated them as the first-born male.
- Their parents didn't rescue them from problems or mistakes, but made them figure out how to cope on their own.
- They were encouraged to ask for ideas by readily available parents.
- Parents were supportive and complimentary and didn't discount the daughter's dreams and goals.
- Both parents (especially Mom) aimed high and worked hard so that the daughters could emulate both of them.

Reality Check: Although the following advice goes for a successor, regardless of gender, it's even more appropriate for a female, who may be judged more critically. Women should not enter the family firm unless they have drive, goals, qualifications, credibility and maturity. They will be steps ahead if they have the right educational background and experience working outside the family firm. Once inside the family company, they should be prepared to prove themselves. If they are career-minded and professional, perceptions of them will change over time and they will be treated with the appropriate respect.

26. What problems might a son encounter working with his parents?

In 1914 when William Dierberg purchased a country store (founded in 1854) in St. Louis County, Mo., an area of thick meadows and farmland, and renamed it Dierbergs Family Market, he never imagined that 85 years later his grandchildren and great grandchildren would work in the business together and expand it from one store to 17.

Today Dierbergs Family Markets, Inc. is a true reflection of a healthy family's culture, a clan with a strong bond between work and home that fosters family harmony. Their stores, located in St. Louis and St. Charles counties, are known for quick and friendly service and unique inventory, from dense flavorful breads, tarts, pies and richly decadent cakes made in their European Pastry Shop to freshly prepared foods and salads from the stores' delis and the best fruit and produce the family and staff can find, all artfully arranged to attract attention.

What has made these stores so successful is the family running the operation behind the scenes. The Dierberg family's fourth generation has followed their father into the business. Togetherness, especially in a physically grueling business that operates from early morning until late at night seven days a week, can be tough on relationships. Not in this family. Today, president and chairman Bob Dierberg, 59, works side-by-side with his son, Greg, 28, who manages the produce, meat, seafood, dairy and bakery divisions.

Bob was 55 when Greg, then 23, came into the business in 1994, which family business therapist John A. Davis considers to be "ages much more conducive to harmonious interactions." However, the fact that the two men are so simpatico goes beyond this. Bob and his wife Sharon have always hoped their children would come into the business, but they never pressured them. "We didn't want to push. Forcing one's children to come into the business can put a strain on family relationships. We are close to all three of our children. Our daughter, Laura, 24, just joined the firm in an aggressive management training program. Our other son, Brian, 26, is also welcome but hasn't expressed any interest yet," Bob adds.

Some business owners believe the emerging generation should work elsewhere first so they may establish their identity away from the family company, and Bob Dierberg subscribes to this dictum. A successor needs more than bloodlines to become a leader in the firm. Greg had credentials, a degree in business administration from the University of Kansas, determination and a good work ethic. He also worked for a Minnesota food wholesaler for more than one year before joining. Laura, who graduated from Vanderbilt University with a degree in human and organizational development, worked for a public relations agency before joining the company last year.

Once Greg came into the business, he started at the bottom working in all divisions. He was mentored by nonfamily employees as well as by his father whose office today is right next door. "We have lunch together at least two days a week and talk most nights on the phone even after work. Since family members in a family business are bound to have overlapping relationships, it's important for all of us to have a healthy rather than competitive relationship," says Greg.

Communication is key if you're going to work with a parent; it's the focal point of any good relationship, Greg adds. "My father and I have a great working relationship. We get together and discuss the strengths and merits of a proposal and if something is wrong, we both have an open mind. I'm in a position that I want to learn from him, and he's really good at pointing out when an idea needs tweaking and then helping me develop it. In a family business there isn't room for a lot of egos. When egos get in the way, it causes a breakdown in communication, a stonewall effect, if you will. There are a lot of things that trickle down from that. A lack of communication means operations suffer and there are gaps where people are misinformed or not informed."

Greg and Laura are also quick to credit their mother for the good communications in the family. "She fostered an environment where we could express ourselves. We are a very close family who really enjoy each other's company."

Father–son relationships are the most typical family pair found among family companies, says John A. Davis, a senior lecturer at Harvard Business School, one of the authors of *Generation to Generation: Life Cycles of the Family Business* (Harvard Business School Press, 1997) and co-author with Renato Tagiuri of the article in *Family Business Review,* "The Influence of Life Stage on Father–Son Work Relationships in Family Companies."

Instead of viewing a father–son relationship as possibly one rife with problems, a son and a parent instead should be aware of potential stress and developmental factors. The more potentially difficult partnership may be between a son and a father rather than a son and a mother based on anecdotal evidence and research, says Davis. Not enough mother–son relationships have existed or been studied to compare the two.

How easy or difficult the parental working relationship becomes hinges to a large extent on several factors, including:

- The history of their prior relationship and chemistry.
- The current context of their relationship and what also occurs around them, such as the presence of siblings and the business' financial state.
- The ages of the son and parent when they began working together and their ages as they continue their partnership, since the relationship changes over the course of time. "When both father and son are in periods of life in which social interactions tend to be difficult, then we expect that their work relationship will be relatively problematic," Davis and Tagiuri say.

  The most difficult age periods for this interpersonal and work relationship are between 17 and 22, 34 and 50, and 61 and 70. In contrast, the age periods between 23 and 33 and 51 and 60 are much more conducive to harmonious interactions. One reason: men beyond the midlife transition (the 40s) are less competitive, idealize and condemn others less, are less controlled by external stimuli, place less emphasis on possessions and are more objective, philosophical and better able to respond to the developmental needs of their children and young adults, Davis explains. Unfortunately, it's impractical to plan to have a father-son relationship only during those few "golden" age ranges!
- The stage of the business when they started working together also plays a role, with the stages described by Davis and his colleagues as startup, expansion and mature level.
- What stage the family is at developmentally. In the book, Davis and his co-authors categorize these as the young business family stage, the working together stage and the passing-the-baton stage.

While all these factors influence harmony or discontent, it is important to remember that no father–son or any familial business relationship can be neatly pegged into one given scenario. Other intangibles come into play, and the dynamics of the business and the family constantly evolve. To look at a scenario in terms of one moment in time is to oversimplify and ignore distinctions that occur and blur lines, Davis says.

The good news is that any problems in a relationship can often be mitigated if the parties involved want to do so. The first thing for a father and son to do is try to determine why they had a troubled past, which may or may not have to do with their behavior. "They may have had an early separation where they didn't see other that much. But it doesn't mean they can't mend the relationship if they come and work together. They may be able to build a sound foundation that is ripe with goodwill and leads to open communications," Davis says. "An exception, however, may be if the early relationship was characterized by abuse or a diminution in self-esteem. If the men are on a path that is troubled, it may lead to distorted communication and mistrust."

Equally important is that the generations should consider not working together until both are beyond their individual periods of identity formation. "Not only must sons have time to establish their own identities away from their families, but the sons' presence might exacerbate the fathers' own questioning and internal conflicts," Davis says.

And although casting blame may not prove useful, the father often is more responsible for determining the ultimate relationship. In many cases, Davis adds, he must decide which child—his son or his company—means more to him.

Reality Check: Difficulty in parent–son working relationships can arise from any number of causes—from stormy growing-up, asserting-identity years to domineering male egos, to tough business pressures. The parties must want to work together to make the relationship successful. Both sides must recognize that the necessary elements of a successful relationship include communication, setting parameters for responsibility and authority, and a recognition of the importance of compromise and mutual respect. Plus, don't forget that you love each other even when discussions become heated!

CHAPTER IV
TRANSITION CHALLENGES FACING THE FAMILY BUSINESS LEADER

27. How does a founder get and keep qualified children interested in the business, especially when he's not yet ready to retire and there's no sign of stepping aside?

The late Donald P. Babson, CEO of Babson-United Cos., in Wellesley Hills, Ma., ran his family's firm with an iron hand. Today, the 94-year-old publishing and investment advisory services firm with about 85 employees and more than 19,000 clients is headed by Donald's son, Richard, 40. For Richard, the youngest of five children, it wasn't an easy decision to make to be the only sibling to come into the family firm.

Although Richard never intended to enter the family enterprise, he did so in 1991, when his father was 67 and clearly had no other successors. "I could have missed a wonderful business opportunity," he says. Richard also knew his father wasn't about to turn the company over to him until Richard went through the paces. Although his father was delighted to have him on board, as were the employees, Richard was never publicly introduced as heir-apparent. He says, "I didn't do anything about a public announcement because I figured that I would outlast him. Why go through the friction of trying to make something happen that would have upset him and would have created more problems and negative fallout."

However, Richard was groomed to take over. He worked in sales almost two years; moved into the editorial department to write copy and to oversee the transition to desktop publishing for the weekly newsletter, the *Babson-United Investment Report*; moved to an administrative-level post; and was named company treasurer, where he worked directly for his father. It was when

Donald was diagnosed with cancer in 1996 that he began a transfer of power to Richard. When Donald passed away, Richard was president of Babson-United Investment Advisors, a subsidiary of Babson-United. The board named him chairman and president of the parent company in June 1997.

There are a few basic human weaknesses that make wooing, grooming and keeping a qualified successor a formidable and sometimes even impossible task. Among them is complaining continually about the business at the dinner table while your children are young. You have to expect it to filter down into their permanent memory bank. Another is the belief that once your family members come into the business, you are immortal and no potential successor can be counted on to run the company nearly as successfully as you.

You may see no reason to worry about grooming a successor. You have no plans to pass on your business to anyone. Your grand plan is to sell for a huge amount of money. That's your prerogative, but cross your fingers that you have something to sell.

If you care about the continuity of your business and keeping it in family hands, however, it's time to think about whether you've given your children a reason to really want to come into the business and continue it, according to *The Family Business Succession Handbook* from the editors of *Family Business* magazine.

There are certain building blocks that you can use beginning when your children are young to inspire them to enter the firm and stay. These techniques need to be added one at a time like the layers of a beautifully baked wedding cake.

First layer: Strive to paint a positive rather than negative picture of the business at home when your children are young. Children react to everything you say and how you say it. They are quick to pick up negative vibes. If you're fatigued and harried when you come home and complain night after night that business is bad, employees don't work hard enough, customers are difficult and vendors are slow and unreliable, your family won't hold a favorable view toward your business. When the time comes for you to pass the reins, they'll be reluctant to take them.

Children are eager to soak up the virtues of what their parents do. If you want them to feel a kinship to the firm, it's up to you to let them hear some good news. If you have a great sales team, excellent customer relationships, or if you just grabbed an important account or made a tremendous sale, say it. Convey to your children the importance of the business to the community and to employees.

You don't have to paint a pseudo-rosy picture. You can be honest and mention the downsides, but don't dwell on them. If you have a bad day, show your children that even in tough times, you can cope.

Here's a case in point. One son of a contractor, who owned his own firm said that while he was growing up, his exposure to his father's business was mostly negative. The business sucked out all of his father's energy, leaving little for his family. The son remembers going out to dinner on Friday evenings and on the way swinging by job sites. On one of these outings, his father found a job had been left uncompleted. He sped the car to the local bar, where he found his workmen and ordered them to return to the job site. After witnessing many scenes like this, none of his three sons chose to go into the business, and the father eventually sold it.

Second layer: Do not treat the company as a playground and babysit your children at the office. It's unprofessional and gives them the wrong impression. Moreover, it alienates your employees. If you do bring your kids to the office when they're young, give them something productive to do such as copying, licking envelopes or filing. Introduce them to the employees, and when they're a little older, expose them to key suppliers, clients, bankers and board members. Let them sit in on a meeting, see what you're working on and contribute an idea. In general, make them feel part of the team. When they're old enough to work, let them do something substantive like selling or working in the warehouse to fill orders to learn the products and staff.

Third layer: Encourage your children to gain outside experience. In most cases, this is crucial. Children who come in right out of school don't learn if they could have made it on their own. It's healthy to earn their spurs elsewhere in a neutral environment where they work hard, are judged on their own merits, and can amass their own ideas and accomplishments. Being responsible for making your own decisions and mistakes is heady and necessary. Also, working away from the family microscope gives your children perspective to make some comparisons and judge if they're in the right spot. Those who have never worked elsewhere might have a distorted picture of your business and their value to it.

However, there can be exceptions to this "work elsewhere" rule. Sometimes you've done such a good job selling the pluses of your firm to your children that they're passionate about your business. They've worked there summers and know this is the only place they want to work full-time, and they're qualified to do so. Other times, a crisis or work conditions may demand immediate entry.

If your children are not interested in joining the business, or worse, are inept, don't pressure them into joining. On the other hand, don't fear that if your children work elsewhere, they won't come home. Quite frankly, a simple rule applies! If they're interested in your business, they'll enter.

Fourth layer: Don't allow key managers to worry that successors entering the business put their jobs at risk. You can remedy this by giving your children a job only if one is available. Don't create one. Explain to employees that your successors are being groomed to take over your job, not theirs, and the best thing that managers can do is to be part of the grooming process. Offer something special—a promotion, raise or perhaps a special bonus—for key managers who mentor your children. Let them know that, if your children are not properly prepared to assume responsibility, the business likely will be sold and the employees may lose their jobs as a result.

Fifth layer: Allow your children to learn from their mistakes rather than have you micromanage all their decisions. This is a basic tenet of good parenting, and the rule applies to children in a family business.

Sixth layer: Deal with the "R" word upfront and honestly. If you plan to retire, time it so you don't discourage your successors into thinking they'll never take over. Don't wait for them to beg you for a stock transfer plan. Beat them to the punch. This will immediately establish trust and goodwill.

Draft a formal and public succession plan with a timetable for leaving. Pick a retirement date and communicate it to the organization. Stick by it. Identify who your successor(s) will be. There's no magic bell that goes off when it's time to leave. You have to pick the time. It's probably best psychologically to peg it to an anniversary of your company or other special event rather than to your 65th or 70th birthday.

If you don't plan to retire, but hope your successors will run the business when you're gone, tell them. That's your prerogative. However, you risk that they will decide not to wait for the opportunity to lead the business. There's no rule that you must step away, but you can transition more authority to successors to keep them on board, interested and learning.

Seventh layer: Avoid the semi-retirement syndrome. It can undermine your successor's authority and cause him to leave. As you get older, you might spend more time away from the business than in the business. Perhaps you go South for the winter for three months and put your successor in charge. The worst thing you can do is to come back for a couple of days and start questioning and overturning the successor's decisions. The employees get confused, start to listen to you, and your successor loses all credibility.

Eighth layer: Don't put your heirs-apparent in positions of authority before they're ready and have appropriate experience. Such a move will doom them in the eyes of management and breed resentment. A good way to keep this from happening is to allow your successor to learn the business by working in various areas and for different key managers in order to get to know the people and the business and vice versa. Parcel out the responsibilities and have a preset timetable. Have your candidate work in the office for a few years, then hook up with the sales team and work in the field a few more years, then do a stint under the general manager. While the heir takes on more responsibility, the founder should begin to step back.

The owner of a large mail-order business made the fatal mistake of placing his 26-year-old son in charge of all warehousing activity. He had no experience, few skills and no education past high school. He came in, took over like a big shot and alienated key managers, who began sabotaging the son. Several of the best managers quit. They wanted to see the successor fail. Eventually, not only did he fail, but so did the business, which went into bankruptcy and was liquidated.

Here are additional smart ways to make you less vulnerable to losing qualified successors and to make them feel more valuable:

- Draft an organization chart for the entire staff to show the chain of command and each relative's responsibilities so that there are no misunderstandings.
- Assign all your children to departments where they don't compete with each other and where you don't supervise them. Make your successors accountable to a key manager rather than to you and avoid any confrontations. Nonfamily members should do the mentoring.
- Offer a formal training program.
- Let family members come in for a three-month trial period and chart their work ethic, work habits, strengths and weaknesses, and how they interact with various managers and employees. Judge their job performance objectively. Keep a record of their accomplishments and shortcomings or have someone in their department report to you about how they fared.

- After they learn the ropes, assuming they are capable, give them a high-visibility job. This way, employees will quickly see their value to the firm and in turn the family members will feel useful.
- Encourage your successors to join trade and professional groups so they continue to build skills and their value to the business. They should also network with other successors by attending seminars and workshops or taking courses.
- Develop clear and mutual understandings of what authority and responsibility you are willing to allow your successors. Then stay out of their way as long as they stay within those bounds.
- Avoid challenging and questioning a successor's decisions and actions in public. Discuss your concerns behind closed doors and let the successor make any agreed-to changes.

Reality Check: To keep qualified successors interested in your business, start when they're young. In most cases, insist that they earn their spurs elsewhere. Once they come into the business, have them work in different areas of the firm for different key managers. They should prove themselves in each position, not simply spend time in it. Make them earn promotions. Years in advance, draft a formal succession plan with a timetable. When you retire, allow your successors autonomy and authority. Don't semi-retire and be a pop-in manager who overrides successors' decisions. Don't put children in positions of authority for which they're not ready and don't have appropriate experience. You need a succession and retirement plan that pays attention to what's in everyone's and the company's long-term interests.

28. How can you avoid morale problems that result from employees' fears of change expected by the involvement and eventual management takeover by your successors?

When Paige Jennings joined Jennings & Company, her parents' advertising and marketing company in Chapel Hill, N.C. two years ago at the age of 27, she was determined to prove that she was more than some ne'er-do-well looking for easy employment. The fact that she was coming into the family firm was unsettling to the other employees of the company her parents had founded 18 years before. She had a college degree from the University of North Carolina and worked five years outside the family firm. To diffuse hostilities, she and her parents agreed she would "come in at the bottom as a secretary-receptionist for at least three months to learn the business. But everyone knew that I would eventually move up. And that was probably resented by some of the staff," she said.

Because she recognized her colleagues' concerns and because of her own drive, she says that she "worked harder than anybody, often stayed until 8 p.m. or 9 p.m., came in on many weekends and did all my work and did it well." Nevertheless, it was probably not by coincidence that three or four staff members resigned within six months of her entry into the company. As the boss' daughter, she had a leg-up to the top. "No one admitted that I was the reason they left, but I think it was in many cases," she says. But she persevered and eventually was promoted first into agency development and then to account executive.

Her advice to others: No matter at what level they enter the firm, family members must be willing to work hard, display a great attitude and separate their family and business lives at work. "Gaining acceptance and being able to motivate others take time. I think I now motivate people by my example and the pride I have in my work." Her parents also did their part by not questioning her in public, yet they did not protect her either. "They let me fight my battles, which validated my presence, and they also didn't show any favoritism toward me, which was more professional." In private, however, they lent their full support and reassurance and patted her on the back when she was doing a good job.

In certain situations, actions speak as loud as words, especially if you bring a successor into the family business and want it to be a smooth transition. It's up to you as the founder to step in and send a clear, forceful message to employees that you plan to keep the company as a family business that will eventually move into the next generation.

At the same time, you need to allay concerns that your successor is going to turn the company upside-down and replace all your people. The worst thing that an heir-apparent can do, or be perceived as doing, is to push aside or fire loyal, hardworking staff who have been at the company a long time. Stress that you and your successor will continue to value and depend on the contributions of nonfamily employees. You can, however, explain that every generation needs to make its own imprint and that your successor eventually is likely to take steps to keep the company competitive amid industry and economic changes.

Besides conveying these messages in words, prove it by letting your heir-apparent get to know your employees better and on a one-on-one basis. Perhaps you can schedule one-on-one lunches or meetings. Or maybe you can arrange a rotation through various departments, but as a trainee, not as a visiting "boss."

Your successor must do his part as well. First, he should do what you told him to do: stay in school and get experience outside the family company. Once he comes in, he must work his tail off—preferably moving up through the ranks, listening well, not being patronizing, knowing the business intimately, and gaining exposure throughout the company.

Finally, a little humility goes a long way toward instilling trust. Your successor cannot brave the transition on his own. He must rely on the expertise of veteran employees and defer to their wisdom. After he is more seasoned, he will be better prepared to make any necessary changes among personnel. Your successor should always keep in mind that great people helped build the company and are still needed to keep it chugging along.

Reality Check: Bringing a successor on board requires a delicate balancing act of teaching him all about your business, keeping him motivated, finding a niche where he's needed and can contribute, and having him respect the nonfamily employees. Employees need to know that your plan is to keep the business within capable family hands, so succession is a natural and healthy event required of every company. Family members need to believe that their roles are valued, in order to ensure their security and avoid distractions that will reduce their performance. Depending on your age, health, financial resources and outside interests, it may well be years before you yield control. In the meantime, your successor can gain employee loyalty and respect by working harder than anyone else and deferring to the expertise of veteran employees.

29. What is the best relationship for a founder or owner to have with the business if he retires?

Jack Krenzen, founder of Krenzen Indoor Auto Mall in Duluth, Mn., was thrilled when his two sons came into the business and developed the skills necessary to continue its success. Now, after turning over most management responsibility to them, he is enjoying retirement. He spends summers at his lake house in Minnesota and winters at his home in the California desert. He talks occasionally by phone with his sons. He sold part of the stock to them and receives retirement income from the company. "As long as the check shows up on the 10th of each month, I leave them alone," he says. "I can't tell you what a joy it is to see the business doing even better than when I was there. And, I've developed a relationship with my sons so that they are comfortable calling me for advice." Now Jack spends time speaking at conventions and counseling other family business owners about the potential joys of a great relationship with successors in the retirement years.

Imagine an architect's pride when his beautiful new building soars to the sky, or a proud parent discovers that his children have matured and can lead independent, successful lives. An aging leader should be equally delighted that the family business can survive and prosper in a successor's able hands.

The best business relationship for a retired leader to have with his company is described by the word "minimal." He should receive enough information to feel confident that all is going well, but not so much that he feels the need to step in and offer unsolicited advice. The elder person needs the discipline not to interfere unless asked, but also the confidence to offer information and counsel when requested or really required. It's hard to define that fine line.

In the best cases, you and your successors set the tone together as you plan for the succession. Here are some suggestions for a game plan. Agree in advance:

- How often the successors will report information;
- What type of information will be made available;
- How often the retiree will come in for lunch, discussions or simply to schmooze.

Ideally, the retired leader should avoid coming into the office, except on special occasions. The idea is not to push him aside, but to avoid the potential for confusion as to who is the boss. Perhaps you can arrange to have periodic meetings outside of business hours or at a different location.

The retired leader should avoid criticizing or questioning a successor's decisions in public. He also should not brag about past achievements or constantly talk about how things used to be done in the old days. Conversely, the successor must learn to accept gracefully constructive criticism and advice. He should evidence humility and respect. In fact, the successor would be smart to seek his elder's worldly advice.

Both sides should periodically get together and discuss how the relationship is progressing. It's easy to get under each other's skin unintentionally. Sit down, close the door and openly discuss concerns and needs. Don't let resentment and tension build. If Dad is getting on your nerves because he seems to challenge you in front of the employees, tell him. He may not realize that he's creating a problem. Conversely, if you think your successor is taking too much risk with the business, raise the issue and discuss it, rather than nitpicking minor decisions or complaining behind his back. The key is open communication, handled with respect and in private.

Reality Check: Retirement can be one of the toughest jobs. It's important for both the retiring leader and the successor to respect each other's needs and positions. However, when you take the plunge and turn over authority and responsibility, you must not take it back. You can inadvertently do so through your actions, comments and body language, with the result of undermining your successor's credibility and self-confidence. The best role for a retired owner is to remain very much in the background. Try staying out of the way and experience the joy of being sought out by your successor for your wisdom, counsel and experience, rather than being resented for your constant intrusions.

30. How does a business leader attract qualified family members and choose the best successor, while screening out those who are not so good?

It was clear to her father that Jodie Tanaka, now president and chief executive officer of Tanaka & Co. Inc./Tanaka Advertising, a Minneapolis-based agency, was his most qualified heir. She had a degree in advertising and experience with other creative firms. Her older brother chose a different career path; he's an airline pilot.

Jodie and her father had worked at the same ad agency, but 10 years ago the two broke away when her father started his own firm and brought her in. "I had an absolutely good feeling about working with Dad. My father did it right to attract and keep me. In my early years of development within this industry, he did not overburden me with responsibility, but was overwhelmingly tough on me. I think it was because he felt that I needed to overcome the opinion that this was a cushy job or that I worked for Daddy who handed his little girl his company."

Jodie admits that it can be "formidable fighting unspoken challenges and perceptions regarding my ability to be a strong leader," particularly since she's a young and petite woman. "For example," says Jodie, "I have been in the front office and a vendor or client will assume that I'm the receptionist." Two years ago, Jodie bought her father's shares of the company and assumed ownership of the 18-employee firm. Jodie made it clear that she bought the company; this was no silver-spoon transition. "Dad was tougher on me than anybody. This made me determined to show everybody. Because I love the work, I expanded my responsibilities, worked harder than anybody, basically learned all aspects of the advertising business and began running it," says Jodie.

The grim-faced family business owner entered the boardroom. He knew he was about to open a can of worms. This was the day he was to announce his successor. He had met with his board to help him decide who would be anointed from among his four children. He prefaced the announcement with a summary of what was happening in the industry which, he said, was tied into his decision. Profits and revenues were down. He needed someone who knew more about world markets and finance than he did to take the helm, if the company were to stay afloat.

The firm would have to position itself for the future: adjust to global markets, automation, technology, and its current crippling debt. This would require a leaner and more flexible work force. He'd have to make cuts, which would extend to relatives as well as to nonfamily employees.

Deciding which family members are in and which are out can be more painful than losing your best friend. You feel boxed in. You're up nights. You cannot concentrate because you're so afraid of showing favoritism. And for successors hovering in the wings, the strain may be worse than waiting to hear if they got into a "good" college.

There are several tacks you can take in dealing with the issues of selecting the next leader as well as encouraging entry only by qualified family members. These range from avoidance—doing nothing at all—to taking the bull by the horns and making tough decisions that may threaten family harmony.

For many older founders, playing paterfamilias is the only role they know. It's too difficult to make a choice between children and risk their wrath, or the wrath of their mother. However, avoidance usually results in secrecy, poor communication and incompetence. It can be a death sentence for the firm, and a harsh and undesired emotional and economic legacy for the up-and-coming generation.

If you have a problem making these decisions, don't just neglect them or toss the ball in somebody else's court. The following are steps you should NOT take when tapping a successor:

- Don't let a nonfamily CEO make the selection, although you can accept any input. If you cannot choose, let your independent board (if you have one) or your advisors help. Their goal should be to pick the highest caliber leader. You, however, must be the one to make the final selection.
- Don't make the decision by default.
- Don't let your firm become a charity for any unemployed and feckless family members. Just because sons or daughters come with blue ribbon bloodlines doesn't mean they're fit for the job. Here's one startling example. The owner of a mid-size firm hired a consultant to help him decide which of his two sons should take over. He wanted to appoint the eldest because he felt that son deserved the job. After all, he was the first born and had worked the longest in the business, he said. However, that son was an alcoholic. In addition, he had alienated everyone in the business. The consultant warned the owner that the eldest son was the wrong choice. He might destroy the firm, but the father, nevertheless, felt obligated to give him the nod.
- Don't let a committee of siblings appoint a successor. This can go one of two ways: either end in an impasse or an ugly fight. If you're really lucky, the natural leader may emerge. But don't expect the family to make the best business decision because its views likely will be tainted by emotions and lack of sufficient business insight.
- Don't let the transition be a rotating one. Some succession arrangements have created revolving bi-annual presidencies among siblings. Sometimes the strategy works; often it doesn't.
- Don't let your need to pass on your firm pressure anyone into joining. If family members choose not to come in, don't push or hold it against them. Tell your children to pursue whatever they want with your blessing and emotional support. Remember, you don't need to offer financial support.

  One owner told his son and daughter that he expected them to join the business. He hadn't even kept track of their strengths or levels of talent, yet forced them to come on board.

They were unhappy pursuing his dream. Tired, feeling out of place, angry and frustrated, both son and daughter left. It was hard for Dad to accept that his children weren't interested and relations became acrimonious. Finally the business was sold.

- Don't let your decision be based on gender. Some older owners still have traditional ideas about women not working and staying home to rear children. Some fathers tend to view their daughters as their little girls. But this is slowly changing as more women start their own firms and name successors, and as more male and female business owners consider qualifications and skills rather than just gender.

How do you ferret out your best-qualified successor and family members to come into your firm? Is this a determination that requires the wisdom of Solomon? Actually, it's often pretty clear cut if you set prerequisites. Judge family on the basis of qualifications, education, leadership abilities and skills, not emotion. Emphasize that your firm is an equal opportunity employer for those who meet the standards set for entry. These should be developed and communicated in writing to your entire family when children are relatively young. Knowing expectations ahead of time makes it easier for the next generation and also easier for elders to say no. When scions are older and ready to join, they should be hired and compete for jobs and promotions on the same basis as other nonfamily employees:

- Education. Does the family member's education meet company needs? Perhaps what is required is a four-year college education, a trade school or a high school diploma, or an advanced degree in a specialized field.
- Work experience. Some companies require family members to gain at least two years of experience elsewhere. It doesn't need to be in the same industry but should be in business rather than academia.
- Competence. Whoever you tap to be your successor should be better than you are and bring special skills, training and education to the table. It's also important to have someone who gets along with key management.
- Interest. Choose successors who have demonstrated an ability to understand the business, and are motivated to expand, manage and maintain the firm for years to come.

- Chemistry. Parents don't necessarily have favorites, but their personalities fit better perhaps with one child than another. If that's the case, look at the different personalities and decide which fits best for what job and with which people in the company.

If the rule is to provide a place for all family members, you won't have to weed out anybody, but make sure the firm can support them all. It's fine to find a place for family members if there's room, but their needs and talents are likely different. As a result, not everyone can or should run the firm or be in a top managerial position. Talented offspring should be given opportunities, not jobs. If you bring in a family member, find an appropriate slot and don't push someone else aside.

Reality Check: Your family business should not be a welfare agency that takes in any and all unemployable relatives. Jobs must be given on the basis of competence, according to clearly worded and written rules, and the family members should be compensated and promoted accordingly. It's important to look at differences in contributions and talents within the clan and place the right person in the right position. It can be tough to select one family member over another or to decide there is no place for an offspring in need of a job. But caving in and making the wrong *business* decision will damage both the company and the family in the long run.

31. Is it ever okay to have two or even three children or in-laws sharing management by serving as co-heads?

Barry Forman, a co-head of his family's Washington D.C.-based wholesale wine and liquor distributorship, Forman Brothers, thought he was going to be the seller of his shares in the family business. He ended up a buyer. It happened because his family firm had too many chiefs.

This story is a prime example of co-ownership between two cousins and an in-law that could have toppled the third-generation firm. The second-generation Forman brothers, Isidore and Maury, each had three children. In the early 80s, they started estate planning by creating preferred stock for themselves and giving equal shares of common stock to their successors.

Barry, Izzy's second-oldest son, (the eldest son owns a bed-and-breakfast inn) was among the third-generation members to enter the business with his newly minted degree from the University of Pennsylvania's Wharton School of Business. Barry was passionate about his family's firm and knew it inside out having worked there summers and holidays. He clearly thought he would run the business some day, but soon he was to be joined by other family members, in fact too many. Barry's younger brother Howard wanted his turn to enter the business and was given a middle-management slot. Next, Maury's eldest son Matthew, six years younger than Barry, wanted to come in and be given a management position. In time, Matt became president of the family distributorship in Virginia, and Barry became president of the D.C.-based business.

But the plot thickened when Matt's brother-in-law Hal, married to his sister Tracy, was interested in coming to work for the family. He had impressive credentials as an antitrust lawyer and went to work with Barry in the Washington, D.C. office. Conflicts erupted from the start about who reported to whom and who handled which accounts."For an in-law not knowing what life in a family business operation is like, it's difficult. Hal came into the firm and he didn't have any history with our family. And he didn't want to be encumbered by any history," says Barry.

The problems that surfaced spilled over into the Virginia operation. Each decision became a battle of wills between Barry, Hal and Matt. All wanted the final say. The friction caused the warehouse operations in both cities to split apart. The family tried to repair relationships by bringing in advisors and therapists. They even tried to form a nonfamily board. Nothing worked. The only way to alleviate the mess, Barry reasoned, was for him to leave.

A financial firm was brought in to value the stock. However, when it came down to the final wire, Hal agreed to sell his wife's shares to the company and leave the firm. Now there were two co-heads and three shareholders. Barry and his brother Howard, who has shares and a limited vote because he is not in senior management, agreed to share voting power on a 50-50 basis with Matt. Matt and Barry also agreed to make the two companies separate businesses, but to consolidate operations. "As long as each of us is meeting his budgetary goals, there is no reason to meddle in each other's business," says Barry.

Is this an ideal situation? Barry chuckles. "You can't get around egos. This arrangement isn't perfectly satisfying. I'm not suggesting anyone in the world should try it. Serving as co-heads is a compromise, given the reality that we have an equal vote. But we have different strengths and styles, which sometimes clash. Also Matt and I are six years apart. Whether brothers or cousins, what the family experience has been in my judgment makes a huge difference in how that family will get along down the road."

It used to be that if you wanted to have only one head of a company, you had to make some hard choices. No more. Today there's a trend in family firms as well as in publicly held nonfamily companies toward having co-heads at the top and sometimes more than two. For example, Sanford Weill of Travelers Group Inc. and John Reed of Citicorp decided they could share the chairman and chief executive's offices when their companies merged. But can it work? Are two or more heads better than one? It may seem like the business version of "The Odd Couple," with two or more leaders at the helm, each with different styles and philosophies. But the differences can make these combinations a natural. When it works, it can create a leadership powerhouse. And when it fails, it can fail terribly.

Apparently, family business leaders think shared leadership is a viable option. The *Arthur Andersen/MassMutual American Family Business Survey '97* found that 42 percent of the more than 3,000 who responded believe that more than one family member may serve as co-CEO in the succeeding generation. A secret ingredient for success is that the next generation of leaders, no matter how many, must be clear about what each expects of the other and for the company, and view themselves as true teammates rather than as adversaries.

The second-generation Fendi sisters of the Fendi Group have had enormous success as five co-heads. They work and own the company together. They have brought on board three third-generation female family members as well. Why has sharing leadership worked for them? The sisters meet on a regular basis to review activities. Contested decisions are made on a majority-rules basis, with each sister having an equal vote. The sisters function professionally as a team. They insist there are no rivalries or jockeying for position. Each assumes a special role. Paola is responsible for the fur department. Anna directs the design division. Franci handles all direct Fendi sales in Rome and oversees purchasing. Carla, president of the board for Fendi Group Companies, heads communications, while Alda runs the fur boutiques in Rome, oversees all production of furs, and serves on the Fendi Group board.

Their mission is the same: to maintain a successful family firm. The sisters' synergy has enabled the third generation to step in, but not on their coattails. Anna's daughters Maria Teresa and Ilarai, and Franci's daughter Federico, started their own label, Fendissime. The cousins grew up in the business and absorbed the family culture and values early.

Sometimes co-leadership (unlike a diamond) doesn't last forever. One or the other leader may leave for greener pastures, or the firm may be sold. For example, the three presidents of Chicago-based Fel-Pro formed a collegial triumvirate until the company was sold. The partnership between Bob and Gene Pressman, grandsons of the founder of Barneys Inc., headquartered in New York City, was dissolved in 1998, 75 years after the company was founded. The two were co-chief executives until the company went bankrupt.

Although sharing leadership can work well, it's doomed if there aren't collegiality, similarities in style among the leaders, planning for the company as a whole and a shared vision. When there's rivalry or conflict between siblings, a parent and child, between cousins and in-laws, working together in business can become explosive. If there was rivalry between siblings in their early years, it may intensify when they work together. Often when two or more competitive persons run the show, it becomes a contest for power, limited resources and final say. There can be backbiting, hatred, fistfights, and even murder threats. Remember the Guccis?

In these situations, old clichés apply: Too many cooks. Too many chiefs. The buck has to stop somewhere. If co-management won't work with the personalities involved, there are healthy compromises to consider. You may have to sacrifice parity by having one family member run the firm and giving the other an almost equal but important role. Or you may have to bite the bullet and have one leave.

Some public companies designate one person as the chairman and another as the CEO, who in some cases is groomed to take over later. It's analogous to playing second chair in an orchestra. When the principal leaves, the second chair moves up. The first chair can't play all the notes, so the second position is extremely important. The same is true in business, meaning there's room for multiple leaders as long as they understand their respective roles.

There are two ways family owners often go about forming a co-leadership situation; both usually backfire. One is to give their successors meaningless titles such as co-executive vice-presidents. But these co-executive vice-presidents never really know what their roles are or who's in charge. The other is to rotate the presidency. This typically isn't a good move either, especially if there's rivalry. When the one in power knows he's going out of office, he may rush too quickly to make changes during his term. The next one enters and proceeds to undo his predecessor's accomplishments.

Here's what you can do to help make co-management work:

- Get an agreement from both parties that co-leadership is acceptable. Don't settle for a set-up that you know won't work.

- Write down the conditions for co-management and have both candidates pledge to stick to those standards. Include a code of ethics, responsibilities and the consequences for defying the rules.
- Outline managerial and financial responsibilities, in addition to details of ownership. This avoids misunderstandings and duplication of each other's efforts, which would be counterproductive.
- Draft a mission statement and use it to test whether the co-managers are on the same wavelength, speak the same language and have a shared vision.
- Dictate that the business comes first and foremost and personal vendettas need to be pushed aside.
- Make sure that tasks are divided, based on each person's special talents and skills.
- Match personalities. Generally, shared leadership will work best if personalities, strengths and management styles are different but not conflicting. Similar management styles can spell disaster because the co-heads may step on each other's toes.
- Set clear policies on compensation, perks, hours, and time off. Most experts advocate compensating differently. If one is doing more work and putting in most of the hours, he should be better paid for it.
- Require the co-managers to take courses on negotiation and communication skills. The senior generation should not serve as corporate referees. The successors need to learn how to duke out disagreements and come to a decision. It's similar to what the parenting books say about negating sibling rivalry. If parents stay out of the fray, the rivalry may dissipate.
- Make sure every family member who's involved with co-management is in the loop when you set policy. Don't hide information.
- Consider dividing responsibilities in the company and have each member stay on his own turf. Each should have a separate budget and duties, but come together at the management or board level to apprise each other. If the firm's too small, divide responsibilities on a project basis.
- Schedule regular formal and informal management meetings to air problems.

- Even if the co-owners get along today, there's no guarantee they will in the future. Develop mechanisms in advance to help resolve the inevitable disagreements that occur in every business. Possible approaches include a board of independent directors, required input from advisors and key managers, and mediation.
- Decide on a mechanism to dissolve all or part of the partnership if conflict becomes untenable. Provide a way for one co-leader to buy out the other, such as a buy–sell agreement.
- Set a policy on how other family members can become eligible to enter the business.
- Make sure that the co-managers understand their responsibilities to shareholders, both active and inactive. Help them develop a sense of stewardship and understand that the business is bigger than just themselves.

Reality Check: Co-management of a family firm must be approached with great caution, especially if the relationship between family members has been acrimonious. But it can work and seems to be a trend today in closely held family and publicly held firms. However, equal "partnerships" are very fragile forms of management. If there are family members who serve as co-heads, there must be a code of ethics and a set of rules to follow to make it workable. Mechanisms must be developed to deal with the inevitable disagreements without destroying family relationships.

32. How does a business leader overcome his reluctance to share information with children in the business?

Allen Bender has always been amenable to sharing information with his family about the construction business he and his late wife Beverly founded in 1971. The reason? "We were scrutinized by surety companies about our continuity or transition plan. They wanted to know who would take over some day, if Allen were to die or be hit by a truck," says Allen's second-eldest son Brian, 36, one of four siblings. From the day the Benders started their Sacramento, Ca.-based business, Allen L. Bender Inc., Allen felt that if he were forthcoming about financials and other important business issues, his two sons and two daughters would be more encouraged to enter the firm some day and take over. He did it right, says Brian. "Allen shared all his philosophies. He was like a coach and we were getting the best MBA program we could. He went to seminars and he sent us to seminars. He educated us and let us get as much experience as possible. I did accounting and was allowed to revamp the company as I saw fit. Allen was good about giving me his advice but letting me do these things. He enabled each of us to see and do everything and to have small failures so we could grow and become independent." And he succeeded in his goal. All four children play some part in the business today. Jennifer, 42, is secretary of the corporation; Blake, 39, and Brian, swap between president and vice president, and Kathryn, 30, is office manager. All four siblings, each of whom has a college degree, are co-owners.

Brian adds that his father, whom all the children call Allen at the office, made them work harder than anyone else. In 1992, Allen started stepping back and giving his children more autonomy and control. Three years ago, he stopped coming in completely. Brian says that his father is busy piloting his plane and playing golf. "Fortunately, because he wasn't secretive about his business, we had confidence when Allen left that, hey, we can do this," adds Brian.

You'd be hard pressed to find one entrepreneur who hasn't occasionally kept a few secrets locked in his desk, briefcase or head. This can, however, wreak havoc on management, employees and the bottom line, not to mention on family morale.

Chances are that if you're being cagey and concealing information, you're undermining your own goal if you want to pass on the firm to your heirs. By being secretive, you might just turn your successors away from your business.

Many entrepreneurs, especially business founders, are reluctant to share information. In the early stages of forming a business, entrepreneurs are worried about people quitting if they realize the precariousness of the business. In the later stages, owners are afraid employees will want too much in salary or perks if they find out the business is doing so well. Children might be less motivated to develop an appropriate work ethic. Some leaders simply don't trust people with the information or think concealing it enhances their power.

Nevertheless, family members may feel hurt and resentful when information is kept from them. If you're hesitant to share information with your children, you should carefully think through the consequences. Admittedly, discussing such sensitive topics as your estate plan is difficult. Upon being advised to share information with her children, one business owner was aghast. "You expect us to share financial information with our kids, employees and management!" she exclaimed. "Our financial officer doesn't even know how much money the family takes out of the business."

This is erroneous thinking. You cannot manage and the children cannot successfully learn the business without access to full information. They can't learn to budget and exercise cost control if they lack a realistic understanding of the firm's and their financial situation.

Some business owners don't want their children to know the value of the business for fear that they will lose motivation and drive. Sometimes this strategy works, but ultimately it backfires. Sooner or later, they will find out. In the meantime, their drive and motivation are a function of how you raise them and of the example that you set. In fact, giving your successors a taste of wealth may motivate them to come into the business and work as hard as you did to continue its success. If you deny them access to information, they inevitably will come to erroneous conclusions about the information they seek. False information and the uninformed conclusions drawn from it typically are worse than the facts and informed conclusions.

Better to communicate openly on all matters. However, how much you divulge to your children depends on you, your children, their maturity level and the way they handle their money. Once you feel they have the maturity and the experience, they should be given access to more information that makes them feel a greater part of the firm.

How does an heir-apparent deal with a secretive parent or in-law? He can schedule a talk with the parent face-to-face. If he isn't yet in the business but has some interest, here's a possible conversation to start a dialogue: "I'm interested in the firm and possibly trying to make a career here, but in order to make this decision, I need facts. How many family members can the firm support, what are the requisites for entry, and what are your expectations of me? Also, where do you see the business headed and how can I make the greatest impact? If I were going to work for another business, I'd expect to receive that information from the company, and I expect it in this particular case."

Reality Check: Entrepreneurs are secretive at heart. It's the nature of what they do, why they choose to be their own boss and why they keep their firms private. However, by not imparting information to the family and key managers you limit their ability to understand the business and eventually weaken their contribution to and love for the firm. Secrecy keeps people from making informed decisions and fosters distrust, potentially with devastating impact on the business, the family or both.

33. How does a boss handle a successor's improper decision-making? How do successors keep the older generation from sabotaging their decisions?

Susan (not her real name), vice president, sales, of her father's 20-year-old Midwestern wholesaling company, was getting frustrated. Her father constantly challenged her decisions. Most recently, he forced her to cancel a sales contract with a large customer because he felt that the company could not make money from the deal. When asked why, he said that the margins were too thin. He then chastised her for not pursuing an account in a city 400 miles away. Susan told him that she didn't think they could compete with a distributor located in that customer's city. When she asked one of the other officers in the company what he thought, he just said that her father seemed to know intuitively what business to take and that you can't quarrel with his prior success.

Just the facts, sir. And, by the way, just do what I say. Decisions are often made poorly or incorrectly by successors who are termed unqualified, which may be a euphemism for saying they're "inexperienced," "inept" or even "dumb." Of course, some training and experience may be all that's needed. However, inexperience and stupidity are not usually the whole story.

Of course, good and frequent communication can help reduce disagreements over decisions. Additionally, the family members should try to establish parameters of authority. Maybe Dad would be willing to back away from reviewing and challenging a successor's decisions within some dollar limit or over specified aspects of the company's operations.

Perhaps there is a broader issue. The "unqualified" family members simply may not have the right information or may not know how to get it. Somehow, Dad must get over his secrecy and the children must figure out how to get Dad's experience out of his head and available to them so that he'll stop questioning or sabotaging their decisions. After all, you can make decisions based only on what you have at hand.

One approach is to try to develop a more "fact-based" decision-making process. It takes some work, but will pay off in spades. It requires a meeting of the minds concerning the business' strategy and complete information about operations. Here is how it works:

- Develop a clearly articulated strategy and business plan.
- Develop a financial management system that includes analytical tools and reports covering major aspects of the operation.
- Make the financial tools and reports available to the appropriate family members working in the business.
- Develop an understanding of the types of decisions that can be delegated without review, as well as those that must be discussed in advance.
- Keep each other well informed.

The process of developing strategic and business plans identifies target markets, objectives and motivations. It educates family members and employees about the company's strengths and weaknesses and develops a mutual understanding about how the company makes money and avoids undue risk. Before decisions are made, they can be tested against the business strategy and plan. If they are consistent with those plans, they are far more likely to be appropriate and far less likely to be challenged.

Developing these plans also requires challenging traditional assumptions and accepted approaches to conducting business. How do you really know whether you make money with certain customers? Do you really know all the costs of servicing an account or are you just comparing the sales price to the projected product and shipping costs?

As your business grows and becomes more complex, it is important for you to be able to analyze operations more thoroughly. Good management systems can provide factual information to support decision-making. You cannot determine the profitability of an account without considering warehouse space, cost of carrying inventory and other indirect costs. Perhaps experienced family members know these things intuitively. However, there's a good chance that their seat-of-the-pants approach is not always correct. Furthermore, successors simply may not have the same intuition and may require analytical approaches to decision-making.

The bottom line is that family members are less likely to question decisions based on facts rather than intuition. Disagreements become more manageable once facts are no longer in dispute. However, differences of opinion inevitably will occur if factual information is unavailable or is not shared. Your company's management information systems should provide what you require. If they only spit out an historical income statement and balance sheet every month, you miss vital information that can be used proactively to support decisions.

If the facts support a decision and it is in line with an agreed-upon plan, the decision-making process becomes less emotional. Both generations can start a debate with a common grounding in the facts and focus their attention on the critical judgmental issues associated with making the call. At this point, referring to the strategy can be a big help. Is every decision in line with the original plan? Is there a supportable justification for departing from the plan?

Reality Check: Stories abound about inept family members who come into the firm, stick their fingers into the proverbial family pie and hurt the company because of bumbling decisions and the senior generation's efforts to sabotage them. In both cases, it often happens not because anyone is unseasoned or vindictive, but because the family members lack a common understanding of the business plan and how the business makes money. There will be disagreements and wrong decisions. Those go with the territory. However, with open communication, a common grounding in facts generated by up-to-date management information systems, and mutual agreement on business strategy and plans, there will be less confusion, frustration and purported sabotage.

34. How does the older generation best delegate responsibility and authority to the younger generation?

Seymour Israel, 65, who heads Universal Engineering Sciences, a $20 million 270-employee firm headquartered in Orlando, Fl., with 11 other branches throughout the state, has made it clear that when he leaves the business, his son Mark, 33, will take over. But this was not a directive. Mark loved the business. He knew it well. "Dad started taking me to the office when I was five. I'd play with the dirt and sit on the big equipment. And we had a big drawing board to sketch on. It was fun. Somehow the idea of working in a family business got drilled into my head. Dad always talked about the business at home, mostly the good things," says Mark. He worked in the firm during high school and college as a technician. "It's typical to have high school graduates in that position that involves lots of field work and heavy lifting," says Mark, who learned the engineering business from the ground up. He also received a degree in engineering and was licensed shortly after. After working for another firm in New York for a year, he joined the family business and worked in all departments. Mark, who is currently vice president, is less involved in the engineering and more in business development, where he puts his MBA to good use. His goal is to take over, but he works hard to earn that right and the respect of the other employees. Another thing his father did right was to prepare employees for the change in ownership and leadership. Seymour has slowly backed away from the day-to-day duties, handing them to Mark.

Nothing in business is static. Running a company is hard nowadays, and you must constantly find new ways to run your business better. Your successors, particularly if they have experience outside your business and a solid education, can be a source of new ideas. But you have to give them room to exercise their knowledge.

Delegating is a skill that must be learned. You have to have reasonable confidence that the person can handle the responsibility and you have to accept the risk that he'll make a mistake. You have to overcome the belief that the world will come to an end if anyone else is allowed to make a decision. The best way to start is slowly. Grant a little authority and see how the family member handles it. With any luck, everything will work out fine and you'll feel comfortable about granting a little more authority the next time.

When is the right time to turn over authority? Apparently, it is not a decision based solely on the age of the owner or the successor. According to the *Arthur Andersen/MassMutual American Family Business Survey '97*, of the more than 3,000 respondents, 11 percent had CEOs aged 71 or older. So it's not a matter of age. But the ultimate question persists: Is the senior generation of these businesses waiting too long to turn over the reins? The child of a 70-year old is probably 40 to 45 years old. Is it reasonable to expect him to wait much longer for a turn to run the business? Conversely, if the successors "aren't quite ready yet," is it reasonable to think that they'll ever be ready?

Here's how you can achieve the peace of mind to step back and let your successors shoulder more duties:

- When your successors enter the business, don't have them work for you. Have them work for key managers. It may be easier for your managers to grant authority than for you. Put a buffer between you and your successors, particularly in the beginning.

- Start them in areas of the business where they can't do much damage.
- Encourage key managers to train your successors, to instill their knowledge of the business and their ways of doing things. These managers should be treated as your partner in educating and training your successors. At the same time, you must assure them that their jobs are secure and that they will not lose them to your successors.
- Communicate frequently with your successors and help them reach appropriate decisions. Ask their opinions and debate issues, but don't squash their creativity.
- Attend family business training sessions, trade seminars and trade shows together. Although the younger generation should be mentored by key executives, it's still necessary to learn the business from a parent. Traveling together is a way to continue to bond and a way for you to share the secrets of your success with your children outside of the office.
- Make sure there's clear communication about the responsibilities that you're delegating and what your expectations are. Have specific tasks. If you put an heir in charge of a sales area, be sure he understands how to execute those duties, whom you expect him to call on, where you expect him to go, and how much time you expect him to put into the job.
- A strict timetable can counteract unrealistic expectations. Your children should be moved into different areas once they've mastered skills in the area they're in. Let their boss evaluate their abilities. When the time is ripe, move them on to another area. The goal is for them to understand the company thoroughly.
- Treat your successors like other employees. Give positive feedback, praise and constructive criticism when appropriate and offer new challenges.

Reality Check: To pass responsibility and authority to the younger generation you must be ready to step back. Take a broad view of family members' talents, qualifications and experience. Start small and increase their responsibility over time. Explain your expectations clearly so there is no confusion. Enable them to make decisions and implement their own ideas in their particular division. Then sit back and experience the joy of watching them succeed, possibly beyond your wildest dreams.

35. What is the best way for a founder to give a successor a sense of well-being and self-worth in the family business?

Tom Mullaney, the second-born of three siblings, cherishes his third-generation family business, Mullaney's Pharmacy in Pleasant Ridge, Oh, like a precious heirloom. Part of the reason is that his father always had confidence in Tom's ability and conveyed the message that the business was there for him, if he wanted it.

Tom grew up in the business and never wanted to leave. As a child, he'd sit on the counter and count pills. Tom received a pharmacy degree from the University of Kentucky and came right in. "The business is in my blood, so to speak," he says.

This family passion has kept the independent pharmacy, founded by his grandfather, afloat despite competition from large conglomerates looming around the corner—Kmart, Wal-Mart and Walgreens. Mullaney's revenues are up. In fact, the pharmacy just had its best year ever, helped by its foray into medical equipment sales, says Tom. Tom was given the autonomy to expand the business into the new niche, which helped ratchet up business. Ten years ago, the operation moved into larger quarters. Today there are two stores and 30 employees. Tom's two brothers have no interest in the family business, so in 1992, Tom took over. His father still works as a full-time pharmacist and owns the majority of the stock. However, Tom is being given more shares and is buying them as well.

When you relinquish authority to your successor, the message empowers. It says: "You can do it." If you believe in him, he will believe in himself. But respect must be earned. Some owners do this early on. If you are willing to give up some control, and if your successor is qualified and ready, doing so can be a wonderful confidence builder and great for the firm. It shows a real vote of trust. Keep in mind that what your heir does is not a contest with you. You need to allow your successor the autonomy to play a major role in what you've built and allow him to continue to build. Choose your timing carefully or you may set him up for failure. The following 10 tips will help:

1. Insist on outside experience before a family member comes to work for your company, and tout its importance. Working elsewhere will enable your successor to have a better perspective, a more professional attitude, a greater sense of self-worth and skills that can be valuable to the business.
2. Openly discuss your expectations and the roles that your successors are expected to play.
3. Develop a clear and mutual understanding of compensation, perks, work hours and habits.
4. Have your successors work for and report to nonfamily managers. Don't let them report directly to you.
5. As your successors gain experience, relinquish authority as they become able to handle it. Give the successor enough autonomy to operate the segment of the business for which he is responsible using his principles and ideas.
6. You must not override your successor's decisions once you delegate authority. Allow him to make mistakes. But don't put the successor in a position to make a big costly mistake that could cripple the business until he has proven himself ready for that much responsibility.
7. Hold periodic meetings to update each other on where the organization is going. You need to communicate openly and candidly, and be as truthful and forthcoming with information as possible. Don't hide news from each other or you'll set a precedent. You will end up doing things behind each other's backs.
8. Have an organized approach to your retirement that's specific and logical. This will show your successor, employees, clients and suppliers that you mean business and that your heir-apparent will be in charge some day. If you are having trouble deciding whom to appoint as successor, keep watch. Analyze strengths and weaknesses of each. The natural successor, the heir who takes on more responsibility and problems, will stand out.
9. Organize a transition team that includes the departing head and the successor as Arthur Ochs Sulzberger did when he retired as chairman and CEO of the New York Times Co. His goal was to "make the changes as seamless as possible," according to an article in the *Times*. Involve your board of independent directors in the evaluation and mentoring of potential successors.

10. Encourage your successors to take external education courses to brush up on business, technology, leadership, communication or whatever skills they may need to manage or to take over successfully. This sends the message that you want them to improve.

Having confidence in your successors from the start makes the task of yielding control and eventually stepping down much easier. Try to let your successor run with his ideas, even if you think he should go in a different direction. He'll learn on his own and that can be a more powerful message than if it comes from you.

Reality Check: Giving autonomy and authority to your successor imbues a sense of self-worth and confidence. If you really believe in your heir-apparent, he'll believe in himself. If you bring him in without experience or the right educational qualifications; give him too much authority too soon; give him some authority and then take it away; or fail to step down, you will help set your successor up for failure.

36. When should successors begin to receive equity? Are there different options? How can the family prevent resentment that can be caused by your estate plans?

George S. Grostern, an accountant and business owner, believes that in most cases only active members of a family business who have proven themselves should receive an ownership stake. But there are exceptions, including his own three children, he says. Twenty-three years ago at age 38, George bought a photo vending business in Montreal that his father Samuel founded with two partners, including a brother-in-law, and of which he owned a portion.

After joining and buying out the partners, George decided that all three of his then young children—8, 10 and 13—should get equity. A minority interest in the common shares was placed in a trust to provide income for George's children and, ultimately, a retirement nest egg. "Unlike a lot of business owners I believe in sharing wealth with my children and not keeping every last dollar for myself. I wanted to help set them up early so they'd have a good start. I've always had a good relationship with them and supported them financially and emotionally. All three today are professionals," he says.

When they were growing up, George also believed that his children needed to offer something in return for his largesse. All three had to work in the business while going to school and even if they had wanted to join him in the business they first had to work elsewhere. If they joined him, they'd also have to prove themselves before receiving additional equity.

As fate would have it, his oldest son Jeffrey, also an accountant, joined him and his grandfather five years ago at age 30. The other two children pursued different careers. One is an investment banker in England; the other, a physician in Chicago.

Because of George's basic philosophy that those working should benefit most, he used capital from the business to help his oldest son buy out his siblings two years ago when he felt Jeffrey had shown his mettle and dedication. "He's got a piece," George, 61, says. "In general, I don't think a child should get equity at age 20 or 25, but by 30, if you're working with them, you should have a good idea whether they have the right stuff. It wouldn't have been fair for my other two children to get all the benefits without working in the firm."

The company, which employs 25 full-time and also contracts out work to independents, has carved out a unique niche with its 400 Canadian outlets, which develop color and black-and-white photographs for IDs, passports and vanity purposes.

Many of you have spent decades building your businesses and working long and hard to make money, but too little time learning whether to hang onto it or share the pie with family members or outsiders. Just like you plan your day, your investments, a meal or a party, why not plan how you'll hand over equity in your company? It should not be a serendipitous act.

There are a couple of reasons to begin transferring stock as early as possible. First, and perhaps foremost, Uncle Sam's estate tax strongly pressures you to give away stock while you're alive. Lifetime estate planning allows you to take advantage of tax-saving exemptions, exclusions and techniques that are not available or as beneficial if you wait until you die. Second, just as public corporations grant stock options to their managers, transferring stock to your successors can provide them with incentives to either work in or work harder at the business.

Before you begin, you need to consider your and your spouse's retirement and other financial objectives. Through financial projections and "what-if" analyses, you can estimate your capital and income needs. If you have built sufficient wealth outside the business, you can afford to transfer the stock, at least from a financial point of view. If you lack sufficient resources, then you might choose to transfer only portions of the stock by gift and, perhaps, sell other portions to your successors in exchange for notes to be paid from future business income.

Next, consider your objectives from the standpoint of control. It is possible to transfer virtually the entire business, yet still retain voting control. One easy approach is to convert most of the stock into nonvoting stock to be transferred, while retaining the resulting small class of voting stock.

The next issue concerns your standard of fairness as it relates to ownership by your heirs. Should heirs working in the business receive all the stock, with none going to those who choose other careers? Or should the inactive heirs receive equal or a somewhat smaller percentage of ownership? How does a parent express equal love for children while recognizing as a businessperson that it may not be fair or appropriate to make them business "partners"?

Many owners conclude that they should give equity to successors in the business only once they have contributed to the company in a positive way and made a long-term commitment. This time frame may occur after a year, if your successor is older and experienced, or after five or 10 years, if young and green when he came aboard.

One major problem with early stock transfers is that you probably cannot predict which children will choose the business as a career. You also cannot know whether your successors will learn to cooperate and prosper as joint owners. You could delay transfer, but you suffer adverse estate tax consequences if the value rises. Moreover, there will always be future uncertainties no matter when you decide to start transferring ownership.

Rather than avoid discussion about your beliefs regarding equity, get rid of this albatross and have a frank talk with your successors. Tell them exactly what they will need to do to begin receiving ownership. You need to be honest and open about whether you plan to give any equity as well to your spouse not working in the business, to inactive children and to any key employees. Any decision should be totally yours, if you're the sole owner, perhaps with some input from a trusted advisor. It is wise to communicate a decision face-to-face rather than let your scions make assumptions, and possibly incorrect ones.

If they don't agree with your decision and discussions become heated, don't feel pushed by your children. They may have unrealistic expectations regarding their fair due or anticipated inheritance, what some term a malady known as "affluenza." Many children of successful entrepreneurs often harbor such thoughts, and well they should based on the lifestyles they have become accustomed to, unfortunately sometimes due to your indulgences since they were children. (It may have seemed cute always putting your daughter in new dresses, but it's another thing to keep funneling money her way when she's a working adult.)

At the same time, you as the parent should not have unrealistic expectations regarding what you hope your children will do with any stock you bequeath. Like an inheritance and child's allowance, equity should be theirs to do with as they see fit. Hopefully, you've reared them to understand such concepts and bear the consequences. One good book dealing with this subject is *Beyond the Grave: The Right and Wrong Way of Leaving Money to Your Children and Others* (Harper Business, 1995) by father and son authors, Gerald M. with Jeffrey L. Condon.

One of the major downsides of giving equity is the risk of resentment among those who don't receive ownership, or receive less than they expect. Again, open communication and explanation are keys to building acceptance. The worst approach is for your children to discover your decision in your lawyer's office after your funeral. Don't leave them to wonder why Dad and Mom did what they did. It is better for you to share some of the "blame" rather than let fellow heirs deal with the fallout and resentment. These discussions allow views to be voiced that you may not have considered. The children may modify their plans or you may modify yours. Ultimately, everyone is likely to be happier than if a situation is forced on them.

Regardless of your decisions, you should create a shareholder agreement that sets forth the terms for a successor to dispose of stock should the need arise in the future. Exercise your best judgment regarding ownership based upon the facts as you know them. Actively work to teach your heirs the business and relationship skills necessary to make them informed and cooperative owners. But have the shareholder agreement as an escape valve, if it becomes necessary for you or your successors to modify the plan based on future developments.

Reality Check: Your company is yours to give away in one fell swoop or to slowly parcel it off to family or key managers as you see fit. You must consider your retirement financial needs, estate taxes, plus your successors' demonstrated ability, commitment and cooperation. You'll be torn between the tax laws' motivation to give stock early and the human-nature desire to delay decisions until the future becomes more certain. However, with open discussion of your thinking and, ultimately, of your plan, it is possible to minimize problems associated with stock transfers. You might even discover your children's objectives and concerns, help deal with them, and position your children for a better future relationship.

37. How long does a good succession process take and exactly how should it begin?

Family business experts could study the kingdom of Jordan as an example of succession planning that started off right and in plenty of time, but needed to be rejiggered because of changed circumstances due to ill health. King Hussein, ruler for 45 years, had battled cancer. Observers were placing bets on who would take over—the king's brother, Prince Hassan, or one of the third-generation princes—Crown Prince Abdullah, Hussein's 37-year-old son, a product of a prior marriage, or Hussein's son from his marriage to American-born Queen Noor.

Originally, Hussein appointed his brother as his successor in 1965 and was careful that he received the necessary training. He made that decision when his sons were young and inexperienced. Later, after his sons learned the ropes and because Hussein's own health became a matter of great doubt, people wondered whether he would change his mind and succession plan. Before he died, he readdressed the issues and circumstances and named son Abdullah to the throne. Obviously, much more was at stake in this case than bottom-line finances—the peace and security of the region and even the world.

In a nutshell, it takes years to plan and implement succession properly in a family business. Exactly how many years depends on how much time you have left and what you've done up to this point. Succession planning is a bit of a contradiction because the more time you have, the longer it should take. If your successor is 45 and you are in your late 60s or 70s, your successor may have to take over literally overnight. But if your successor is 30 and you are in your late 50s, succession planning may be a much more gradual process, which is the preferred route.

Just think about the many important things that must come together to make succession occur smoothly. Here are some examples:

- The successor must be competent, capable and experienced in all aspects of the business.
- The family members must accept and support the successor.

- Your key managers must support and respect the successor, and they must be capable of helping lead the business in an increasingly competitive environment.
- The business must be viable and have the potential for future growth.
- You must be willing to retire and turn over responsibility and authority.
- Your and your spouse's financial security in your retirement years must be assured.
- Your successors must have a mechanism to resolve inevitable disagreements and reach consensus on objectives.
- Your estate plan, particularly as it relates to the business, must be understood and accepted by your heirs and be consistent with their future objectives.
- Your estate tax bill must be funded without undue financial stress on the business.
- Your heirs need to understand their rights and responsibilities as owners.
- You must make sure your successor and other family members know and respect your advisors so that they can help provide continuity and help ensure proper action after you're gone.

It almost boggles the mind how intricate this process can be. And it explains why it takes so long. If you only focus on getting the successor trained in business operations, you will miss many of the potential problems that cause the downfall of so many family businesses.

Undoubtedly, you are ahead of the game in some respects and behind the eight ball in others. The key to getting started is to sit down and thoughtfully and realistically assess the situation. You'll need to develop a game plan to move the meter forward on many fronts over time. Seek input and help from advisors, independent directors, family members and others.

You will have some setbacks along the way. You'll need to periodically readdress where you stand and make changes as needed. If it were easy, a far greater percentage of family businesses would make it through the tough transition.

Setting a specific time frame for your departure may be your toughest personal challenge, but doing so will convey to your successor that he has your backing. Each year, perhaps on one of your birthdays or the anniversary of the company's founding, talk over where each of you is in the process. Be honest and forthright with each other. The successor needs to be blunt and ask, "Hey, what are my prospects?" "Are they still doable?" You need to be equally open, perhaps saying, "I'm not yet comfortable stepping away, but you're handling such-and-such much better."

Reality Check: A good succession process may take years, but exactly how many depends on how much time you have left and what groundwork has been laid. You can never have too much time to adequately prepare your successor, family, employees and others to make the transition as seamless as possible. Take stock of your situation and thoughtfully consider your objectives. Then methodically address each issue that might stand in the way of those objectives. It's a tough task, but it's not insurmountable, especially if you begin now.

CHAPTER V

THE BENEFITS OF AN INDEPENDENT BOARD AND FAMILY COUNCIL

38. When is the proper time to organize an independent board? Does the company have to be a certain size in terms of revenue or employees to do so?

Hatfield Quality Meats, a 103-year-old Philadelphia pork processing firm headed by Philip A. Clemens, 49, a distant relative of Mark Twain, was founded in 1895 and continues to grow, moving into new geographic areas and markets. The 1,500-plus employee firm is now in its fifth generation with 46 family members working in the business and sales of more than $386 million. This is a company that accepts any family member for life, as long as the family member is qualified. But with so many, it's easy to blend family and business issues. To delineate between them, an advisory board of eight members was formed last year. They elected Clemens president. Three outsiders and five family members represent 182 family shareholders plus 75 nonfamily shareholders. Clemens says that one of the advantages of the board is to keep him from feeling that he's running the firm in a vacuum. Ostensibly, the board provides impartial feedback and keeps Clemens on his toes. They advise him on business matters and family issues as they relate to the business, giving him more time to focus on business concerns. Clemens believes that "a family business must be a business-first company and a family company second."

Today it is difficult for a head of any company to succeed without the benefit of outside advice. It helps to rely on the experience and expertise of others. In public companies, CEOs can engage consultants and access knowledgeable members of their board of directors. However, one of the problems in many family firms is a dearth of unbiased people to talk to about your business, family and management. Everyone is willing to provide advice, but whose opinions can you trust and respect? The employees most likely will nod and say what you want to hear. The same is true of top managers who are beholden to you. Family members have their own agendas and often lack sufficient experience beyond their own sphere.

You could hire consultants, but your company may not be able to afford an expensive advisor to handle each dilemma. Furthermore, consultants may not have the necessary level of commitment or first-hand experience. Accountants, lawyers, insurance agents and bankers are paid for their advice. But is their input the most objective advice possible, or might they hold their punches for fear of jeopardizing their professional relationship with you and your company? They also may be uncomfortable addressing emotional issues.

So the bottom line is that you may not have anybody to stand up to you or for you. Wouldn't it be nice to have a group of people who are unquestionably in your court, but will speak up for what they believe, even if it might jeopardize their relationship with you, other family members and the company? When they do offer constructive, supportive suggestions and feedback, without ulterior motives, you would listen.

One of your toughest tasks in gaining true, independent input, however, is shedding those layers of possessiveness and secrecy that shield your business. That's why most boards in family firms are comprised of family, friends, employees, and sometimes-loyal advisors, and also why they rarely meet. Their role usually exists strictly on paper, which makes it about as useful as a discussion with your bartender or hairdresser. Feedback from this legal fiction is anything but objective. As a result, neither the company nor you benefit.

An independent board of directors comprised of "non-self-interested, risk-understanding, mutually respectful peers" is the best way to gain impartial, experienced guidance. This group becomes a forum in which members don't have a personal agenda. They serve as a court of last resort, which examines hot issues objectively.

For an independent board to work it must have parameters, focus and a mission; otherwise it may flounder. Some boards take on one or two goals a year, perhaps a succession plan or a strategic mission. If organized and operated effectively, the board can help keep your company on target, help people mature, set policies and strategies, and communicate the company's vision.

The board can help make sure the successor whom you have chosen with your board's approval stays on track to take over. It can also help with challenges concerning business expansion, diverse capital demands, retirement and much more.

Virtually any time is the right time to organize an independent board. In fact, the sooner the better. But it's not cost effective for all companies. As a rule, a business should have a few million dollars of sales and a net income of several hundred thousand dollars before it is practical to incur the cost. However, a desire to grow and a willingness to listen to the board's input are more important than size.

If you're too small, there are viable alternatives. Turn to organizations such as the Young Presidents Organization, World Presidents Organization or similar organizations formed by trade associations. Some of these create small peer groups, get together and serve as each other's sounding board. They provide at least some feedback that owners need and often crave. Typically, common threads exist in any of these peer groups: they meet monthly and are comprised of companies with the same mix of operations and sales but without competitors in the same group. Once formed, the group names officers and sets ground rules.

In a larger company, accepting a board of independent directors is a bit of a religious experience. You must reach the point where you feel you don't have all the answers to your business' or family's future. Forming the board will mean gradually letting go of some control. Virtually all business owners who take the step of setting up a board say it's the best thing they have done for their business' future.

It's important to note that the function of a board is not static. It changes as the business enters different growth levels and subsequent generations. More structure and organization are needed as more family members enter the company, as the company grows, and as the company's challenges become more complex.

Reality Check: Sooner rather than later is the propitious time to form an independent board. One packed with family often is no more effective than the paper it's written on. An independent board is a healthy, professional way to gain objective feedback about issues concerning the business and the family's role in it. A board puts the business first. It can help establish much-needed policies and offer creative solutions and objective opinions about business decisions, succession, liquidity, advisors and more. As a rule, a firm should have at least a few million dollars in sales before it's cost effective to set up an independent board because directors should be compensated for their time and input. If the company cannot afford a board, a peer group can offer objective feedback.

39. What type of people should serve on a board? How many should the owner know well—professional advisors, family, friends and employees—or to what extent should they be true independents? How do you find independent directors?

Talk about a business and board of directors top heavy with family. David Runk, 39, is one of the heads of such a company. He's a co-vice president of his family's second-generation Lima, Oh.-based firm, CSS Publishing Company, which publishes books used by the clergy. David shares power with two siblings; all three work for their father Wesley, 64, president and chairman of the board. David, who has a degree in education, is responsible for commercial printing sales, purchasing and estimating. He is a co-vice president with his sister Ellen, administrative vice president, who also has a teaching degree, and brother Tim, head of Books on Demand, who holds a degree in political science and worked for another company before joining the family business.

When their father decides to retire, the triumvirate will serve as co-presidents. All three have been given shares and now hold the majority interest. "But Dad's still in charge. Each of us has special talents that make us a good team," says David. "In this family, our life is our business and our business is our life."

But how to separate the family from the business out of the office? The firm does not have an independent board and doesn't feel it needs one. Those who serve on the board are Wesley, David, Tim, Ellen, their mother and two nonfamily employees. They've found that having this board enables them to chart strategic goals, gain a better perspective of where the business should go and how to get it there. So far, this has worked for them.

Without an independent board, whom do they turn to for objective advice? David notes that his father consults with peers who own their own companies, as well as a close friend who works for the firm as a part-time acquisitions editor. David adds, "We're a pretty close family and personal issues are discussed at the same time as business problems. If there's a problem, we talk about it until everyone is satisfied with the results. We have on occasion called in an outside consultant, but that's not long-lived. They usually end up saying, 'You already know what the problem is, and I think you know what to do to solve it.'"

Back in the early days when your business was a simple Mom-and-Pop shop, a board of directors was one of those details you never had to consider. But as your business grew, life became more complicated. You incorporated, and by law in your state you were required to form a board. To you it probably was an annoyance or inconvenience. So you made it as simple and non-threatening as possible and stacked it with family, friends and employees. This story is typical of many fast-growing family companies.

However, a professional board can keep your company marching ahead, provide a new paradigm for decision-making, and infuse the company with fresh ideas, according to *The Family Business Advisor* newsletter. Forming an independent board requires you to let go a bit to allow others to come up with management and operational ideas while you focus your energy on your areas of expertise. It also creates a natural barrier between the business and the family so you don't let the two overlap too much in your business decision-making.

According to the *Arthur Andersen/MassMutual American Family Business Survey '97,* respondents described their boards as a strong, positive component of their firms. But do they really take full advantage of their boards' potential contribution? More than half meet only one to two times a year, while nearly one-fifth do not meet at all. Only about 17 percent meet three or four times per annum, while the remaining 11 percent meet five or more times annually. More than two-thirds of family businesses do not compensate directors, which probably indicates the owners' true view of the boards' value.

Can a family business' board then really serve a purpose? Absolutely, but only if it's formed and used properly and meets on a regular basis to discuss substantive issues. Its primary role is to be a "sounding board" for family business leaders to review and test management decisions; evaluate advisors and their suggestions; and pinpoint the effects of changes in markets and the economy on your business, according to *Family Business Governance: Maximizing Family and Business Potential* by Craig E. Aronoff and John L. Ward (Business Owner Resources, 1996).

WHO SHOULD NOT SERVE?

A board has a clear function, which is to represent the interests of *all* shareholders, not special interest groups. It should be structured and operated with that objective in mind. Stacking the board with family is not savvy management. Family members who are shareholders have an emotional connection to the firm, which is unlike owning stock in a public company. One family business advisor described a good board as a device that serves as a mediator to help family analyze decisions and look at options from all vantage points. If the board is all family, how can this be accomplished? Not very well. It's permissible to have a family member or two or even three on the board, but in no instance should the board be top-heavy with family. In fact, preferably less than half the board members should be comprised of relatives. A board should not be a training ground to expose your inexperienced family members to the business or to other business people. That will prevent the board from functioning properly.

Here are some thoughts about the types of people often found on family business boards, but whose involvement might not be consistent with the board's role:

- Typically, the senior owner's spouse should be on the board only if active in senior management. Informal discussions and family meetings are better ways to keep spouses informed.
- A minority shareholder with a substantial interest in the business should be entitled to representation on the board. But clearly that board member should be qualified. Aunt Wilma, who knits during the meetings, should not serve even if she owns 30 percent of the stock. A qualified, independent business person would protect her and the company's interests far better than she can.
- If you have two or three children in the business, but they're not in key management positions, there is no need for them to be on the board. They could be permitted to attend board meetings as silent guests. A clear-cut successor in a position of high authority in the business often should be invited on the board.
- Your professional advisors—lawyer, accountant, banker, insurance agent—don't belong on the board. You should pick up the phone when you need their advice, and they should feel comfortable sending you a bill. They typically don't make good board members because they depend on you for their business. In addition, having advisors serve on your board is a conflict of interest because one of the board's duties is to evaluate advisors' performance. That doesn't preclude advisors attending board meetings or making presentations when appropriate.

- Academicians don't necessarily have practical hands-on business experience and may tend to intellectualize issues. They should be periodically called on for counsel.
- Your key management people typically should not be on your board, although they may make presentations to the board and may participate in meetings as guests. The board is not a substitute for management meetings. A key role for the board is to evaluate your managers' strengths and weaknesses. It can't do that objectively if the managers are members of the board.
- Your close friends typically should not be invited to serve. They may temper their input to avoid offending you. Plus, other family members may question your friends' objectivity.

WHO SHOULD SERVE?

What are the ideal characteristics for board members? They should be non-self-interested, risk-understanding, mutually respectful peers. They should comprise the majority of members. "Non-self-interested" means that a candidate has no personal financial or emotional stake in the issues you face. That way, you know the advice is completely objective. "Risk understanding" means that the candidate has made tough business decisions himself, perhaps similar to those you must make. More important, the candidate had to live with the results of his decision. That differentiates a board candidate from most professional advisors, who go home after dispensing their advice and leave you to clean up after you make your decision. "Mutually respectful" means that you and your family respect the candidate and that the candidate respects you. "Peer" means an individual who is at least as successful in the business world as you. You and your family will listen carefully to the views of people with these characteristics. You will trust their advice, which is the key to a meaningful and successful board of directors.

The best size for a family business board is five to seven people, more than half of whom are independent people with these characteristics. You will find them in various circles:

- Retired businesspeople are possibilities, but be sure you tap those with current market-relevant experience. Limit the number of retirees so their advice is not out-of-date.

- Middle- and upper-management employees in larger companies, such as a vice president of marketing or of operations, also make competent board members. They will bring discipline and structure to your organization.
- Owners of businesses as large or larger than yours can make excellent directors, particularly if they have personally experienced and successfully navigated through the types of issues you and your business face.

Here are some suggestions about how to form a board and find qualified directors, some of which are outlined in *Family Business Governance* by Aronoff and Ward:

- Interview shareholders and key executives and assess your business' strengths and weaknesses. Develop a profile of people who can strengthen company weaknesses. If your company's weak link is finance, find a financial expert. If inventory management skills are minimal in your organization, find a board member with particular strength in this area. If you are contemplating expanding to other countries, find a person who has successfully helped a company start operations overseas.
- Define your culture. Find personalities consistent with your culture. If your daughter may be your successor, it might behoove you to find some female entrepreneurs to serve who may relate to and even mentor her. Perhaps you should have a director who is the same age as your successor.
- Draft a board prospectus, which is a document that describes the purpose and goals of your board. It should explain the type of people you want, company history, size, employees, locations, sales, markets served, market share, customer information, organizational structure, background on the industry and information on the composition of the board. If you don't have a written document that communicates the culture of the business and what you do, plus some history, you don't have anything to entice people to serve.
- Find potential candidates through referrals. Go to your key advisors like your accountant, lawyer or banker who work with other businesses and ask for their suggestions. Other sources include business owners, members of organizations such as the Young

Presidents Organization or a trade association, members of your church or synagogue, or other social organizations. Draft a letter of introduction, interview them, go see them at their place of business, get references, give them some idea of what they'll do and introduce them to family so they may have some input.

Most people are flattered to be asked to serve on boards. Board members don't serve because they need the director's fee to enhance their standard of living. Rather, they are enticed by the opportunity to interact with peers to discuss business and share their insights and experience.

Reality Check: Most states' laws require a board of directors if your business is incorporated. Most founders, however, tend to stack their boards with family members and employees who pose no threat to their control. However, you overlook a valuable resource that could help you grow and professionalize your firm if you don't go outside this small circle. Ideally, fewer than half the board members should be family and management people. The rest of the board should be filled with non-self-interested, risk-understanding, mutually respectful peers, many of whom are entrepreneurs or business owners like you. The ideal candidates are CEOs of other family firms or mid- and upper-level managers from large public companies. Avoid people who would not offer you objective feedback or represent your shareholders objectively, or who do not have current or relevant experience. Avoid placing your accountant, banker, lawyer, spouse or key managers in this important role.

40. What are the responsibilities and liabilities of an independent board? Should the board be indemnified and how much should directors be paid? Can the board disagree with the founder/owner or the children?

As G.H. Busch & Sons Inc. in Cleveland, Oh., grew, the family knew it could use some unbiased outside advice. The business used to conduct 450 funerals a year from two locations, until fourth-generation members Mark, 38, and Jim, 34, stepped in and bought the parent company from their father John in 1990. Their father agreed to the transaction for tax and estate planning purposes. The firm, a regional family-owned funeral service founded in 1905, now conducts 1,500 funerals annually from eight locations, and owns 11 different companies. Two years ago, the family also formed an independent advisory board, which has been a boon to their business and their family.

The brothers started acquiring funeral firms in 1986. When the two bought the parent company, they divided the pie 50-50. Jim, now president, heads operations, and Mark, vice president, oversees development. Their father remained on board, but it soon became apparent that the brothers were faced with some mild family conflict between themselves and their father in terms of philosophy, management styles, accountability, areas of responsibility and performance, says Mark. "We were having unproductive corporate meetings among ourselves with key management people and we were getting nowhere. So we brought in an outside advisor, an organizational development specialist. He identified our work habits and different personality and management styles. One of his recommendations was that in addition to corporate meetings, we establish an advisory board of leaders outside our industry," Mark says.

They soon learned how important a company's independent board could be. Members include a retirement investment counselor, a retail specialist, the CPA of a private firm in Cleveland, two key senior managers—a vice president of finance and a vice president of service, and the three family members, Mark, Jim and John. The three outside board members serve three years and receive an honorarium of $200 per meeting. The board is indemnified for liability as a safeguard, a recommendation of the company's attorney and insurance company, says Mark. "But I don't see where any decision would come back to haunt them." The board meets every other month and two weeks prior to each meeting, members receive a packet of information. "We analyze our areas of responsibility, discuss marketing issues, research and development, advertising strategies, public relations opportunities, pricing, consumer perception and more. The board members give their thoughts."

Most important, the board has modified the family's behavior through accountability. "It elevated the level of interaction among the three of us from siblings and a father to one of a business and professional level. The board has clearly allowed us to separate the family emotional issues from the business and professional issues. We've learned how to steer the boat together," Mark adds.

Once a crisis hits a family business, there's usually a quick scramble to put the pieces back together. Perhaps the business owner is ill and unable to work. Maybe the company faces a cash-flow problem or unusually high turnover. Who can you as an owner turn to for objective help? In tough times—and good times—an independent board can be invaluable. But how?

An independent board provides a focus and forum that can draw all components and people in your business together and make them—and you—accountable to one impartial body, which places the needs of your company first.

PURPOSE

An independent board will not run your company; it is not an operational arm. It won't decide which products your business should manufacture or sell, and it won't tell you how many shifts to run. Instead, it typically deals with broader issues that affect your company's success and growth, such as successor selection, business strategy and the quality of your professional advisors. It provides objective opinions on managers, including a review of you, the owner. Having a group that provides honest feedback is essential to professionalize your family firm.

When your board assists in grooming and choosing your successors, it's healthy for them to get to know your and others' strengths and weaknesses. Even if your children are not on the board, they can be exposed to the directors through casual get-togethers. The board needs to see them, hear about their plans and find out how they conduct themselves in social and business situations. Board members can also serve as mentors and role models to young scions and help bridge the generation gap. If you're 65 and your children are in their 30s, board members in their 40s and early 50s can fill the age and experience niche.

In addition, an independent board can help map a strategic plan for the business and the family, and set long-range goals. The board can help you examine the advantages and disadvantages of expanding into new markets, acquiring other businesses, selling pieces of your business that are not critical to your company's growth, and recapitalizing your business.

Other issues the board might address are: the decision to continue or sell the firm after your retirement, the family's value system, employment guidelines for family members, dividend and compensation policies, wealth transfer funding, participation of in-laws and inactive family members in key business decisions.

To address these issues, a board should convene about four times a year, meet with a planned agenda and priority list and have an opportunity to peruse materials, including financial statements and business plans, well in advance of meetings.

These days, owners can encounter difficulty in filling slots on their boards because of candidates' fear of personal liability in serving as directors. However, these fears typically are based upon perceptions of risk arising from suits against public company directors. Fortunately, there are few documented cases of lawsuits against board members of family-owned businesses. How risky the role is depends on your company. Directors are unlikely to be held liable if they perform their responsibilities with reasonable, diligent care. Some firms buy officer and director liability insurance, but that can be expensive. Most companies indemnify board members. In most cases, the potential for lawsuits against directors comes primarily from shareholders. Corporate and even shareholder indemnification is a strong deterrent against such suits.

Another obstacle is the time commitment. Try to hold no more than four meetings a year plus occasional conference calls. Set the meeting dates a year in advance. Depending on company and industry trends and crises, emergency meetings may sometimes be needed. Board meetings usually last one day and may be preceded by a dinner the night before to give members a chance to interact and discuss more far-ranging issues.

These evening dinners can be a good time to involve your children, whether active or inactive, so board members can speak to them in a more informal setting. Consider occasionally inviting spouses and significant others. Doing so will make them more aware of what goes on in the business. Plus, they are far more likely to trust the judgment of people they have met and with whom they are comfortable.

It doesn't matter where board meetings are held, though it's best to have them in an accessible city or at the company itself. Some companies like to hold at least one meeting a year in a resort or more exotic site with conference facilities.

You'll need to pay directors some sort of honorarium, which can range from $250 to $5,000 per meeting. A good rule of thumb is that you should value your directors' time as much as you value your own. Assuming you are the top officer in your company, try dividing your total compensation by 2,000 hours. Multiply the result by about 50 hours, which represents four full-day meetings, plus some preparation and telephone time. That may be a good indication of the annual amount to pay each director. For emergency meetings, you may be smart to pay extra to enhance the directors' willingness to rearrange their busy schedules. Of course, you should also reimburse travel expenses. Your respect for your directors' involvement should be reflected in the fairness of the fee.

Some business owners put off establishing a board of directors for fear of being rejected. You may wonder why anyone might want to serve on the board of your company. Most of those asked are flattered and honored that you think so highly of their skills and knowledge. Those who say "yes" consider serving on a board fun, challenging and an opportunity to hone their business skills.

If you're afraid you'll make a bad choice, remember that board terms are limited, usually to two or three years. So that all directors' terms do not expire at the same time, be sure to structure directors' appointments carefully. If you're just starting to establish a board, you may want to appoint a core group of directors at the outset—two or three, for example—and then add more members a year later. Their terms then will end at different times.

It is not absolutely critical that you accept your board's suggestions, but if you keep rejecting their ideas, you run the risk that some may eventually quit. Remember a few key points: The board's obligation is to your shareholders, and it cannot overturn the decision of its owners/shareholders. If you are the sole owner of your business, the board is obligated to you. You can call a shareholder meeting to remove board members. If your children are minority shareholders, the board can't override you in their favor. Nevertheless, keep in mind that you and your company will benefit most if the board is allowed to voice its opinion and, when appropriate, exercise its judgment. If you have the right people on your board, heated discussions may arise. But, in the end, it is unlikely that you and the board will disagree. Reasonable, unbiased people will make the best decision after all views are aired.

Some business owners just can't stand giving up legal control. So they create an "advisory board," which lacks the legal authority of a true board of directors. An advisory board also can be used if your business' legal liability risks are too high to attract real directors. However, try to avoid falling back on an advisory board. There is an emotional difference, a bit like the difference between a marriage and simply a long-term relationship. Commitment is the key. You need to be truly committed to listening to and respecting all members' input.

Reality Check: A board of directors can help your company set long-range goals as well as address pressing business issues. To get the most value from a board, compensate directors fairly for their time and related expenses, hold meetings at least four times a year, and give careful thought to directors' recommendations. Typically, indemnifying directors from legal liability is sufficient to attract qualified candidates, although some companies buy officer and director liability insurance as added protection. As a last resort, you should consider an advisory board, which functions like a legal board of directors, but lacks legal authority and liability.

41. What is a family council and what is its purpose? Who should belong on it, and how often should it meet? How does a family council differ from a board of directors?

Now in the fourth generation with hundreds of family and nonfamily shareholders, the Sweasy family of Red Wing Shoe Co., a domestic manufacturer of shoes for the occupational market, headquartered in Red Wing, Mn., has to keep its large family informed of what's happening in the firm. Chairman Bill Sweasy, 45, is third-generation head of the company his grandfather Jess (J.R.) Sweasy bought into in the early part of the century. Bill's father William D. took over from his father in 1949, and pared his responsibilities to those of chairman in 1973. His son Bill was still in college so he brought in an interim nonfamily president. Bill entered in 1976 and worked his way up the ranks. Ten years later, he was tapped to take over. But he was still accountable to his family. He formed a family council in 1986 to keep the family updated on the business through quarterly meetings at the company office. Although it does not use an outside facilitator, it adheres to a family creed that spells out rules which family members have agreed to honor.

The family charter stipulates that any member of the family over age 14 may attend the family meetings. This encompasses three generations of Sweasys—"too many to count," says Bill. The family council has grappled with many difficult succession and shareholder issues that could have become untenable situations if the entire family had not been informed and involved.

Call it family communication, education or public relations. Many families hold meetings that gather all family shareholders from multiple generations to share information, ideas and criticism.

A family council is important for a first-generation family enterprise, but even more so in subsequent generations when the family circle expands so much that it's impossible for family members to know much about the firm except through hands-on involvement. Because of the Byzantine web of family in subsequent generations, few know exactly how much they have at stake. But they know one thing for certain: they have been bequeathed stock in their company and desperately want accurate information about their firm's performance and whether their shares are appreciating, declining or stagnant.

A family council or meeting provides a two-way street: its purpose is to educate your family and to gain feedback from your relatives about matters important to them. Members typically listen and ask lots of questions about what is going on and whether management is doing its job well. Meetings can be used to provide information about company financials and new product lines or services. They also provide a forum to air family concerns, ideas and even feuds and to design ways to resolve conflict. Most important is that all members hear the same information at the same time, whatever its content, so that rumors are dispelled, hidden agendas tossed aside and everyone's fears allayed. As a result of improved communications, the meetings provide not just important data, but extend goodwill to all who have a stake in your business.

One important caveat: a family council is not to be confused with a board of directors. While both significantly change the way your family firm has been historically managed, the two organizations have different roles. Your board is focused on the business, its strategy and management. It is a business organization. The family council addresses family matters and issues of importance to owners. It is a forum to inform the owners about the business and for owners to express views about the business' overall objectives. Through the family council, the owners can determine and nourish the appropriate culture under which the business should operate, including broad perspectives about the business' role in the community, ethical operations, overall profit objectives and more. You can express these views in an organized way and provide them to the board of directors through the family council. The council also provides a mechanism for educating younger family members and for developing and maintaining commitment to the business. It is a place to voice family concerns and share ideas.

A family council is really a tool to provide structure to your family meetings. The amount of formality typically is a function of the size of your family, with larger families opting for greater structure and strictness. Your family council may elect officers, keep minutes of your meetings and sponsor a family newsletter to foster knowledge of family members' activities. It may designate specific members who will serve as a liaison to your board of directors.

The best-structured councils hold meetings at regular intervals, typically once or twice a year in larger families and more frequently for smaller ones. Meetings should last a predetermined period of time, typically one or two days. A respected family member or an impartial outsider often serves as moderator or facilitator.

Ideally, each family member should receive material in advance of the meeting. Materials should include a mission statement, agenda, list of attendees, changes in short- or long-term business strategy, and a discussion of any particular problems the business faces within its industry or because of the economy. Some meetings can be more educational in nature and discuss pertinent tax or estate planning issues, business valuation matters and succession issues. For these, certain reading may be suggested in advance.

Other meetings can include recreation and social activities to encourage distantly related relatives to learn about each other's interests and concerns. One family business held its 40th anniversary meeting at the Canyon Ranch in Tucson, Az., as a way for the CEO to show his commitment to a healthy lifestyle, which he has tried to instill in his children and their spouses. All participants received cardiac stress tests and everyone had an appointment with a physician. The family also attended a consultation on behavioral health and a lecture on good eating habits.

ADVANCE PREPARATION

Before any meetings, ask family members to do their homework by making a list of issues they want discussed, read industry-related articles and attend lectures on business and family business matters.

You may also ask your members to come to each meeting with a nonbusiness-related story. In advance of a meeting, a facilitator might pose an icebreaker such as: "What are your fondest and happiest memories of the family and of the business?" or "What would you like to learn about the company?" Storytelling can loosen up your most serious, crusty relatives.

In spite of so many potentially positive results, many owners still balk at the idea of organizing a family council. They may feel it's nobody's business, not even of family members, to know what goes on in the firm, or they don't want anyone else's opinion. They may claim that meetings provide no substantive help and function more as a holiday gathering. Some owners fear they will have to yield some or all of their leadership and, consequently, rationalize that a council would duplicate their board, especially if it is jam-packed with family. Keeping family members totally in the dark is counterproductive in the long run. You cannot expect them to be willing, supportive owners of a business that is kept secret from them.

To make the distinction between a council and board clear to your family, your family council may want to develop a charter. The charter describes the purpose of the council and establishes policies for how meetings are to be conducted, how often they are to be held and who may attend. Charters can set other guidelines, such as whether or not a facilitator should be used, how long a particular matter can be debated and what kind of follow-up is required.

Reality Check: Lack of formal communication among family members is perhaps the single biggest problem in family firms. The best way to avoid backbiting and politics, which can easily arise in any family business, is to dispel misconceptions before they become ugly rumors. Many feel having informal chats about the business around a swimming pool or dinner table are sufficient, but what is really needed is a formal channel of communication where everyone hears the same information at the same time. A family council is an organized way for family members to debate issues, learn about the family and business, and provide constructive input to the board of directors. That type of governance is healthy for all members of your family and for your business.

CHAPTER VI
PLANNING FOR YOUR ESTATE

42. When should estate planning begin and how should you start a discussion, particularly if you're the spouse or heir?

More than 25 years ago Samuel and Sally Pennington started the monthly publication, *Maine Antique Digest,* in Waldoboro, Me. But the couple waited until a decade ago when they were in their late 50s to do serious estate planning. "We wanted to wait until there was something worth passing on," says Sam. But he also didn't want to wait too long since he says that all around him he has seen great antique businesses that have failed after the principal's death. "I don't know what will happen with Israel Sack Inc., the famous American antiques dealer in New York City, when the three second-generation brothers die," he says.

In the Penningtons' case, they had no difficulty broaching the subject of estate planning with their five children since they had always conducted frank, open discussions. They had also given each child six percent of the firm's non-voting stock, which pays dividends used to help fund each child's college education. The elder generation, which holds the remaining 70 percent jointly, has resisted naming a successor leader from among the three children who work in the business since they believe that's the responsibility of that generation. "It's up to them since we don't think we should speak from the grave," says Sam.

In our society, it seems taboo for anyone to raise the estate planning question. If you mention it, your spouse may worry that you've discovered a grave illness. If your spouse questions you, you might wonder whether there is a "friend" in the wings. And if the children raise it, they might be perceived to be greedy. Unfortunately, if no one raises the issue, it never gets discussed. The result may well be that your estate planning is not accepted by those affected after you're gone.

ASAP, *as soon as possible,* the senior generation should draft a plan and then the different generations should sit down and discuss it. Most successful plans take a long time to implement because they involve far more than simply writing a will. For example, you may need to create wealth outside your business both for your retirement security and to provide for children who do not want to be, or should not be, business owners. Think of it as similar to planting a tree. You plant the seeds but a large oak will not sprout and offer shade overnight.

After you do your initial digging—the equivalent of researching and developing a plan—you're only partway there. You need to water and nurture your tree regularly and perhaps even make changes, maybe replant it or prune scraggly branches. Like the tree, an estate plan must be nurtured and its elements must grow over time. In a family business, the corollary is making adjustments as the business and family members change or as the overall economy necessitates. And just as sometimes the tree doesn't survive in a bad climate or poor soil, the same may be true of a family business estate plan, which must be modified due to uncontrolled rivalry, unexpected family developments, conflicting objectives and the like.

An early start to estate planning is recommended, but when is that right moment? Experts advise starting when the business shows a profit and proves that it's going to survive. No matter what the owner envisions happening with the business—moving into another generation or being sold—he needs to plan smartly to minimize his heirs' estate taxes. Fatal illnesses and terrible accidents such as plane and car crashes occur. In these worst-case scenarios, a business may have to be sold to pay taxes if planning hasn't been done and sufficient funds are not available. More likely, the passage of time, coupled with business growth, simply makes the planning process more difficult.

In addition to being sure that taxes can be paid, other critical issues need to be addressed:

- Who will take over the business or be in charge of selling it? Does that person have credibility and experience or will an interim head need to be selected? It's too late to start training someone in a crisis; good management succession requires years of mentoring and grooming.

- Has a qualified executor been named to handle the estate and oversee inheritances?
- Are wills current or do they reflect old family ties and out-of-date finances? Perhaps the owner has been divorced and his new spouse's needs haven't been considered, or maybe the company has grown like topsy, requiring adjustments to the overall plan.
- Has adequate income been provided for your and your surviving spouse's retirement needs?
- Have you determined whether business ownership is desired by each of your heirs? If not, have you worked out a way to bequeath them different assets to enable them to accomplish their legitimate objectives without infringing on the business' needs?
- Have available gift, estate and generation-skipping tax exclusions and exemptions been utilized effectively, especially given Congress' penchant for making and phasing in changes to the tax system?

The best way to start planning is to assemble a small multidisciplinary team of experienced estate planning advisors. This team can help you define the company's and family's long-term objectives and be sure that all critical issues are addressed. They can provide objective input not only on the estate tax implications of alternatives, but also the willingness and ability of your heirs to handle the responsibilities associated with the property you choose to give them.

Family members should not hesitate to raise questions about others' estate plans. Of course, they need to be careful and respectful, and they should avoid prying into matters that do not concern them. Sometimes, you can trigger discussion by sharing a well-chosen article or attending an estate planning seminar together. It is appropriate to ask questions like:

- "Dad, I am concerned about whether the business can afford to pay the estate taxes if something happens to you or Mom. Can we discuss what planning you have done and whether additional ways exist to reduce the estate tax burden?"
- "Sister, I love your husband, but I'm not sure that we should become business partners if something happens to you and your stock passes to him. Can we discuss our estate plans and determine ways to deal with potential issues before they become problems?"

- "Mom, I really respect the business that you have built. However, I want to start my own business. What are your thoughts about how I might finance my business without putting a potential financial strain on either your business or my siblings after you're gone?"
- "Uncle, I sense that there may be problems between your children and me after you retire. Family harmony is really important to me. Can we discuss ways to arrange business ownership that will reduce the potential for conflict in the future?"

Reality Check: You're racing along, running a highly successful family business, but you may have been so busy or so cavalier that you forgot one critical step—determining and preparing successor owners. Even if you think you'll always work in the business or are so young you can't imagine retiring, it's time to rejigger your thoughts and the planning process. Crises and tragedies occur and it's better to be prepared and ready to hand over the reins, even if that step is not imminent. More important, preparing your heirs and your estate takes time. Most likely, you'll be active for years. You must use that time to implement your plan. Start discussions early. Your advisors can help you understand the many implications of the plan they help develop and you'll be able to begin preparing your family appropriately.

43. What are the basics of transfer tax planning? What is the value of my business for transfer tax purposes? Where should the funds come from to pay these taxes?

Although 71, Stella Skonieczny, widow of founder Walter, still comes twice a week to the family business, Tesko Enterprises in Norridge, Il., a custom metal fabricator. Chairman of the board, Stella handles the payroll and accompanies her daughter, Barbara, treasurer and head of the concrete accessories division, on business trips. In spite of Barbara's pleas to begin giving stock to those active in the business, Stella still retains a majority, 52-percent control, of the $7-million-a-year business with 85 employees and seven family members. The four heirs in management positions—Bob, 52, president; Lester, 62, a vice president; Theresa, 40, who was vice president of operations and is no longer active; and Barbara, 39—were each given 12 percent of the company stock before Walter passed away three years ago.

"My mother doesn't see the need to begin giving assets and cash to the relatives working in the business—me, another child, a stepson, two sisters-in-law and a grandson," says Barbara. "I've tried to talk her into it, particularly now that the company has WBE (Women's Business Enterprise) status, which means that it is owned by a minority. You have to have more women owning the stock than men for it to retain that status and I'm the only other female active in the business. The status gives us access to government projects."

Why does Barbara think her mother is reluctant and hasn't even made provisions for distribution of the stock? "She's afraid of causing personal animosity between me and those in the business, and those not working in the company. Some of the wives will feel their spouses didn't get their due." So, as a result, her mother does nothing, Barbara explains. "Her inertia has in effect become a decision." Barbara isn't totally pessimistic for the long term, however. "I think she'll eventually come around since it makes sense estate-wise and since she knows she's getting older and without a woman owning a majority of shares, the firm will lose its minority status. But it will take more time." Time may not be on her side, however.

Your goal is to have Uncle Sam get as little of your estate as possible upon your death. There are two basic types of transfer taxes that need to be considered if you're thinking about doing some smart estate planning. The gift tax applies to transfers during life, while the estate tax applies to transfers at death. Most states also assess transfer taxes, although there usually is a credit allowed against the federal estate tax for the state inheritance tax.

Generally, it is wiser to transfer assets to the next generation through gifts during life rather than through bequests or inheritances after death. There are four reasons:

1. The federal government allows each person to make a tax-free gift of $10,000 (increased for inflation) per year to each and every person he desires. Your spouse may also use this annual exclusion, meaning a husband and wife may give $20,000 per year to as many people as they wish. That wealth escapes estate tax at the donor's death, thereby saving up to 55 percent of everything they give through these exclusions. The annual exclusions may be used by giving cash, public company stock, real estate, voting or nonvoting stock in the family business, or anything else. In each case, the gift is measured by the fair market value of the asset, not its historical cost.
2. Post-gift appreciation and income are not taxed in the donor's estate. Imagine the potential estate tax you can avoid by giving $20,000 to each child, child-in-law and grandchild every year, plus the income and appreciation on those gifts. In addition to

your annual exclusions, you may give up to $650,000 during your lifetime, spread among your heirs or others as you choose, without paying gift taxes. Your spouse may do the same. The potential estate tax savings from shifting future growth and income on that sum is huge. Plus, the $650,000 exemption increases annually to $1 million from 1999 through 2006. Your and your spouse's wills should be structured to utilize any part of your $650,000 exemptions not used during your lives.

3. If gifts exceed the available annual exclusions and the $650,000 lifetime exemption, the gift tax is relatively less than the estate tax. Why? The estate tax is calculated on the entire value of the estate, including the money used to pay the tax. On the other hand, the gift tax is assessed on the amount of the gift, not on the money used to pay the gift tax.
4. More sophisticated planning techniques are available during life than through your will at death. An experienced estate planner can explain the array of available options.

Gift and estate taxes are among the highest taxes in our country. Any transfers in excess of the annual exclusions and lifetime $650,000 exemption are taxed at rates beginning at about 40 percent and escalating rapidly to 55 percent. Imagine your successors having to run a business saddled with a debt equal to 55 percent of its fair market value. The family might well be forced to sell the business.

You can defer the tax by leaving your estate to your spouse because gifts and bequests to a spouse are not taxed if structured properly. However, since your spouse will be taxed at his or her death, this deferral may just compound the problem if the business' value and the resulting tax burden grow during your spouse's life.

The government does allow an additional exemption for estate taxes on family businesses and farms. However, there are extremely complex qualification rules and requirements. Plus these additional exemptions may be of modest benefit relative to the size of your business, the added complexities and the costs inherent in their use.

VALUE SUBJECT TO TAX

Gift and estate taxes are assessed based on the "fair market value" (FMV) of your assets, including your family business stock. FMV is a nebulous term. According to IRS regulations, FMV "is the price at which the property would change hands between a willing buyer and a willing seller, neither being under any compulsion to buy or to sell and both having reasonable knowledge of relevant facts." Quite a mouthful. No wonder it is one of the most frequently litigated issues in the federal tax law.

Absent actual sales of family business stock between unrelated parties near the time of a gift or death, determining FMV requires consideration of numerous factors. However, valuation of operating businesses places great weight on future earnings potential, while investment and holding companies typically are valued by reference to the values of their underlying assets.

A valuation by a reputable appraisal firm is the best way to make sure that you have a realistic sense of the company's worth. However, you typically can approximate the value by comparing your company to comparable public companies. Of course, your business is different from any public company. But it is a starting point. Here is a series of steps to roughly estimate the value of your business:

- Step 1: Identify public companies that are in businesses similar to yours. Perhaps they are competitors. Find their price-to-earnings (PE) ratios in the stock quote section of your newspaper.
- Step 2: Add up these companies' ratios and divide the total by the number of companies to give you an average PE ratio.
- Step 3: Estimate your next 12 months' earnings and adjust them to eliminate expenses that another owner would not incur. An example of these expenses might include compensation of family members in excess of what would be paid for replacement personnel hired by a buyer.
- Step 4: Multiply your adjusted earnings estimate by the average PE ratio of the public companies to get an initial estimated value.
- Step 5: Next you have to adjust this estimated value for major differences between your company and the public companies. You might increase your value if, unlike the public companies, your company owns its real estate. You might decrease your value if you have a smaller market share than the comparable companies. This is part science and part art, which is why a professional appraisal can help.

- Step 6: The resulting value is commonly referred to as the "freely traded minority market value" because the public companies' PE ratios are calculated using the values of small blocks of stock sold on the stock exchange. Your company's stock is not "freely traded" because you can't call a broker and sell it instantaneously. Therefore, you can discount your stock's value for "lack of marketability." The marketability discount typically ranges from 20 percent to 35 percent.
- Step 7: Multiply the discounted value by the percentage of the corporation's outstanding stock being transferred.

The result is an estimate of the value of the stock if you make gifts of noncontrolling interests, meaning 50 percent or less of the voting stock, to one or more people. It also is an estimate of the value if you die owning 50 percent or less of the voting stock. However, if you die owning more than half of the voting stock, you must add a control premium, which often ranges from 15 percent to 30 percent. Avoiding this premium at death is another reason for making lifetime gifts of minority stock and for trying to reduce your stock ownership below half of the voting stock before your death.

Although determining the business' value can open Pandora's box, that information is critical to making informed estate planning decisions. Family members typically have an unrealistic view of the business' value; whether it is high or low, factual knowledge is better than the unreasonable expectations ignorance creates. You must have a clear view of value to assess your estate tax burden and take advantage of planning opportunities.

SOURCE OF FUNDS

Where does the money come from to pay the tax? Obviously, the best plan is to minimize the tax while you are alive. Unless you build substantial wealth outside the business, the business is the obvious source for payment. The business' ability to pay the tax is partly a function of when the estate tax is due. Although the tax technically is due nine months after death, the government grants extensions of time for up to 15 years for the tax on closely held businesses. However, numerous requirements must be met both before and after death. Unfortunately, the government charges interest, albeit at a reasonably low rate, on the deferred tax. The extended payment terms create an opportunity for the business to generate the earnings necessary to pay Uncle Sam his share, but it can still put a real crimp in business operations and growth plans. In any event, there should be no need for a sacrificial sale to pay the taxes.

Insurance can be a source of funds to pay estate taxes. However, it can be dangerous to rely solely on insurance because the business' value hopefully will grow over time. The resulting tax can outpace your willingness to pay the increasing premiums necessary to maintain sufficient insurance. Furthermore, insurance can get very expensive as you get older. Note that insurance proceeds are subject to estate tax unless you plan appropriately to remove them from your estate. Properly drafted life insurance trusts are an ideal way to avoid tax on the proceeds.

Some families sell part or all of the business, either privately or through an initial public offering, in order to raise the cash to pay the tax. Other businesses are forced to sell divisions or cut expenses to raise money. If these approaches are undesirable, an early start to your estate planning often can avoid them.

Reality Check: There's no question about it. Estate taxes are a major and expensive problem. The gift and estate taxes are calculated on the fair market value of the transferred stock. The problem is best mitigated through aggressive lifetime transfers that reduce the tax burden. Lifetime planning takes time to maximize the use of available exclusions and exemptions. You must start early to take full advantage. Leaving the problem to your heirs significantly increases the odds that the tax burden will severely hamper the business or require its sale.

44. What types of insurance should you consider to help pay estate taxes and provide funds for your heirs? How much insurance do you need? Who should be the owner and beneficiary of the policy?

In 1983 when they went into business together as architects and had the first of their five children, Nancy and Richard Becker purchased individual whole life insurance policies. After consulting with their agent, they decided that whole life would be a good way to provide for their children as well as save for retirement in a tax-sheltered vehicle. As their family grew and they felt the need for extra coverage, they supplemented the whole life with term."The natural tendency is to buy one type and keep your life as simple as possible, but buying the amount of whole life we needed was too expensive and the term was a relatively inexpensive solution. You can buy term for different-length periods and lock in your premiums," says Richard, whose firm Becker Architects Ltd. is based in Highland Park, Il. "We wanted to be sure we could afford their college educations and support the family, in case something happened to us or one of us," he adds.

About two years ago, the couple set up separate irrevocable life insurance trusts that own 20-year term policies so that proceeds flow to the trust and not their estates, thereby escaping estate taxes. These trusts are for the benefit of the surviving spouse and the children. A year later, the couple established a third trust for the purpose of owning a whole life second-to-die policy that pays off upon the death of the second of the two of them. It was established solely for the benefit of the children who survive both parents. As a parallel exercise, they rewrote their wills to coordinate all the insurance and trusts. They keep all the estate information in a binder in their office, as well as with their insurance agents and attorney."I feel we've done everything we should do with the exception of planning for succession of business ownership. I haven't done so yet, but may explore it in the future,"Richard says.

Most family business owners have automobile, homeowner's and business liability insurance to protect against worst-case scenarios. However, many find something distasteful about another useful tool—life insurance. It requires them to face mortality and address other difficult issues. Yet it can be an important device to ensure your business' continuation and your family's financial security after you're gone.

Should you buy the cheapest available policy? How much do you need? Which insurance company should you use and who should be the owner of the policy? The nature of your needs and the time frame over which they will exist are critical to answering these questions. Here are some sample needs:

- Creating wealth or a safety net to support your spouse and children if your other means are insufficient. This may be a potentially long-term need, though it could be shorter term if you are reasonably confident that you will create that support from other sources.
- Funding a buy–sell agreement, another potentially long-term need unless you plan to sell your company within the next decade or so.
- Creating liquidity to pay estate taxes on the business, which usually is a long-term need.

- A permanent feature of your estate planning with the goal of shifting wealth to your heirs at reduced tax costs, a long-term need.

When it comes to buying life insurance, especially for longer-term needs, don't skimp and just buy the policy with the cheapest premium. Premiums on most insurance policies are not guaranteed and can become onerous as you get older or if the insurance company is not as successful in investing the premiums as it originally hoped. On top of that, the insurance company itself may go belly-up, leaving you with no insurance. If the insurance company survives, and you keep paying the premiums, the government may collect more than half of the proceeds. Plus inflation in the value of your business and of your dependents' support needs might make the proceeds seem a mere pittance when you die decades from now.

Dealing with these issues requires great care in selecting the type of insurance and insurance company, determining the extent to which your overall estate plan will rely on insurance, and structuring the ownership and funding of your policy. You should involve an advisor who is knowledgeable in insurance products and structuring, but who is not compensated based on your insurance decisions. Truly objective advice is a must. Some considerations include:

TYPE OF INSURANCE. Term insurance looks really cheap compared to whole, variable, universal and other types of "permanent" insurance products. That's because the insurance company bets that you'll live a long time. As you get older, term premiums go through the roof, and you may drop the policy long before the insurance company pays off. As a result, insurance companies are more competitive on pricing term premiums until you get into your late 60s. A common rule of thumb is that if you expect to keep the policy in force for more than 10 years, particularly if you are in your 40s, steer away from term and toward a form of permanent insurance.

What's different about "permanent" insurance, which typically is far more expensive? Why pay higher premiums to buy something other than a term policy? Permanent policies are like a mysterious black box. You put money into the box. The insurance company takes some out for a variety of purposes every year, including:

- A mortality charge equivalent to a term policy.
- Heftier commissions for the agent.
- Money to cover overhead expenses and profit.

The latter two charges usually are higher than for term insurance. Any remaining money is invested, hopefully at a profit. In some forms of policies, you are given some say in the nature of the investments; however, only a minimal rate of return typically is guaranteed. If you add the investment earnings to your premiums and subtract all the amounts that the company extracts, the remainder continues in the policy and can be applied to future years' costs. So, if you pay higher premiums and/or the policy's investment earnings are large enough, considerable value can grow inside the policy.

If you read the contract, the insurance company has broad discretion over the amounts going into and out of the box. For example, the earnings within the policy are subject to how well the insurance company invests the money. If it invests poorly, you may need to increase your premiums to maintain the coverage. The amount taken out for mortality costs is based on the company's risk experience, so the charge rises if the company is not careful in deciding who else it will insure. The insurance company also decides its overhead and profit charges against your policy. All of this means that you have to have a great deal of confidence in the company's integrity and financial strength.

Why subject yourself to the vagaries of a permanent policy? The primary reason is that the earnings within the policy are not subject to income taxation. This gives you a clear advantage over buying cheaper term insurance and investing the premium savings yourself with the intention of using those savings to pay term insurance's increasing premiums. Stated differently, the mortality charges in permanent insurance go up every year just as they do for term insurance. However, the expectation is that the permanent policy's income tax-free earnings will accumulate and can be used later in life to fund part or all of those increased charges.

Here are some additional considerations as you ponder your life insurance needs:

INSURANCE COMPANY. Think of insurance as an investment. In fact, it may be an investment that you'll hold longer than most anything else. As such, you need to consider the quality and strength of the insurance company and choose your agent carefully. In most cases, buy only from long-standing, highly rated companies. You may not initially get the lowest premium, but the policy will more likely perform the way you expected when you first looked at the complicated illustrations and projections when you bought it. If your plan is heavily dependent on life insurance, you should consider diversifying your risk by buying from more than one company.

SENSITIVITY TO POLICY ASSUMPTIONS. Since the insurance company can increase premium requirements on most types of insurance policies, it is extremely important that you question the company's projections and assumptions. In the early 1980s, many people bought policies in which the insurance companies projected double-digit returns on their investment of policy premiums. When interest rates declined, most of these people were shocked when the companies came back demanding higher premiums to keep the policies in force. You need to understand and plan for the potential for increased premiums.

OWNERSHIP. To avoid the government taking up to 55 percent of the proceeds, most people place their insurance policies in irrevocable life insurance trusts. You must carefully address the trust instrument provisions and the gift and generation-skipping tax consequences of getting money to the trust to pay the premiums each year. You must understand those tax consequences if the insurance premiums unexpectedly go up due to poor investment performance within the policy. You may consider a "split-dollar" ownership arrangement in which the business funds much of the premiums through what amounts to an interest-free loan. However, split-dollar arrangements have income and gift tax consequences that must be carefully addressed because those tax consequences can become burdensome as you get older.

TIME. If your business and investing are successful, your insurance needs will likely grow, making that policy you bought years ago look rather puny. Assuming you are insurable, you can buy more. However, in the longer term, insurance probably should be considered only a partial solution to the needs that motivate you to buy it in the first place. Be sure to factor that into your planning and consider using additional techniques to accomplish your objectives.

One strong caveat: Get an independent opinion by using an experienced advisor who is not compensated based on the type or amount of insurance bought. Most insurance agents are reputable, but they may not be totally unbiased or knowledgeable in the broad range of available estate planning alternatives.

Reality Check: The need for a means to pay future estate taxes is perhaps as pressing as protecting yourself from disaster with homeowner's, health and automobile insurance. Unfortunately, no one has been able to escape death or taxes. The right type of insurance, when integrated into your overall estate plan, may keep the family from having to sell or liquidate the business. It also can be used to cash out some shareholders and support your dependents. Inexpensive term premiums can be enticing. However, depending on the nature of your need, a form of permanent insurance may best suit you and your business. You will need to consider far more than a few years' premiums to make an informed buying decision. Relying solely on a fixed amount of insurance is problematic as your business grows, so insurance typically should only be a part of an overall estate plan. It's a big, complicated investment, and you should get competent, unbiased advice on all aspects of your insurance considerations.

45. When does a family limited partnership (FLP) make sense and when is it not a good idea?

Sue and George Smith (not their real names) heeded their consultant's advice and built up significant wealth outside of their business to enhance their financial security. Meanwhile, they became increasingly concerned over how their children would manage their growing wealth. Their teenagers were good children, but who knows how a teenager will turn out in the future? "There are just too many chances for them to go astray as they make their way through their late teens and 20s," says Sue. But the Smiths know that it is important to do some estate planning to reduce the tax burden if something were to happen to them. Wouldn't it be nice if they could give part of their wealth to the children, but keep the youngsters from getting their grubby hands on it until they are mature enough to handle the responsibility? "Age 50 should be about right," thought Sue. "I want to control the investment of the money since I know more about handling a portfolio than my children," says George.

So they put part of their wealth into a family limited partnership and transferred limited partnership interests to their children. Since the Smiths kept the general partnership interests, they could retain control over the investment of the funds and could decide when and whether to make distributions. That satisfied their nontax objectives. Plus, because the partnership interests are nonmarketable and do not allow the children to exercise any control over the partnership's activities, they were able to discount the gift tax value when they transferred the interests. That allowed the Smiths to transfer more wealth using their annual gift tax exclusions and lifetime exemption.

A family limited partnership, also known as a FLP (pronounced"flip"), can be the centerpiece of a family's estate planning. It's fairly simple in concept and can provide great benefits. But there are numerous tax, legal and other details to consider. The basic premise is that the older generation puts assets into a newly created limited partnership, receiving both general and limited partnership interests in return. General partners have management control, while limited partnerships have virtually no say over partnership activities. Typically, the limited partnership interest accounts for the lion's share, say 95 percent of the total, with the general partnership interest having the right to the remaining five percent of all income, capital and appreciation. Later, the older-generation family members start giving limited partnership interests to younger-generation family members.

FLPs have increased exponentially in popularity in recent years, in part because Congress outlawed many other estate planning techniques in 1990. Some of the benefits include:

RETAINED CONTROL. To avoid estate tax on an asset, you generally must give it away and not retain any control over it. Unfortunately, the desire to retain control often is a primary stumbling block in convincing a family business owner to undertake estate planning. However, a FLP's general partner, typically an older-generation family member, can retain almost complete control over the partnership's activities without being subject to estate tax on the partnership interest that he gave away.

Perhaps even more important, the younger generation, as limited partners, does not have a right to demand distributions of cash or other property from the partnership. The general partner determines when and whether to make distributions. Furthermore, as a practical matter the limited partners cannot sell or borrow against their partnership interests. So parents can be assured that their children will not get access to significant sums of money.

COORDINATED MANAGEMENT. It can be extremely helpful from a management standpoint to keep wealth together in one place. There can be economies of scale relative to each family member separately managing smaller blocks of assets. Some assets, like real estate, simply cannot be managed effectively with multiple co-owners who must agree to and sign off on every decision. The partnership agreement can be written to place control in one or a limited number of general partners.

TRANSFER TAX REDUCTION. For gift and estate tax purposes, partnership interests are valued at a discount from their proportionate shares of the partnership's assets' values. That means they can be transferred to the children at a cheaper gift or estate tax cost than transferring the assets outside the partnership. The reason is that a limited partnership interest is not readily marketable, and it lacks control over the management of the partnership. Those restrictions make them less valuable. The valuation discounts often range from 20 percent to 50 percent or more, depending upon the partnership agreement provisions and the nature of the assets held by the partnership.

There are also disadvantages to FLPs. First, because of their popularity, the IRS has mounted a major campaign to challenge the estate and gift tax benefits. Legislative proposals have been suggested to repeal those benefits. Second, family members may resent being controlled and may not want to be partners. Third, there are administrative costs associated with the creation and operation of the partnership.

Family partnerships generally can be used for most business and investment assets, including stock of the family's business. However, Subchapter S corporation stock may not be placed in a partnership. Through general partnership interests, control can be vested in, and later transferred to, those who manage the business while passing limited partnership interests to those who should receive only the economic benefits of ownership.

The magnitude of gift tax valuation discounts and the estate tax consequences varies with the terms of the partnership agreement, the nature of the assets placed in the partnership and the way in which the partnership is operated. As with any estate planning, competent advice is critical.

Reality Check: A FLP can resolve numerous tax and nontax estate planning objectives. It allows the older generation to separate management from the beneficial ownership of the assets placed in the partnership. As a result, the older generation can transfer wealth while retaining control over it or passing control only to selected family members. It also provides centralized management for diverse assets, potentially creating economies of scale and providing better structure for management functions. With careful structuring, FLPs can substantially reduce gift and estate tax costs due to valuation reductions for lack of marketability and control. No wonder FLPs seem to have become the technique of choice for so many family business owners.

46. Is it fair to give equal ownership to both active and inactive children?

The second-generation owners of a small publishing firm in suburban New York decided to give each of their three grown children equal nonvoting shares of the business. However, only their middle son works there, having joined after a career as a trader on Wall Street. "We're a close-knit family and felt it was fairest for all three to share equally," says the wife, whose husband's family started the company in 1928. "It was also the way my husband's family had dealt with shares. He and his two siblings shared equally, until he and I bought them out 15 years ago. In essence, this tack has been family policy."

How does the active son feel about sharing the nonvoting stock with his brother and sister? A vice president of operations and production, who oversees the office infrastructure, he says that's quite fine. "I recognize it's a family business and as such the entire family owns it. I get other benefits working here—a place of employment, a salary, a bonus, a pension fund."

What's more of an issue, he says, is what happens when his parents retire, and he shares the voting stock with two nonworking siblings. "I wouldn't want the two of them to gang up and fire me if they don't think I'm doing a good job," he says. What he has suggested is that his parents begin to give him some of their voting stock so that he will have real control over the firm some day. He also wants a buy–sell agreement put into place so that if either sibling gets divorced, the ex-spouse won't get an ownership stake. The parents are wrestling with the right course to take in a company with a future that may be more interesting than its past.

Are you working in a family business that has suddenly taken on all kinds of inactive family shareholders? You question: "Should those not working in the business have ownership?" Many parents believe that, when it comes to the treatment of their children, what's fair is equal ownership and what's equal is fair. Is it? After all, when the children were young, the parents bent over backward not to show favoritism. It's just the way families behave. But is equal ownership for the next generation really fair?

Most parents love their children equally. They translate this equal love into equal treatment. They think everyone in the family is entitled to an equal stake whether they work in the business or pursue another career. They think it is their right to leave the business that they created any way they choose. To them, disinheriting one or more kids from business ownership would be inappropriate favoritism.

Those who argue the flip side believe that fair need not mean equal. They are adamant that only those who work in the business should own a stake. Otherwise, the parents bequeath the future sweat-equity of the active children to the inactive ones. Don't leave your more successful children an obligation to support their less fortunate siblings, they say. You can decide to support a child, but should not leave this duty to your heirs. Unless you are careful, your plan may have this effect or be perceived to do so. How can that be fair? It is a disincentive to those who build the business if a significant portion of their efforts benefit another owner who opted not to contribute. Inactive owners can interfere with the business' management and cause significant distractions. On top of that, there can be no assurance that having only active owners will mean that the shareholders always agree on all business issues and challenges.

So how does a parent decide? Unfortunately, there isn't an easy answer, or, necessarily, a "right" one. You may be the fairest person in the world, but unwittingly may be doing your children a disservice, whatever course you take. Whatever you do, the situation may end up in a knockdown, drag-out fight or may leave some children feeling they've been cheated. They may be resentful of their parents and siblings.

Stop and catch your breath. Assess your specific situation. There may be a "simple" answer when children don't get along together. In that case, it makes little sense for a parent to make them business partners. The parents simply have to find another way to be fair with their heirs other than through equal division of the business.

The answer also may be obvious if you talk with your children. While parents should not let children make the decision as to what they will inherit, it is a good idea to seek their views. One daughter and her three brothers each inherited an equal quarter of their parents' stock. She was distraught. She wanted to start her own business, but her only capital was the family business' stock. The stock could not be sold. When asked whether her brothers would buy her stock, she said that she thought selling the stock would betray her parents' dream that their children continue in business together. However, that was not her dream. Wouldn't it have been better for the parents to have learned her dream while they were alive, rather than leaving her tormented with her situation? They probably would have helped her accomplish her dream, which they undoubtedly would have believed to be at least as important as their own.

Many older family businesses, with a long history of inactive owners understand how to accommodate the different needs of active and inactive owners and develop appropriate policies. For long-term success, there must be some critical ideologies within the family, regardless of whether the owners are active, inactive or some combination of the two. These beliefs must be created, verbalized and nurtured within the family. Parents who teach these values leave their children a greater legacy than mere ownership, regardless of their ultimate stand on the fair-versus-equal issue.

Here are some examples of a family credo that addresses these important ideologies.

FAMILY MEMBERS IN THE BUSINESS

Family members working in the business must:

- View their roles as being stewards of the business for all owners.
- Avoid receiving compensation and perks above market rates.
- Believe that their compensation is the reward for their services and that growth in the business' value is attributable to the owners as a result of their invested capital.
- Provide complete information to all owners about the performance and strategies of the company.
- Recognize the right for owners to receive a fair, current return (i.e., dividends) on their investment.
- Provide a forum for all owners to have input on the major operating philosophies and strategies of the company.
- Respect and respond to the input and questions of owners.
- Submit to oversight and review, preferably by a board of independent directors.

FAMILY MEMBERS NOT IN THE BUSINESS

Family members not working in the business must:

- Respect the operational decisions of, and avoid unduly interfering with, management.
- Understand enough about business to recognize that they are not entitled to current distribution of all of the business' operating income, since businesses must invest a portion of that income for current operations and growth.
- Avoid relying on dividends or other distributions for their day-to-day lifestyle and recognize that there may be times when those distributions must be reduced or suspended.
- Recognize that they do not have a right to serve on the board of directors or try to elect someone who will be their surrogate to accomplish personal objectives.

OWNERS: ACTIVE AND INACTIVE

All owners, whether active or inactive, must:

- Listen to and respect the views of their fellow owners.
- Develop communication and negotiation skills.
- Deal honestly and openly with each other.
- Avoid putting their self-interest and individual objectives above the needs of the business.
- Be willing to sell their stock (or buy the stock of a shareholder that wants out) on reasonable terms, rather than foster a feud that can destroy the business and the family.

Open discussions about the fair-versus-equal issue are critical. Keeping family members' opinions under wraps only delays and probably exacerbates the ultimate problems that will arise by failing to address the question. You'll probably be surprised at family members' ability to rise to the occasion and help resolve the issue. If they don't, it's better that you know now so that you can take appropriate action rather than leave the decision for them to sort out without your guidance.

Reality Check: The age-old premise that you have to share equally to be fair and prove your love for all your children—active and inactive in the firm—is still held by many family business owners. To do otherwise is divisive and unfair, they rationalize. Others disagree because they view family business ownership as a right only for those who devote their lives to it. Those who pursue other interests simply aren't entitled to a stake in the business, they say. Problems can arise either way unless your heirs understand and agree with the decision. Even then, your heirs must develop the ability to deal with the inevitable disagreements and challenges that the business will throw their way in the future. Rather than focus on the imponderable fair-versus-equal issue, consider focusing on developing the relationships, understanding and skills that will be required of co-owners, regardless of the decision that you make. Your heirs' ability to develop these attributes, or their inability to do so, will go a long way toward telling you the best answer for your own particular family situation and for your family members' needs and wishes.

47. How can you be both fair and equal when it comes to estate planning if you decide that some children should not receive stock?

Ann Stettner Schreiber, 37, works with her husband Neil, 35, in the business her mother Enid started in the mid-80s, Wild Thymes, a specialty food manufacturing company based in Medusa, N.Y. She was given 50 percent of the stock in her mother's firm last year. Ann and Neil head the sales, marketing and public relations divisions of the company and have been designated to take over the firm some day. However, Ann has two younger siblings, neither of whom works in the company. Her brother, Adam, has a technology consulting business and manages a technology mutual fund, and her sister, Nina, was a fashion director in women's wear who now works as a designer in her father-in-law's diamond business.

In doing estate planning, Ann says that her mother wanted to be fair and equal to all her children. "My mother's will stipulates that the three of us will divide my mother's 50 percent of the business into thirds. However, according to the will, at the time of my mother's death, my brother and sister must sell out to me at fair market value. This way they receive something from the business, but I won't feel that I'm doing all the work and they'll benefit from future growth and profits without putting any funds or time into the business."

Figuring out how to be fair in your estate planning is tricky, especially if you decide that it is inappropriate to leave your stock equally to your children. You probably want to treat the children equally because you love them equally. But you also may want to treat them differently because of their inability to get along or their varying financial circumstances, talents at managing wealth, interests and the like. The last thing that you want is for one or more of them to resent you or their siblings because of how you and your spouse decide to divide your estate.

It's a real dilemma for parents if they've given it some thought or, if they haven't, it should be. That's the key: you have to think about estate distribution, then plan for it. Upon reflection, you may decide that "fair" means leaving all children an equal share of the value of your estate, not necessarily of the value of your business.

Some ways to leave equal value to those who should not receive family business stock include:

- Give them different assets, such as real estate, marketable securities, antiques and jewelry.
- Buy life insurance to provide proceeds.
- Give business real estate to the inactives, which they can lease to the actives.
- Engineer the terms of a post-death buyout of the stock that you leave to inactive children, funded with income generated after you die.
- You could compromise. How about giving more stock to actives and less to inactives? Or, how about leaving a small class of voting stock to active children, and dividing a large class of nonvoting stock equally among active and inactive children? That can provide equal inheritances, and avoids forcing those who run the business to seek the votes of those who aspire to be successful beach bums.

Seek professional advice and consider a combination of strategies to accomplish your goal, rather than relying on a single one that might not pan out over time.

If you are like many business owners, you lack sufficient wealth outside the business to accomplish this strategy. Plus your nonbusiness assets may be what you expect your heirs to use to pay your estate taxes. With time and creativity, you may be able to pull off an appropriate and fair division of your estate. Starting early enables you to shift wealth before gift and estate taxes get out of control.

Don't forget the big "C"—communication. You should discuss the vagaries of the future with your children. Everyone may accept the plan now. However, if the shareholding children later sell the business for a lot of money, making them far wealthier than their siblings, tensions can arise. Conversely, if the business goes belly-up, those who inherited nonbusiness assets will come out being much richer. You and your children must understand that equality is transitory. Differences in future spending and earning, plus economic and business changes, will make them unequal in the future. That's the game of life. If they anticipate and understand this fact, they are less likely to challenge your plan or their siblings in the future. It also will enable you to divide your estate earlier without concern for future changes that will affect the children's relative wealth between now and the time you die.

You should always leave wealth to your children out of love, not spite. So it's important that they understand the love with which you make your decision. Your estate is part of the legacy you leave behind. Think through all the ramifications carefully. Finally, remember, there is no right or wrong answer; your business and personal assets are yours to bequeath as you see fit, but don't leave your heirs to wonder about your intentions either before or after you're gone. It may be too late for explanations.

Reality Check: Here's a potentially tough call—divvying up the family jewels in your estate planning. There's no right or wrong way. You may decide to divide by need, giving more of the business to your less well-off child or children. Or you may decide to give away all equally, or pass on shares only to active family members, or leave everything to charity. The decision is your call entirely but consider the message and legacy you want to leave behind. Sometimes by doing nothing, you leave an even more powerful message. Take the high ground and tell your children your decision while you're alive. You and your heirs will greatly appreciate and benefit from the give-and-take.

48. Should a spouse or children not active in the business receive any stock or other assets?

Richard Babson, chairman and president of Babson-United Inc., a real estate management, publishing and investment advisory services company in Wellesley Hills, Ma., was the only one of his siblings who opted to go into the family business. He stepped into the firm in 1991. After Richard's father passed away in 1997, the company board voted him to head the firm. He was at that point president of Babson-United Investment Advisors, Inc., a subsidiary of Babson-United. So the question was who would receive the company's shares? All of the siblings, or just Richard who was working in the family business? Richard's grandfather Paul T. Babson, who founded the company, answered the main part of this question. Grandfather Paul had placed the family's shares into a "long-bomb" trust and had given his son Donald both the right to vote the shares during Donald's lifetime and a power of appointment that could be executed by will. Through this power of appointment, Donald expanded the number of trustees to include two professionals as well as the four children and gave Richard the right to vote 100 percent of the shares, subject to certain constraints. As one of the checks and balances, he stipulated that the other five trustees, acting in unanimity, could strip Richard of his voting power. How did Richard's siblings react to this arrangement? He says that, while some of them were not overjoyed, there were more than enough other assets to go around. "Due to my grandfather's planning, the business was not part of my father's estate. My father's estate was divided among the four of us equally, but the company stock cannot be touched," says Richard. In this family and for at least another generation, management and operating control go hand-in-hand.

In any family business, it's especially crucial to define the role of inactive shareholders. They must understand that their role does not include day-to-day involvement in management decisions. They should not be called in to resolve disagreements between the business' managers.

How should ownership and voting power be divided in the next generation? There is no right or wrong answer, but the following are some common arrangements found among family-owned businesses:

EQUAL PARTNERSHIP. This involves giving equal ownership and equal voting power to everyone in the next generation, whether or not they're in the business. Equal, however, doesn't necessarily mean equitable. Here's a prime example. A Midwest business was owned equally by seven children, but only one was active. The firm paid $10 million in dividends split evenly. The son who worked in the firm, owner of one-seventh of the stock, was paid $75,000 a year, a salary far below what a nonfamily employee would be paid for the same job. The father said the son should be satisfied because he also received dividends. In reality, the father created an unworkable situation. Eventually, the active son wanted to leave because he felt used. He believed that his father unfairly bequeathed his labor to his siblings because his salary did not appropriately reflect his leadership role and responsibilities. He also did not believe he should be required to get his family members' input on major decisions because they were not intimately involved in operations.

THE VOTING/NONVOTING ARRANGEMENT. In this arrangement, all family members receive stock, but those who work in the business have all the voting power. Inactive family members receive nonvoting stock. Alternatively, the inactive family members receive a lesser share of ownership and the actives receive control.

Be careful about disenfranchising inactive owners. Wars have been fought over the right to vote. When some family members work in the business and others don't, it's not unusual for inactive members to view the actives as abusing their power (through purported excessive compensation and the like). Conversely, those in power sometimes feel they're doing all the work, while the inactive members sit back and collect their dividends. The voting/nonvoting arrangement works when the people in control understand that their jobs are not an entitlement, and that they were put in charge for the good of the business and the family. Conversely, nonworking owners must understand that they should not interfere with management. Oversight structures, like a board of independent directors and a family council, are critical to ensure that the inactives feel enfranchised (and heard) despite their lack of vote.

SOLELY ACTIVE OWNERSHIP. Under this structure, only family members working in the business have ownership and voting rights. Family members not active in the business receive other, typically passive, assets such as real estate leased to the business. Some parents bequeath preferred stock to inactive children, so that the actives get all the potential appreciation in value generated by their efforts. Before adopting this arrangement, you should hold a meeting to explain your plan and hear all opinions. Make clear, however, that you have final say. Potential for problems: The ones in the business may do better financially than those not in, breeding resentment in the future.

Ownership and management issues can be resolved if the company structure is based on a public company model, with shareholders' meetings and formation of a family council where active and inactive family members can share information and air concerns. If the active family members want to keep the inactives from interfering with management, they should establish a board of independent directors. That way the inactives may feel that unbiased and qualified businesspeople are looking out for all shareholders' best interests.

No matter the split, a shareholder agreement is critical. If any owner decides that he cannot tolerate the way the business is being run, that agreement will provide the terms under which he can sell his stock. Co-owners and co-managers must not be held hostage to each other if relationships go south. A buy–sell agreement is the ultimate pressure relief valve that can keep the family from blowing up.

One of the worst results of voting-control structuring involved a business inherited by two brothers from their father. The active brother held control, with 50.5 percent of the stock. The business paid no dividends because it needed to retain earnings for growth. His brother, a doctor, held 49.5 percent of the stock. The business had a value of some $50 million, which made them both extremely wealthy, at least on paper. The brother in the company lived lavishly on his $2 million annual salary, while the other brother received nothing from the business. Needless to say, the two siblings didn't get along well. The arrangement created such disharmony that the brothers spoke only through their lawyers.

Reality Check: Active family members must understand their stewardship roles and responsibilities toward all shareholders. Inactive family members must resist the urge to meddle in business affairs. Communication is a must and full disclosure of business affairs should be given to all shareholders. The older generation should discuss plans for distribution of ownership and management and seek input.

49. What other estate planning techniques should you consider for shifting ownership to the next generation(s)?

After analyzing their funeral industry's long-term outlook and their own family's estate planning needs, brothers Matt and Dick Lamb decided to sell the three-generation family funeral business, Blake-Lamb Funeral Homes, which was founded in Chicago in 1880. "We realized that an increasing number of customers preferred to purchase preplanned, prepaid funeral services funded by insurance, which froze the costs at a particular time and rate. But because these customers were highly mobile, they'd want to take their funeral instructions and preferences with them from one location to another in the same way they can get the same prescription through Walgreens, whether they're in Chicago, Miami or San Diego," says Matt Lamb, 66, and eight years his brother's senior.

The brothers also realized that it would be difficult for one of them to continue the firm if the other died. "We were so highly leveraged in real estate that it would be hard financially for one to continue. The government would come in and want its share and the surviving member would have to pay estate taxes and buy the other side off, which would have been a reach." Furthermore, only half of what they had to sell consisted of a tangible asset with a marketable dollar value. The company's reputation and good will, while important, could not be quantified monetarily.

In addition, each had changing career objectives and ideas about risk, expansion and debt. Matt had become very involved in his emerging art career. Dick was interested in expanding the funeral business.

As a result of their analysis, they realized that the most likely candidate to buy their business was one of the large conglomerates that had been helping to consolidate small chains and independent funeral homes. Their final decision was to fold their company into Service Corporation International (SCI) in Houston, the nation's largest funeral home business, which had instituted a "Partners Program" to entice entrepreneurial owners to affiliate. It created incentives for former owners to stay and expand their business and ultimately buy back a portion of the newly enlarged firm.

The brothers received SCI stock for the transaction. "We feel we bought in rather than sold. All that we gave up was our egos of being the sole decision-makers," says Matt, who continues to serve as a paid consultant. Several of his children and a son-in-law also work for SCI.

Dick and his wife Sue, assisted by a daughter and a son-in-law, eventually opened a new funeral business, Richard Lamb Funeral Services after his noncompete contract with SCI expired. They have attempted to give the public a cost-effective, consumer-friendly atmosphere in which to make funeral arrangements.

"We call it 'demystifying the funeral business,'" says Dick. "In fact, the ambiance is more Barnes & Noble than funeral home. We carry several hundred titles on all aspects of death, dying and bereavement. We also carry custom sympathy and thank-you cards, plus all the products one would find in a funeral home such as caskets, vaults, urns and flowers. The major difference is that we do not have facilities at the location for wakes or funerals. We work with the family to find a location. In this way, the family gets more choices, and since we don't have a large fixed overhead, we can pass the cost savings on to the family."

While many families do indeed sell their businesses to stanch their estate tax burden, family businesses should know that they have many other less drastic options. In fact, there probably are more estate tax planning techniques than ways to save income taxes. Selecting the right technique or combination requires consideration of the older generation's financial needs, the size of the estate (both now and projected into the future), your views about retaining control over your assets, the younger generation's ability to handle wealth responsibly and more.

People with smaller estates probably are best served with simple annual gifts and making sure that their wills properly utilize the $650,000 lifetime exemption (that escalates to $1 million over the next several years). Larger estates typically require a combination of techniques, both to handle more complex objectives and to diversify the risk that any single technique may not work. What are the risks? To name a few, the IRS may successfully attack all or part of any particular technique, unexpected changes in your financial and business situation, and changes in family members' objectives.

Some more commonly used estate planning techniques for family business owners include:

OPPORTUNITY TRANSFERS. These allow the younger generation to buy into new investment opportunities before they skyrocket in value so that the expected value increase never gets into the older generation's estates.

GIFTS OF NONVOTING, RATHER THAN VOTING, STOCK. This technique allows a slightly larger valuation discount for gift tax purposes than gifts of minority interests. More important, it allows the older generation to transfer more than 49 percent of the equity, while still retaining voting control.

INSTALLMENT SALES. Permits the younger generation to purchase shares and pay for them from future business earnings. Provides cash flow to the older generation for retirement needs, while shifting growth (in excess of the interest rate on the note) to the younger generation. Unfortunately, a sale triggers capital gains tax, although it usually can be paid as the note principal is collected.

INSTALLMENT SALE TO A GRANTOR TRUST. A technique similar to the installment sale, except that a trust buys the stock. The trust is designed to be ignored for income tax purposes while respected for transfer tax purposes. That permits the older generation to avoid capital gains taxes.

GRANTOR RETAINED ANNUITY TRUST (GRAT). This technique is widely used because Congress specifically authorized it. It is similar to but not as advantageous as an installment sale to a grantor trust. Instead of "selling" the stock to a trust for a note, the older generation transfers the stock to a trust while retaining an annuity, which is an obligation to pay a fixed dollar amount for a period of years (like your home mortgage note). The GRAT's downsides compared to the installment sale to a grantor trust technique include 1) the older generation must outlive the annuity term to keep the stock from being subject to estate tax, 2) the installment sale technique's note requires a lower interest rate, so the trust pays less overall for the stock, and 3) unlike the GRAT, the installment sale technique can incorporate generation-skipping planning. The GRAT's primary advantage over the installment sale technique is that you can eliminate gift tax exposure if you undervalue the stock when transferring it to the trust.

REDEMPTION. If the younger generation already owns stock, the older generation may redeem all or part of its remaining shares, thereby increasing the younger generation's ownership. In a partial redemption, the proceeds are taxable as ordinary income. A complete redemption of the older generation's shares can be taxable at lower capital gains rates, but there are several requirements, including prohibitions against the older generation continuing to be employed by the business. If you are structured as an S corporation, a partial redemption can be totally income tax free to the extent of the older generation's share of undistributed S corporation earnings and stock basis.

PRIVATE ANNUITY. The younger generation can buy stock from the older generation in exchange for a promise to pay a fixed amount to the older generation, usually for the rest of their lives. The technique can work extremely well from the standpoint of providing retirement income, but is best for estate tax purposes if the older generation dies prematurely so that the children do not have to pay as much.

SALE LEASEBACK. This technique involves the older generation selling assets (like real estate) to the younger generation and then renting it back from them. The technique removes future appreciation and the cash rentals from the older generation's estate, although the sales proceeds and related rental earnings add to the taxable estate (unless spent before death). Taxable gain may be triggered because of the sale.

FAMILY LIMITED PARTNERSHIPS. These are covered previously in Question 45.

TRUSTS. Many people use trusts for management reasons. Instead of giving stock outright to children who may not manage it properly, a trustee is named for that purpose. Trusts also can provide protection from creditors and divorcing spouses. When carefully designed, they can permit stock or other property to avoid estate tax when younger-generation family members die.

DYNASTY TRUSTS AND OTHER GENERATION-SKIPPING PLANNING. Wealthier individuals view estate planning over a longer time horizon than just how to shift wealth to their children. The problem is that wealth transferred by gift or bequest is taxed as it passes from generation to generation. Congress allows each person to transfer up to $1 million (increased for inflation) to grandchildren or beyond with only one tax (the gift or estate tax at the initial transfer). Placing the $1 million in a long-term trust allows the property to escape transfer tax for multiple generations. In fact, one of the newest techniques is to create a so-called "dynasty trust" in a state that allows the trust to last forever, potentially preventing the property and all future income and appreciation from ever again being subject to transfer tax. Even more sophisticated planning allows you to leverage far more than $1 million into these long-term trusts.

CHARITABLE TRUST TECHNIQUES. There are a variety of techniques that use charitable objectives to leverage additional wealth to the younger generation or to avoid capital gains taxes. For example, charitable lead trusts commit a cash-flow stream to charity for a period of years, with the remainder passing to your heirs. The charitable contribution aspect of the technique discounts the value of the property for gift tax purposes. On the other hand, charitable remainder trusts are primarily used to defer or avoid capital gains taxes on the sale of an asset, like the family business stock. The trust sells the asset and reinvests the proceeds income tax free. It pays the older generation a cash-flow stream, usually for life, with anything remaining in the trust passing to charity.

PRIVATE FOUNDATIONS. A private foundation does not shift wealth to the younger generation. Everything goes ultimately to charity. However, for wealthy families, the ability to retain control over and invest the wealth in the foundation may be more important than the ability to spend it for personal consumption.

Of course, Congress and the IRS constantly tinker with the law. Get competent help from advisors who are experienced in estate planning. Discuss the current status and the pros, cons and risks of these and other techniques. Always make sure that you thoroughly consider the cash flow and economics of the techniques before you use them. Projections under varying assumptions of future economic events are extremely helpful.

Reality Check: The world of estate planning is extremely complex. But with that complexity comes great opportunity. You can not only save estate taxes, but also accomplish a wide range of nontax objectives. The best estate planners will take the time to understand your concerns and goals, and then select and tailor the right techniques for you, your family and business.

50. What kind of planning and other actions should be undertaken in the event of the owner's death so the family feels the company is poised to be successful over the long term?

Bernard Freelander was the owner of Richards Homewares Inc., a company that manufactured closet storage accessories and protective covers for outdoor furniture. Almost no planning had been done before he died of a terminal illness in 1985. As the second-generation head, he did not feel it necessary because the company, started by his father Myron in 1939 and originally known as Richards Plastics Co., was financially sound. Other reasons accounted for his mindset. Bernard had purchased some token life insurance policies and his son Robert was well equipped to take over, having worked in the business for nine years and elsewhere as well.

Once Robert took over, he slowly came to a different point of view after discussions with his attorney. He decided he needed to plan better to protect his wife Karen and four young children. He decided the corporation needed to purchase keyman life insurance so that the business could continue, would not have to be sold, and so that his family would be financially cared for. "The last thing I wanted was for my wife to be under pressure," he says. Robert did not select a successor, however, in part because his children were too young and in part because he had no idea whether any would want to follow in his footsteps. Instead, in a worst-case scenario of his death his goal was for his trusted employees to keep the business going until a buyer could be found. But he has done far more. He moved the company, originally located in Los

Angeles, to Portland, Or., five years ago. It had outgrown its facility, and Robert considered the Oregon location a better long-term fit. He also went deeper into closet accessories such as wooden hangers, canvas garment bags, garment racks and shoe racks, a shift his father had started when he moved out of the company's original niche of round vinyl covers for dental chair headrests. Robert also found that the burgeoning large linen and bath companies nationwide were healthy outlets when department stores gave up their notions sections, the company's original distribution channel.

The death of a family business leader obviously is traumatic for the family. It also can be extremely unsettling for employees, customers, suppliers, bankers and others who have a stake in the business' ongoing viability. It is a time for compassion and cooperation. It is a time for all those involved to pull together and work through their grief, attempt to fill the huge hole left by the untimely departure and take the steps necessary to carry on.

Obviously, the actions required are very much dependent upon the plans put in place and agreements reached before the leader's death. There may be a very smooth transfer of power and leadership, or a vacuum filled with distrust, greed and power-grabbing.

Unless there are serious business problems, it typically is best to avoid rapid change immediately following the leader's death. Change is always tough for people to accept and implement. It can be even more unsettling after a long-time leader's death, particularly if untested leadership takes control.

The initial task is to "stabilize" the situation. The surviving owners should quickly provide assurances to employees that the business will survive and that their jobs are secure, at least during the transition period. It's a good idea for senior family members or managers to meet with major customers and suppliers shortly after the leader's death. Those dependent upon the business will need assurances that it will not "fall apart" and that the business' life will carry on uninterrupted.

After a brief mourning period, the family should meet and openly discuss the transition. This meeting should be a simple reaffirmation of agreements reached previously concerning successor leadership. If this is not the case, the owners should decide quickly who will take the leadership role and then announce the decision. Family members must set aside personal agendas and agree on either transitional or permanent leadership as soon as possible. If appropriate, the successor leader should stress his or her intent to continue the philosophies and business practices that have been successful in the past. Assuming the goal is continued family ownership, that fact also should be included.

If the deceased leader was overly secretive and kept the successor and family in the dark about business operations, the survivors must act quickly to develop a clear understanding of the business and its financial status. Interview key managers, outside advisors and independent directors. Identify current strengths and potential threats. Make sure that day-to-day operations can run smoothly during the transition. If the deceased leader tightly controlled the business, it is possible that the employees will feel powerless or incapable of making even the minor decisions needed daily.

Within the first several months after the death, determine the estate tax and other capital demands that must be borne by the business. The surviving widow or widower must be confident of an income stream for support. Inheritors or other owners who do not want to be owners may need to be bought out. These demands must be considered in the context of ongoing business operations.

After a suitable period, when all those involved have become comfortable with the business' continued viability, the successor leaders can begin the steps necessary to implement their vision and strategies for the future. It may take several years for them to develop credibility and to gain the esteem previously held for their predecessor. Patience and consensus building often are critical.

Reality Check: The death of a leader is the ultimate test of whether sufficient planning was done to assure the continuation of the business and the family's ability to be accommodating and supportive owners. True visionary leaders play "what if" games to simulate what should and will happen when they leave the scene. These activities provide assurance to family members and employees that they can successfully continue the aging leader's dreams. Many leaders, however, will not address their mortality or take the necessary steps to assure as smooth a transition of management and ownership as possible. The survivors must fill the resulting leadership vacuum, unfortunately at the same time that they must cope with their grief. They must rise to this tough occasion or suffer a worse fate—the ultimate loss of the business and the disintegration of family relationships.

CHAPTER VII

FINANCIAL AND CHARITABLE PLANNING FOR FAMILY BUSINESS OWNERS

51. Should you have a shareholder (buy-sell) agreement?

H. Greenberg & Son in Northbrook, Il., was founded in 1924 by Hyman Greenberg. Today the business is headed by third-generation member Lee Greenberg, chairman, and his fourth-generation son Scott, president. The company employs 100 and manufactures ready-made textiles for mass merchants such as J.C. Penney, Target and Sears, Roebuck and Co. Concerned about having the uncertainties over future ownership if one were to die unexpectedly, the father and son sat down a few years ago and created a buy-sell agreement.

A shareholder's agreement is an absolute must in any business when more than one person is an owner. Depending upon its terms, the agreement can assure continued family ownership and provide an "escape" mechanism for disgruntled owners. The wording and terms of shareholder agreements can vary greatly, but they most commonly address the following issues:

- Who may or may not own shares and what happens if shares intentionally or unintentionally fall into the "wrong" hands due to divorce, death, credit problems, lifetime transfer or otherwise.
- Events permitting or requiring a sale, such as leaving the company to pursue another profession, retiring, being disabled, funding estate taxes or getting divorced from a family member.

- The price for which shares can be bought or sold and how that price is modified over time.
- The payment terms, including downpayment, length of note and interest rate.

Many buy–sells give the company and existing shareholders a right of first refusal to buy shares that a family member transfers to a prohibited person, such as a spouse or friend. The right of first refusal gives the company and family flexibility to determine whether to buy the stock. If they don't exercise the right, then the transfer is permitted.

One caveat: The IRS typically is not bound to accept the shareholder agreement's determination of value for estate or gift tax purposes. If the agreement sets an artificially low price for the stock, the IRS may still assert taxes on actual fair market value. The potentially increased tax can eat up other assets and wreak havoc on your overall plan's intended use for those funds.

Reality Check: Going into business with a parent, child, sibling, in-law or cousin demands a certain level of trust. But you need more than good faith, a firm handshake and a look straight into the other person's eyes. Future disagreements and unexpected events can occur and tear apart relationships—and businesses. How do you avoid splitting up a company and deciding who gets what in the heat of battle? You may not be able to think in a level-headed manner when screaming is at the highest decibel and doors are being slammed. What's better is to plan for the worst cases, hoping they never happen. A shareholder agreement legally determines how to handle a host of what-ifs. For example, if you don't want your sister's shares to go to your brother-in-law, you need to put that in writing. Remember the adage, better safe than sorry.

52. How does the business provide for the economic security of the founder if he wants to retire, and for a spouse after the founder dies?

The head of O & H Danish Bakery of Racine, Wi., Raymond Olesen, now 65, began entrusting more responsibility to his three sons who had come into the family business in the mid-1980s. He cooked up a plan to retire by 65 and hand the bakery over to his sons. Ray's only hesitation about stepping away completely was tied to concern over how he would afford retirement. He had been receiving a nice paycheck and there would be a big adjustment when he left. Once he sat down with his advisors, they drafted a financial plan with some viable options so he could safely bow out and continue to receive a comfortable annual income. First of all, Ray and his wife Myrna accumulated substantial savings, which they invested wisely. Second, they own the property on which their bakery is located, so the sons agreed that the business would pay rent to their parents. The third move was to set up a deferred compensation plan. The three sons are buying some shares; this, too, is generating cash flow for their parents.

Those who want to have a successful retirement surround themselves with the best advice for an important reason. It takes the guesswork out of this major life decision.

If you're contemplating retirement, the first order of business is to take an honest look at your lifestyle, savings and the financial state of your business. Determine a realistic income stream that you'll need for retirement, based on your current income, or more or less depending on what type of retirement you envision. Then decide the best ways to balance securing sufficient funds for retirement against draining the company of important resources.

The following are the most common options, many of which can be used in combination. However, be sure to consult competent advisors about income tax and other consequences:

- If the real estate used by your company is owned by you outside the corporation, you can lease it to the company to create a passive income stream. Using a net lease can shift the burden for maintenance, insurance and taxes to the company.
- The company can award you an unfunded nonqualified pension as part of your compensation package. An advantage is that the money is deductible by the company when paid out and taxable to you only when you receive it. A disadvantage is that you become an unsecured creditor so if your company falters you may not get paid. Problems for the company are that it must record the amount as a liability on its financial statements, which may create problems with banking relationships.
- You can sell stock back to the company or to your children on easy terms. They fund the purchase out of future business income while providing you with cash flow for retirement needs.

- If your company is an S corporation, it can declare tax-free dividends to you (and the other shareholders) so that you can build up wealth away from the risks of business operations. Of course, a major downside is that the company will have less capital, and this method should only be used if the company is in good financial shape and doesn't need the funds for capital and other expenditures.
- You can stay on as a member of the board of directors or as an advisor and be paid director's or consultant's fees. The major caveat: Be sure that you are paid only a fair amount for the services rendered, which you may have to prove to the IRS.

Whatever the approach or approaches, you certainly have the right to arrange your financial affairs to provide adequately, if not generously, for you and your spouse after you retire. To avoid excessive estate taxes and be sure something is left over for your spouse, your will should be checked carefully before you die. You can leave your entire estate to your spouse and defer any estate taxes until your spouse's death.

Uncertainty over your financial future can be a major stumbling block to passing management authority and control to your successors. Even though your children are capable operators, there may be fear in the back of your mind that, to protect your retirement funds, you need to retain control to be able to come back in and bail out your successors if problems arise. Yet your failure to fully vest control and authority in them can confuse employees, frustrate successors and prevent you from undertaking proper lifetime estate planning. Consequently, the earlier you start to create retirement financial security that is not totally dependent upon your business, the better both you and your spouse will feel and the more readily you will vest authority in the children while you are alive.

Reality Check: Numerous options exist so you can afford to retire. Some owners place continuing obligations on their company, which subjects them to the risks of the business' future success, while others create a nest egg separate from their business. Many business owners use a combination. This issue is an ideal one to discuss with experienced advisors. Be sure to involve your successors in this process, since the decision undoubtedly will influence company finances. Start as early as possible to address funding your retirement because many solutions require time.

53. How can family members address the use of prenuptial agreements to reduce the risk of problems in the event of a divorce?

When Chris Pisani and Emily Johnson decided to marry, Emily's mother, who had been divorced, suggested to the couple, each of whom worked in their respective family businesses, that they sign a prenuptial agreement. After discussing it, the couple, who both are in their late 20s, vetoed the idea. "We decided that it was too involved—we'd have to value each of our businesses, decide how we'd divide any stock. Instead, we shook hands and promised that if anything happened between us we'd go our separate ways and keep our hands off each other's companies," says Chris, a vice president at Awards International, a Chicago firm started by his grandfather that provides custom recognition and signage. Emily is a vice president at the Chicago public relations and marketing firm Taylor Johnson Associates, started by her mother, Deborah Taylor Johnson. Chris doesn't yet hold stock in his family firm; Emily has eight percent of her mother's business.

Family business owners typically have great interest in keeping the company within the family. They worked hard to build the business for themselves and their successors. To them, "family" means bloodlines and adopted children. The business is a family legacy and they want to maintain family control. Frankly, imagine how difficult it would be to have an ex-spouse as a business "partner." Since one-third of all marriages end in divorce, the logical step is to decide in advance how property, including the family business, will be divided. In theory, that's far easier to do when couples are in love rather than in the heat of divorce.

Bringing up the subject of a prenuptial agreement is far more difficult than many imagine. It's a negative way to start a new marriage, and it raises the issues of trust, independence and the possibility that the union may not succeed. Suddenly, the notion of "we" and "ours" gets divided into "yours" and "mine." The subject can cause great consternation and may put the starry-eyed couple and their families on the defensive.

The idea of keeping the business in the family should be introduced to children when they're young, preferably before they begin dating. Later, before anyone seems to be seriously considering marriage, the family should address prenuptials with a view towards everyone understanding the document's role in maintaining family ownership. Prenuptial agreements should be urged for everyone marrying into the clan, not selectively. Parents need to avoid threatening ultimatums like "Do this or you're cut out of the will" or "Don't sign and you'll have to leave the business."

In the absence of a prenuptial agreement, your state's law determines the property rights of each spouse. Those property rights in turn determine who gets what in the event of a divorce. They also determine which property each spouse may give away during life and bequeath at death. For example, if local law determines that part of your business' stock belongs to your spouse, he can give or bequeath it to his relatives.

A prenuptial agreement is a contractual arrangement that overrides state law determinations of property rights. It is an agreement between two people concerning who owns current and future property, which in turn determines how it is divided in the event of divorce. The agreement can be signed before marriage (a "prenuptial" agreement) or at any time after the marriage occurs (a "postnuptial" agreement).

Exactly what the agreement says and how it must be executed is a function of state law (which varies from state to state) and negotiation between the parties. Full disclosure of each person's assets typically is required, violating the typical business-owning family's desire to maintain privacy concerning the business and family finances. Many states' laws require each side to be represented by separate counsel and not be under duress when signing. Unfortunately, the lawyers' involvement can strain relationships as they strive to "protect" and maximize their clients' interests.

No wonder so few family businesses reported in Arthur Andersen's American Family Business Surveys that they had prenuptials. In 1995, 81 percent of all family businesses surveyed said no family members had prenuptial agreements; the number dropped only slightly to 79.6 percent two years later in 1997. Yet a large number of these families had experienced divorces.

The best way to foster a long-term healthy relationship between spouses is by frank discussions and disclosure. If a relationship can't survive a healthy give-and-take about the future disposition of the family business, it will have a tough time surviving the many pressures and challenges that newlyweds are bound to face.

Pending newlyweds should bite the proverbial bullet and broach the subject of a prenuptial when they become seriously involved and contemplate marriage. The couple should have an honest talk about a prenuptial agreement months in advance of the wedding rather than days before. This should not be done under pressure from family lawyers or older relatives who threaten to boycott the wedding and disinherit the family member if he or she doesn't follow their wishes.

The couple's conversation should start with an explanation of the emotional importance of the family business legacy to blood relatives—why they love the company, what it has meant through the years. It can move on to an explanation of the business reasons behind the family's tradition of not allowing nonfamily member ownership. Incidentally, the best time for a family to develop a policy about in-laws is long before a family member gets engaged. Imagine how your child and future spouse will feel if the subject first comes up after announcing an engagement.

It is important to explain that other family members are not marrying the future in-law. They may love their future son- or daughter-in-law, but they are not the ones agreeing to be bound in matrimony or in business partnership. Furthermore, the rest of the family is not a party to the decision to join the two families together. It is not fair to subject them to the possible claims of the in-law's family through their potential to inherit from the in-law. It also is not fair to the business to expose it to a possible disagreement over ownership in the event of a divorce.

You may want to add that you and your family view the business as more than an asset. Many families view their role more as stewards for future generations than as owners of a financial asset to be divided or spent. You might explain that you were not given the equity as a personal asset that can be divided and passed outside the family. Rather, the family's intent is for the business to continue for descendants of the founder.

At the same time the family member makes his case for a prenuptial, the couple should emphasize their faith in the longevity of the forthcoming union by outlining how they want to share other assets they each bring to the marriage. These may include real estate, personal savings and nonfamily business stock holdings. In addition, the couple should decide then and there how they would share any future assets between them. Some couples prefer to pool their salaries and savings; others prefer to keep them separate and funnel some into a joint account. Whatever you decide, you should recognize that a successful marriage requires the commitment and efforts of both spouses. It may be very helpful for the discussion and the property division to recognize the sacrifices inherent in the in-law's future contribution to the marriage, which may include attending family business functions and going to business retreats.

Only after this conversation—and possibly several conversations—are held and the nonfamily member has had time to mull over the ideas bandied about, study the prenuptial document and consult an attorney, should the future in-law sign any legal documents.

Quick tips before signing:

- Let the future in-law know well ahead of time about the family's posture on prenuptials.
- Discuss why and what would be included in the agreement.
- Find a lawyer experienced in prenuptial agreements as well as estate, trust and tax matters. Both the family member and intended spouse should have separate lawyers who meet to discuss the terms.
- Stick to the assets of the business in the prenuptial, if that's your main concern.
- Encourage your fiancé or fiancée to state his or her feelings.

And beware. Here's what can happen without a prenuptial. A son-in-law who worked in his wife's father's lumber business, but owned no equity, had been having an affair. The founder was deeply hurt. What should he do with the son-in-law? Fire him? Keep him on? Admonish and warn him since he's worried about looking at him every day? One of four children, the owner's daughter owned 25 percent of the company's stock. If the couple were to divorce, the son-in-law might receive half his daughter's assets. In addition, the daughter was incredulous that the family business, which had been such a large part of her life, could continue to give this louse of a guy a lifestyle that would enable him to lavishly entertain his female friends. A prenuptial would not have eased the pain, but it would have blocked the in-law from owning shares.

If a prenuptial agreement was never signed, a postnuptial can be created. It's much harder to implement, however. Not surprisingly, many spouses are reluctant and unwilling to give up rights or possible rights that they have developed up to that point.

Reality Check: Divvying up assets into "yours" and "mine" does not lend itself to marital harmony. Yet in a day and age when divorce ultimately splits apart one-third of all marriages, it can make great business sense to do so if family members want to retain sole ownership of the family firm. A discussion on prenuptial agreements should take place early in a relationship, without attorneys and family members issuing ultimatums. Approach the discussion with a great deal of love, compassion, honesty and openness. A carefully crafted agreement should be drawn well in advance of the wedding day, rather than a few days before vows are exchanged.

54. Besides prenuptial agreements, what other approaches can be used to protect family business stock in the event of a divorce? What kind of financial and other considerations should be addressed in the event of a divorce?

With the odds of one in three marriages ending in divorce, you can never be too careful about protecting a family business, even when couples seem blissfully happy. A soon-to-be ex can quickly make the business one of the assets to divide up, even if he or she never worked a day there. Legal steps can be taken in advance to shield the business from the courts. Business founder Joseph "Jim" Greenbaum shares ownership and management with Ellen, his wife of 37 years, at Greenbaum Interiors, a 47-year-old furniture and design resource in Patterson, N.J. He recommends that a couple working together or an owner working on his own take several steps. First, they should be certain the business has sufficient liquid capital or that they own other assets they can split so the business doesn't get destroyed and torn up in the process of dividing assets. Second, they should have a buy–sell agreement that the spouse not active in the business or one of them, if both are active, agrees to sell their stock back to the other or to the company in the event of a divorce. Third, any in-laws, particularly those not involved in the business, should not own any stock. The Greenbaums' two children both now work in the business, which manufactures many of its home and office furnishings in its eight-building campus. The firm also imports many well-known lines and employs 19 designers, some part-time, to help clients.

Ellen is in charge of a separate division that works with the interior design and architecture trade; daughter Susan oversees day-to-day operations and financial matters, and son David handles marketing, advertising and merchandising. Neither child, both of whom first worked elsewhere in the industry, currently owns stock; nor do their spouses. "Eventually, we'll give our children stock, but we'll be careful so that their spouses can't gain access to it," says Jim who knows that an extra level of protection will be necessary. Even though he hasn't yet initiated a buy–sell for the next generation, a prior one has already helped him keep the business in his grasp. He and his late brother Alvin, after founding the business together in 1952, had agreed to one, and with Alvin's death Jim was able to buy the business for his immediate family, thereby keeping it within a smaller circle of hands.

You have a responsibility and moral obligation to make sure that your parents, siblings and other family members are not drawn into your potential divorce problems. Under ideal conditions, you signed a prenuptial agreement so that your ex has no claims on your stake in the family's business. Since so few people actually sign these agreements, it's important to have some type of plan that will protect your legacy from being dismantled in case of a divorce.

If a divorce is imminent, you will first need to consult competent legal counsel to determine whether your spouse may have some legal claim against your stock. Different states' laws address this issue differently. It is often difficult to quantify what a divorce court may do with respect to awarding custody of the business "baby." If there is a risk that partial ownership may pass to your soon-to-be ex-spouse, your next steps will be to have the business valued by an independent expert, total your other assets and be prepared to work out an equitable settlement that will not include business stock. That may mean that you'll have to give a disproportionately large share of other wealth to your ex, or possibly to pay more alimony. Either way, the fleeing dollars may pose a drag on you and, possibly, the business.

Could you have taken other steps to protect the business' stock? There are some possibilities if you prepare in advance. Here are some:

- Perhaps your parents could have given you stock in trust, rather than outright. With properly written trust agreements, that stock can be protected from the beneficiaries' spouses and other potential creditors.
- The stockholders could have signed a shareholder's agreement, which states that nonfamily members who receive or hold shares agree to sell them back to other family members or back to the business in case of a divorce. The agreement can set forth the

terms for the purchase to reduce the cash-flow strain on the company and other family members.

- In some cases, fairly simple bookkeeping and asset-separation strategies implemented during marriage could have helped you maintain ownership through the divorce proceedings.
- It also may be possible to structure your divorce agreement to shift stock to your mutual children, rather than have it pass to your ex.

All these options should be discussed with your attorney, preferably before you get married.

Reality Check: Even without a prenuptial agreement, you can take steps to safeguard your business in case of divorce. Without question, a shareholder's agreement is critical to assure that any stock that finds its way outside the bloodlines can at least be retrieved under reasonable terms. Trusts may be used to protect stock from donees' creditors and ex-spouses. Like many issues, advance planning with competent advisors is critical to reducing the risk of the jewels falling into the wrong hands or at least to help make sure that they can be returned to the rightful owner under reasonable terms.

55. Why do some families set up a foundation? What are the pros and cons? When should it be set up? Should the entire family be involved in its operation?

The LaFetra Family Foundation in San Francisco, Ca., was established in the early 1990s as a way for a philanthropic family to maintain family unity. "We saw it as a way to do something together, even though we were advised against it because we were only going to set aside about $250,000," says Suzanne LaFetra, daughter of the founder who along with a brother and her father run the foundation in their spare time.

In its first few years of operation, the foundation gave $15,000 grants. "We decided that each of us got so many personal requests for $100 here and there, but if we were going to have some meaningful impact—more bang for our buck—we should give more to one organization. And we decided the best way to do so was to contribute operating support grants in the form of unrestricted funds so that the groups could do anything with the money. It goes right to their bottom line, helping to pay salaries, train workers, pay the rent and light bills. I knew from fundraising work that that's the hard money to come up with since so many foundations want to give to programs."

The LaFetras hold quarterly family meetings to discuss their Mexican art retail business, with shops in San Francisco and Tulum, Mexico. At least two of the meetings center around the philanthropic side of the business. Each family member sends in a list of suggestions. They sometimes make site visits to assess the charities that might benefit from the family's largess.

There are more than 42,000 grant-making foundations in this country, according to the Foundation Center, a nonprofit organization in New York that tracks giving. The vast majority, or 88.7 percent, are independent foundations, which includes those created by family business owners. The remainder are corporate, community and operating foundations. Foundations serve many purposes such as giving back to a community, unifying family members for a common good cause, and making your company distinctive through generosity of spirit and pocketbook. At the same time, if you are considering establishing one, you need to heed a few of the negative aspects as well.

THE BENEFITS OF A FOUNDATION

A foundation allows a family business and family members to take current income tax deductions for funds or other property set aside for future charitable giving. The foundation later parcels out money to charities or charitable causes. Although the Internal Revenue Code sets a minimum that the foundation must actually use for charitable purposes each year (typically five percent of its asset value), most foundations tend to grow in size and can remain in existence for decades. While the individuals and business could just as easily give money directly to public charities, many feel that their own foundation gives them better control over their funds compared to giving directly to a third-party organization.

A foundation accomplishes much more than tax deductions, however. It can provide a smart form of succession planning by creating a meaningful way for an elderly owner to spend time directing the family's charitable activities during retirement. It becomes a legacy that can survive long after founders leave the scene. Foundations can teach younger members the importance of giving back financially to a community, which can trigger the beginning of a lifelong charitable commitment.

A foundation can also become an avenue to bring other family members indirectly into the family business network without involving them in daily business decisions. This can be a particularly good way to develop inactive family members' commitment to the business even though they may not be interested in or capable of pursuing a career in it. The reason is that they can take pride in the fact that the business provides the foundation's capital and is the source of the funding to accomplish important charitable objectives. Moreover, some of these family members may get personal enjoyment from being involved in the foundation's charitable and investment activities.

Tracy Gary, now in her 40s, found this to be the case. After inheriting a large sum of money on her 21st birthday (her mother was part of the Pillsbury family and her father's family also had money), she made it a career to help other women take an active role in making the most of their wealth, as well as in understanding financial terms. She set up an organization, Resourceful Women, for women with money to learn about managing and giving some away.

Gary says, "Philanthropy is a way to get the entire family involved in a creative way and enliven the business, which often becomes the opposite—a source of conflict. It allows both generations to talk about more than making money—the value of sharing their riches with those less fortunate. But most people need help. When I received my money, there were no peer groups to confide in and people hid their wealth."

HOW TO SET UP A FOUNDATION

Legally, a foundation may be created and funded without specifying any particular cause or charitable recipient. Public charities may be selected annually by the foundation's directors. However, many families prefer to spell out specific types of causes, like religious-based organizations or care for disadvantaged children.

If you want your children to be involved, and that's usually a great idea, it's important that you have them participate in finding mutually agreeable causes. You can work together to draft a mission statement and approve grant applications. Otherwise, many heirs feel excluded and never gain their parents' sense of generosity and social commitment.

Setting up a foundation is not complicated initially, though to be cost-effective it typically should have a minimum of several hundred thousand dollars in permanent funding. Whatever the amount, the foundation must heed certain operating and tax rules. Your attorney will draft a charter and your tax advisor can file the request for tax-exempt status. You can set up the foundation as a trust or non-stock corporation. Different states have slightly different rules.

THE DISADVANTAGES OF FOUNDATIONS

Individuals' income tax deductions for gifts to private foundations are more restricted than for gifts to public charities. A deduction for gifts of nonpublicly traded stock is limited to tax basis, while a gift of the same stock to a public charity generates a fair market value deduction. Private foundations also are taxed at a one or two percent rate on their investment income and must avoid business income. It also is extremely important that you avoid "self-dealing" transactions, which can result in major tax penalties. Examples of these transactions include sales, loans and leases between the foundation and the family or between the foundation and the business. Another disincentive is that you may need staff to handle correspondence and bookkeeping, if you're not willing to do it yourself. These costs can mount. Annual tax filings also are required.

A foundation can make you an even bigger target for solicitation by people and organizations that assume that you have very deep pockets. On the other hand, a foundation can offer the perfect excuse, allowing you to gently turn down requests. Callers can be told that your giving is handled by your foundation, which is a focused organization that may already have committed all its funds for the year.

If you're interested in charitable gifts, but are not ready for a private foundation, you should consider giving to a community foundation that's already up and running. It can be a wise way to start since it allows a family time to hone its goals without the same commitment of funds and staff. They provide many of the benefits of a private foundation, but with fewer hassles and costs. The community foundation is a public charity in the eyes of the IRS (so tax deductions are far less restrictive). It need not dole out your contributions each year, but can accumulate them for later disposition. Although you have no legal say over its use of the money, it typically will follow your recommendations regarding the ultimate recipient of your contributions. However, the community foundation probably will want to dispose of remaining funds after your death, so it does not create the long-term legacy potential of a private foundation.

GETTING THE REST OF THE FAMILY INVOLVED

Every few years, the family may change its tune and want to refocus its charitable efforts. Of course, foundation meetings are a healthy way for a family to discuss individual, family and charitable goals. The foundation can provide structure to meetings that were once loose and perhaps even a bit disjointed and disorganized. The meetings can become a way for children to gain a sense of responsibility, develop leadership skills and demonstrate these to their elders, even before they're ready or willing to join the business. Even if they don't join the business, such talents can prove useful in other work and nonprofit situations.

RESOURCES

There are several organizations that help families develop charitable goals and set up foundations. Examples include The Council on Foundations in Washington, D.C.; The Philanthropic Initiative in Boston; and Resourceful Women in San Francisco. They can recommend outside consultants, or your accountant and lawyer can help.

Two useful books to read are philanthropist Tracy Gary's *Inspired Philanthropy, Creating a Giving Plan* (Chardon Press, 1998) and Claude Rosenberg, Jr.'s *Wealthy & Wise: How You and America Can Get the Most Out of Your Giving* (Little Brown & Co., 1994). Also, the reference departments of many public libraries have the book *The Foundation Directory* published by The Foundation Center, which lists thousands of foundations, mostly in the United States, with their addresses, phone and fax numbers, endowments and what they fund. And, of course, you can check the Internet.

Reality Check: You may be interested in setting up a foundation to help a cause you or other family members are particularly interested in supporting. It's not quite as simple as hanging out a sign that says Smith Family Foundation on the front door. You need to comply with certain governmental regulations. Larger foundations also often need to tap an outside manager to parcel out funds and manage administrative tasks. The benefits can be numerous: family members typically have a zest and an outlet for sharing their riches according to their wishes, they come together to discuss different opportunities, and they leave a legacy to their community. The foundation can lead to enthusiasm and support for the business that is the source of the foundation's funding.

CHAPTER VIII

YOUR SUPPORTING CAST: IN-LAWS, COUSINS, SIBLINGS AND EMPLOYEES

56. What is the role of an in-law in a family business? How does his role differ from that of blood or adopted heirs? What about the in-law who's not active in the business?

Martha Lerman eased into her role as daughter-in-law in a family business more effortlessly than most do. When she and her husband Bill were married in 1983, she joined him in the boys' sleepaway camp business in Waterville, Me. Her in-laws Evelyn and Albert had bought the camp in 1967, 45 years after another family founded it. It was a natural fit, Martha says, since she had majored in camp administration and recreation in college and had met her future spouse when she worked for the American Camping Association. "My in-laws were incredibly supportive, probably because they knew I was a natural at being in the camp business, which is so much more personal and humane than other types of companies. They saw how happy their son was as well. Also their daughter wasn't interested in the business," Martha says.

Lerman was smart, knowing to listen rather than talk initially and offering feedback once her in-laws were comfortable with her presence. "I had to be sensitive to their needs," she says. She and her husband suggested changes gradually, although the senior Lermans sometimes were leery. The younger couple expanded enrollment from 120 to 190 and pumped profits back in to improve facilities. "You have to spend money to make money was our philosophy. We won them over as they saw results," she says.

Over the last decade, Martha and Bill gradually purchased the camp, which they now own completely. The senior Lermans are retired and living in Florida, and return to Camp Caribou to spend summers in an A-frame on the campgrounds.

Working with family may be tough enough, but being an in-law can breed numerous additional issues. Some people may assume that you married into the family for the wealth and the opportunity to get a piece of the action, either through potential ownership or a favored job. You also may have to deal with your parents-in-law's perception that they have lost their "baby" to you.

Too often, in-laws feel that they are in a state of limbo. At times you are a quasi-family member, who is more "invested" in the family and business than a nonfamily employee. At other times, you're a quasi-outsider who is not perceived as being as committed as a blood relative and who doesn't have a history with the family. Moreover, many periodically feel the threat of the sword of Damocles hanging over them. They think that if the marriage breaks up, they'll be dismissed from the broader family and from their employment position if they work for the family's business.

Ruling out in-laws, as some families do, precludes a firm from gaining a valuable resource, one that can provide fresh ideas and talent and have less of a sense of entitlement than many blood relatives have. Some families fail to recognize that in-laws have a vested interest in the business for a variety of reasons, including the potential for their children to one day come work for the firm.

It's important that you recognize the fact that your spouse married you. The family did not. While they should welcome you into the family with open arms, you must earn their respect and confidence. If you want to work in the business, you should do so only according to the same criteria used to allow other family and nonfamily members into the firm. For example, you should join only if there's a specific position that needs to be filled and you have appropriate prior education and relevant work experience for the position. Equally important, you should raise potentially sensitive issues before they become problems. What happens if, heaven forbid, your marriage doesn't work out? Or on what basis will your performance be judged and by whom? Setting ground rules early will make everyone more comfortable and ease any future problems.

Don't join if you are simply looking for an easy leg up in the work world or because of the lure of a good salary, club memberships, company cars and easy hours. After all, those are bad reasons for everyone, including blood relatives.

Psychologically, the in-law must continually summon all his determination to prove that he has a long-term affiliation to the firm. The possibility of full or partial ownership can be addressed at some point but should not be part of the initial discussions.

The in-law who decides not to join the business, or who isn't asked, has often been portrayed as a negative influence on family and business relationships—hence the description of "outlaw." To make him a positive influence, the family needs to make him feel included by educating him about the business, being sensitive to the outsider role, and including him in family council meetings, retreats and business social events.

Your spouse must be careful to present a balanced view of the family and business. Too often, in-laws hear only bad things about family members and develop distorted or biased views of the family and business. These negative perceptions can build and create severe problems in the future.

It's possible that the family will not allow you to work in the business. Many don't permit in-laws under any circumstances. They may have a history or a policy against it. Or they may not have addressed the question and do so only after you raise the issue. Either way, if the decision is to prohibit in-laws, you should not take it personally. Most likely, they did not reject you. Rather, they probably can't grapple with some of the potentially uncomfortable problems that may arise in the future. Hard as it may be, don't let it affect your willingness to support your spouse and the business that he holds dear. You should not feel that you are competing with the business for your spouse's love or for the family's acceptance.

Reality Check: If you think it's tough being a family member, consider the plight of an in-law in a family business. Viewed by family as a quasi-outsider and by nonfamily as a quasi-insider, the in-law is scrutinized more intensely and may be considered a lucky person who sneaked into the firm through marriage. The family should be open and candid about whether in-laws are allowed to work in the business and should address potentially difficult issues that may arise in the future. Ideally, both topics should be addressed long before the first family member becomes engaged. Regardless of the employment decision, the family should do its best to include in-laws, rather than exclude them, from business-related discussions. Most in-laws don't walk on water, but can provide a valuable, fresh point-of-view. A final word to parents: your son- or daughter-in-law will form opinions about the family business on the basis of what they hear. Forced to pick sides, they will inevitably side with their spouses and vice versa, if they know only what their spouses tell them. You need friends, not enemies. Treat them accordingly.

57. What is the best role for spouses in the business?

All the chatter about the role of spouses in the business may make you forget that if your spouse works in the firm, you hope he is there because he's qualified to help make the business grow. But this is just half the equation . . . and the challenge. Getting along with your spouse in your family business can be more difficult than climbing the Matterhorn. Too often spouses who work together step on each other's toes, says Ann Stettner Schreiber, 37, who works with her husband, Neil Schreiber, 35. Both came into the business that Ann's mother Enid, started in the mid-1980s. Wild Thymes is a specialty foods manufacturer of mustards, preserves, chutneys, vinegars, sauces and salad dressings, headquartered in Medusa, N.Y.

Having spouses work together was not new for this family firm. When Enid started the company, she brought her husband Fred into it to oversee operations such as shipping and manufacturing, allowing Enid more time to focus on research and development. About two years ago, she asked Ann and Neil, who weren't yet married, to head up sales, marketing and public relations. "We came into the business to help my parents re-launch the company and launch a new line of products," says Ann, whose background is in television and sports marketing. Quickly the wife–husband duo has beefed up sales with a more eye-catching label and better national distribution into stores such as Williams–Sonoma and catalogues such as Dean & Deluca.

Ann works in the business day-to-day. Neil, who had worked for the State Department and in the business side of publishing, does long-term projects for the company, including strategic and business planning. Both couples learned early on that to work successfully with a spouse there must be a delineation of responsibilities. "We all do very different things, but there is some overlap," adds Ann.

There are pros and cons about working with a spouse, Ann says. "In terms of a lifestyle, it's great. It enables you to have a complementary schedule, which allows a tremendous amount of freedom. However, it can be difficult to define who is doing what." Ann adds that it's also important to respect each other's opinions and separate them from anything personal. "If you have a problem over the weekend with your spouse, working together forces you to resolve it more quickly—before the work week begins. You have to respect your spouse's knowledge as a person rather than a spouse. I would recommend working together if basically you have a good relationship and a good communication system. We do."

Do spouses and family business mix or are they like oil and water? Some owners feel that spouses have no business knowing about their business or working in it, including sitting on the board. This attitude is most common among older founders who started their companies right after World War II and built them while their wives stayed home to manage the household and rear children. Today, as more women earn degrees and achieve success in the workplace, they are likely to be as educated as their spouses. In fact, today's younger entrepreneurs, both men and women, tend to involve their spouses. Many even work side-by-side and share responsibilities. It's a shame to dismiss this pool of potentially highly dedicated talent simply because it happens to be married to a family member.

Overall, the pundits say that owners and family business members who don't include spouses in some way are headed for trouble. It's a huge oversight not to listen to a significant other's input. This doesn't mean a spouse has to be put on the payroll. Spouses who are supportive of their partners and have an understanding of what goes on in the firm can be a real boon to family harmony. An angry, jealous spouse who feels slighted can split apart siblings and cause horrific family friction.

In-laws' frustration is often exacerbated by their lack of information about the business. Most of what spouses learn about the company is parceled out by their partner, often in a one-sided and distorted manner. This can be a breeding ground for trouble. A better way is to bring your spouse into the fold so that he or she feels like a valued member of the family business team.

Before you balk about whether to involve spouses, let's strip away the layers. It isn't a black or white issue; they don't need to be either in or out. Pretend that spousal involvement looks like a ladder and that each rung up connotes a higher level of involvement that ranges from keeping your partner informed on a regular and formal basis about business goings-on to bringing your spouse into the firm to work either part- or full-time. Each family should decide as early as possible where it wants to be on the ladder of potential spousal involvement.

Consider spousal involvement to be a public relations campaign. Businesses do public relations to improve their image. The same is true here; the plan simple. You need spouses' support because you don't want them working behind the scenes counter to the business' or the family's objectives. You should establish a code for spouses and set some boundaries for their role. Are they allowed in to work or not? Be consistent. What applies to one applies to all. Without a clear-cut policy, such battles as the following can arise.

After Jane's children were out of the house, many already working in the family business, Jane began thinking she'd enter the firm as well. She talked to her husband Tim. He said she'd have to ask their son, Adam, who was head of human resources. He couldn't undermine his son's authority. Adam told his mother there was no job available for which she was qualified and that hiring relatives created too many headaches. A year later, the wife of a different family member wanted a job in the firm. She was told the same thing as Jane. But she persisted, saying that she needed the money to send her youngest child to a special school. Adam relented and found her a slot. His decision caused a major family split, which could have been avoided if he had applied the rules consistently.

If there are pre-set guidelines, the next step is to communicate persuasively the rules to spouses. In fact, the key to keeping spouses content at home and/or at work is open and regular communication. Many just want to be heard and want to understand the business. Here are some suggestions for how this may be accomplished:

- Include spouses in regularly scheduled meetings, even if predominantly about business. This will help to dispel rumors and put all family members on equal footing in terms of information they receive. Family meetings are a good way to get together, to make members feel in the loop, and receive news from the horse's mouth to obviate backbiting and rumor mongering.
- Augment these discussions with informal periodic social gatherings. The spouses will be friendlier with each other in this setting. Furthermore, it's fun to get together, particularly if you serve good food and drink.
- Don't hide information from your spouse, particularly your exact job and title, benefits, vacations, compensation and the roles of other family members. Make clear the company's succession

plan. Explain how these decisions were made. Remember, secrets breed divisiveness.

- Consider having spouses sign prenuptial agreements. Without them, angry spouses can divorce and take with them some of the company assets, which could financially cripple the family and the business. Create prenuptials for all spouses, not just for some.
- Pledge not to complain to spouses about siblings or parents. This means there must be some vehicle for airing differences at work rather than ranting and raving at home.
- Encourage your spouse to get to know your entire family better. One of the ways is to have fun together around non-business events such as family vacations, holidays, dinners, parties and barbecues where business is not discussed.
- Don't feel just because you work for your family that your spouse doesn't have his or her own family. Make time to have dinner with your spouse's family at holiday time and other important occasions.
- Don't ignore the strengths of a spouse who's not in the firm. Show interest in your partner's work and encourage the rest of the family to do so, too. It makes the spouse feel like an important member of the clan, even if not a contributor to the business.
- Insist that your spouse stay out of your battles at work with your family. These should be off limits and certain decisions are not open for discussion.
- Recommend that your spouse learn more about your business by taking courses or reading books, trade journals and information on the Internet.
- Continue to communicate the company vision and what that means for the family. It's important to help spouses see the big picture.

Now, for one of the touchiest issues concerning spouses who work in the business. What happens if a family member gets divorced and the ex-spouse is an employee in the family firm? There is no easy answer. However, it is clear that a policy should be created to deal with this possibility, preferably long before any spouse comes to work for the firm and certainly before a divorce is pending. Clearly, it can be uncomfortable for all if an ex-spouse remains in the business. Conversely, if the ex-spouse plays an important role, the business can suffer if the ex is forced to leave. Some families have a hard-and-fast rule that the ex must tender his or her resignation in the event of a divorce. Others leave the decision to the board of directors, although that works well only if there are unbiased, nonfamily board members. Whatever the decision, the family should discuss the issue openly and the policy should be communicated to spouses, preferably before they make the decision to come to work for the business.

Reality Check: Spouses of owners of family firms often feel like they're on an island. Many know what happens in the firm only from what their partner chooses to tell them. There are ways to bring spouses who do not work in the firm into the fold, so to speak, so they don't feel left out, resentful or angry. Involving them in some way is critical to ensure that they are supportive of your family, business and you. You can include them in regular formal family meetings and periodic gatherings. Your company also needs to have an across-the-board policy on employing and terminating spouses. There also should be a clearly stated policy for what will happen to a working spouse in the event of a divorce. Preferably, family business members should have prenuptial agreements with their spouses to avoid the risk that they and their family members must remain business partners in that event. Communicate this and other decisions upfront and before such a crisis occurs.

58. What is the best way to bring on board another family member (child, sibling, in-law or cousin), particularly if he's more qualified than the one already working in the business?

Marcy Syms brought leadership, teamwork and people management skills to her job. For more than 20 years, she has been involved in the retail business Syms, founded by her father Sy in 1959 and headquartered in Secaucus, N.J. While she attended college in New York as an English literature major, she worked at the company, which retails off-price, in-season tailored clothing and accessories for men, women and children. She also worked there in between college and graduate school where she studied public relations. She went to work at the company full time in 1978 and her timing could not have been better. A brother already worked there, but after the company went public in 1983, he left. "He had his own career he wanted to pursue," she says. Marcy, who worked without a title, was named president in 1983.

Marcy learned several lessons through the years about ways to bring on board family members, how to keep them and help them take the business to another level. It's important for family companies to have generic rules about joining the business. Once a family member has passed muster, it is crucial for him to find the niche where he's most appreciated and can do the best job."Everyone has a particular talent that they can bring to the business, assuming the company is big enough. And if it's not, then there are often ways to expand it to make room so everyone doesn't get on each other's nerves," Marcy says. In those cases, when there is absolutely no room and no way to expand, the family member should not be allowed to enter the business, she says. "The business has to be able to support the people already there and remain a business."

When it comes to drafting rules, each company needs to establish its own set. "Perhaps," she says, "the company insists that everyone has a four-year college degree, prior experience of a certain number of years, one promotion or a certain major that relates to what they're doing."

Once on board, the offspring should be evaluated the same as any employee, although many children of successful entrepreneurs never get the proper feedback which can help them improve skills and grow, she adds. "The kids have to earn their right—to take their place in your company, and then perform and produce their way to the top," she wrote in her book *Mind Your Own Business and Keep It in the Family* (Mastermedia Ltd., 1992).

In Marcy's case, she was never shown the ropes. Her father never critiqued her because he felt uncomfortable doing so, and the company lacked the management structure of a full-service human resource department where someone else could have evaluated her performance.

She was, however, able to take on more authority herself as the business moved from an entrepreneurial to professional environment. "I was doing the president's job initially with no title." Now she is CEO and her Dad remains chairman of the board. The chain has grown to employ 3,000 and operates 44 stores in 16 states.

". . . the larger the family, the greater the difficulty in achieving total harmony," writes Marcy Syms in her book, *Mind Your Own Business and Keep It in the Family.* And woe be it to any family business that hasn't planned in advance how to accommodate a host of members. The best tack is to have written policies about how to bring in family members. Some firms insist that family candidates have relevant academic credentials, possibly a college and even graduate degree, and minimum grade point averages. Some require prior work experience elsewhere to enhance maturity, gain useful expertise, and experience both success and failure without the spotlight that typically exists in the family's business. Still other family businesses require the family candidate to go through the same interviewing process as nonfamily members and permit entry only when a suitable position exists. With clear guidelines, it becomes harder to take on board someone who's either not qualified at all or not qualified for an existing opening.

The reasons many family businesses have set up such parameters are multifaceted. Some owners have worked in public companies and seen the advantage of professionalization and meritocracy winning out over mediocracy. Many have witnessed, read or heard about the disasters that occur when unqualified heirs-apparent come on board or when there's no true slot for even a qualified one. Typically, guilt prevails with the owner debating what to do, so he welcomes the second scion, particularly when a sibling already works in the business. Even if rivalries never existed or have been dormant since childhood, they may suddenly fester, then explode. Mom or Dad may get caught in the crossfire, everyone may start to fight and the business may ultimately suffer.

The owner can avoid this quandary by viewing his role as the one to place the best people in the right jobs, even if it means that primogeniture won't rule or that one sibling is in and another is kept out. Undoubtedly, there are other ways you can help an heir find meaningful work when your business is not the right place for him. Principally: educate them, call in your chits with fellow business people who may require their skills, help family members decide what they're best equipped to do and want to do outside the company.

Likewise, the second or third sibling considering entering the business needs to think through the ramifications of doing so. Arthur Pine presents some good questions to ponder in his book *Your Family Business* (Poseidon Press, 1990):

- Is there really room for all of us? For all concerned to get their fair share of responsibility and money?
- Am I prepared to work with my brother and sister?
- Can we all get along? What about sibling rivalry?
- Will my sister or brother and I eventually be able to manage the business without our parents?

Inevitably, there will be disagreements among family members, just as unrelated businesspeople argue from time to time. However, you'll need to address some special critical issues when the second and subsequent relatives come to work in the family's business:

- Will the specific family members' egos permit one to report to or work for the other? Ideally, family members, especially early in their careers, should report to nonfamily managers.
- Do family members have the ability to argue and debate, come to a decision and then put the disagreement behind them? If family members are likely to bear grudges, the situation obviously will not work in the long run.
- Who will ultimately pick the leader from among family members? Will family members believe that they have equal decision-making authority despite their differing abilities and roles, or will they accept a single leader? If not, is joint leadership a realistic alternative?

Inevitably, one family member will show better potential for advancement and leadership than another. Of course, the one that got there first will have a head start, but what if he's less qualified? If you believe in meritocracy, the one who's best for the job, including the presidency, should get it. However, that requires the tough decision of picking one family member over another. Resentments can arise when you do that. The alternative is to manage by committee or even to accept the less-than-qualified candidate. Those often aren't great alternatives, either. The best approach to dealing with these issues is to raise them as early as possible. Get all family members to understand the issues and alternatives. Involving your board of independent directors in evaluating family members also can play a crucial and calming role. Hopefully, good sense will prevail.

Reality Check: While no parent wants to favor one child over another, allowing entrance into the family business should not be automatic. Owners can avoid a sure-fire recipe for disaster by setting clear guidelines on entrance requirements, including education, work experience and specific job placement. In some cases, the early bird may catch the worm and the scion hesitating may have to find employment elsewhere. You'll need to think ahead and anticipate the issues that may arise when multiple family members work together. That will help you decide whether to hire the candidate. More important, it should force you to take additional steps to head off potential problems.

59. What guidelines can you offer to help siblings or cousins working together?

For six generations, the Hancock Lumber Company in Casco, Me., has prospered, increasing annual revenue to the current $82 million. One reason for the company's success is that it has adapted to the economy of the times, but another is the family members' genuine belief in a shared heritage. The late David Hancock, who was the fifth generation to run the company, perhaps expressed it best when he said it was his responsibility to pass on the business in better shape than it was when he found it.

He firmly passed on that commitment to his sons Kevin and Matt, who developed a realistic plan in June 1998 to work together and avoid competition. "We're close in age, very good friends, respect one another but are also very competitive," says Kevin. "We went into meetings one-on-one for several months, and while we knew we could run a company together, that wasn't on top of our list. Neither was one of us working for the other."

Their decision was for Kevin to take the helm of Hancock Lumber, one of the nation's largest producers of Eastern white pine, which owns nine lumberyards and two saw mills. Matt, younger by a year, took control of M.S. Hancock, the largest private timberland owner in Southern Maine with 15,000 acres. M.S. Hancock had been a passive company until the death of their father pushed the siblings to find separate outlets for their talents. They also decided that managing the timberland business more aggressively would be smart long term since their biggest challenge would be access to quality timber.

The companies operate from separate headquarters. The family owns 55 percent of Hancock Lumber with nonfamily managers holding the remaining stock, and owns 100 percent of M.S. Hancock, with all the stock held in a voting trust. The brothers hold a minority stake in each other's firms. Their Mother is chair of their stockholder's council. Their next order of business is to decide on a regular meeting schedule.

A family business needs to be run like a nonfamily company. Nobody should have a sense of entitlement when it comes to job titles, responsibilities, authority or perks, and each relative should be evaluated as every other employee in the business—according to a predetermined set of criteria. Siblings and cousins should not have to report to or be judged by each other.

Problems can arise, however, when no single person takes charge and is the final voice. In one company, which prefers to remain anonymous, the generation that owns the company consists of two warring factions made up of six siblings and one cousin. The two sides can never agree, undermining each other's decisions on everything from tactics to long-term strategy and trying to take advantage to push their own agendas. The result is that the current leader plans to resign. Says one observer, "The former head took the easy way out and left the business equally to everyone. That may have been fine when he was alive but not now when he's gone. He should have thought about what would happen when he was gone. Now, the only solutions are for one side to buy out the other or for the sides to agree to bring in an outside CEO and board to run the company."

Even when siblings and/or cousins work well together they need to follow certain golden rules to keep the company running smoothly:

- Deal with problems privately, out of earshot of employees.
- Try to define and segregate each relative's responsibilities and authority.
- Avoid meddling in each other's responsibilities and decisions, unless asked for input.
- Develop mechanisms to resolve differences of opinion before you experience the inevitable disagreements.
- Agree on family member employment, evaluation, compensation and dismissal policies.
- Establish a board of independent directors to help provide guidance.
- Require all family members to develop communication and negotiation skills.
- Foster strong family relationships outside the business through periodic family social activities and gatherings.
- Work hard to develop a common sense of belonging and a belief in the importance of the business to the family.
- Foster a sense within the family that family members are stewards of the business and have the responsibility to see that it survives and prospers for future generations.
- Discourage interfering with other family members' personal lives and respect the bounds between individual families, the extended family and the business.
- Avoid bringing complaints home so that spouses don't take sides and fuel problems in relationships.

Reality Check: Having more than one family member in a firm offers strength in numbers—or problems if rivalries abound. All sorts of reasons can fuel conflict—inappropriate pay, perks and titles; differing responsibilities; and plain-out favoritism by the head of the company, just to name a few instigating factors. Small fights can escalate quickly and pull in additional family, employees and customers. It's important to develop policies, and support for the policies, to deal with potential future problems. The bottom line: Everyone should work at working together for the good of the business, and the long-term happiness of the family.

60. How does the founder deal with long-time nonfamily employees when a family member comes into the business and, later, becomes the successor CEO?

Even when a successor is eminently qualified to come into the family business and take over, it may spell mayhem for nonfamily employees who have been with the company a long time. Of course, if William E. Maritz, 70, hadn't stepped down as CEO of Maritz Inc., a fourth-generation employee-motivation firm headquartered in Fenton, Mo., and turned the job over to his son Steve, 40, he would not have had to deal with this issue. Fortuitously, Steve's installment was met with the invigorating reception of its employees. Why? The succession was handled the right way. William Maritz told employees that he would relinquish the presidency when he was 65, and at 70, he'd turn over the CEO job but stay on as chairman. He never said who his successor would be, but he stuck to his schedule. Five years ago he named a nonfamily member president, and in November 1998, his son was tapped to be CEO.

Steve, who has a degree in psychology from Princeton University, is the only one of four siblings to enter the business. He never expected to be named CEO or for that matter to enter the family business at all. Founded by his great grandfather Edouard in 1894 as a watchmaking company, the company expanded into a broader line of wholesale jewelry. However, during the Depression, when no one was buying jewelry and the company was in the second generation, Steve's grandfather James A. came up with the idea of selling inventory to companies as service awards such as the proverbial retirement gold watch. And from there the more modern form of the company was born. Forty-five years ago William came on board. But would one of his children follow in his footsteps?

Steve says, "For a long time I felt like I didn't want to work in the family business. It wasn't appealing. A lot of expectations and pressures go along with being a family member in a family business. You don't have the same freedom as nonfamily and there are lots of sacrifices." So, the first time Steve was asked to join Maritz's East Coast branch office, he turned down the offer. He finally joined in 1983, but it was not a foregone conclusion that he'd take over for his father some day. He'd have to prove himself, which he did.

The reason the succession process was so smooth is twofold, says Steve. "My first job was not with Maritz, but as a salesman with a small marketing company focusing on banks in the Northeast." The second reason he was so well accepted by nonfamily employees, he says, is that he joined the company as a salesperson, not as a successor. "Of course the last name meant special career advantages; nevertheless, I had to do the job." He also worked in Detroit as a regional manager, transferred to St. Louis to serve as an area manager in the Quality and Productivity Division, was director of sales of the Performance Improvement Company, and served as chief operating officer of Maritz Inc. before he earned his stripes as CEO.

One of the most important aspects of this succession, or any succession for that matter, is that Maritz employees, which number 3,500 in the St. Louis area and another 3,000 outside the US, feel their future is in the capable hands of a scion who cares about the company. Also, Steve's appointment to CEO was never kept under wraps, but was announced publicly to all employees.

When you've made the quantum leap to bring a family member on board, it's not the time to be coy or secretive. Be honest and above board with employees before the news leaks out and company rumors run as rampant as those about politicians in Washington, D.C. Explain why you're bringing the family member in at this particular juncture and state your objectives. Say what he'll be doing and whether any employees' jobs will change. Explain the family member's credentials and why he deserves the slot. Try to win over your employees and encourage them to stay. Let them know they shouldn't feel threatened and that you'll need them to help you groom your successor and continue the success of the company.

Many successful nonfamily business executives are quite content to play second fiddle. What keeps them loyal to the company can be any mix of factors: significant responsibility and authority; outstanding work environment; good compensation and benefits; visibility within and outside the company; a chance to remain a contender for the top position; and a secure ego. No. 2 isn't necessarily such a bad place to be.

There are several specific steps you should take when you bring aboard an heir-apparent:

- Talk candidly with senior managers before they perceive family members as a threat to their security. Get them on your side long before anyone comes on board. If you want a family member to take over your leadership role one day, you should candidly discuss your plans with senior managers. Presumably, you view your successor's role as critical to continued family ownership. Your senior managers should view family ownership and the resulting stability as a plus, rather than as a minus.
- Never push the family member into a role or give him a title for which he or she is not qualified.
- Create a task force of key managers to determine how to train the family member in the new role. Let this group suggest where to start the new hire and how to manage rotation throughout the firm. Convince them that it is in their best interest to have a fully trained and competent leader. Explain that you'll need their help and cooperation. If you hope that the family member will lead the firm one day, openly discuss this objective with your key managers. Help them to understand that yours is a family business. Its future and, therefore, your employees' future and security are dependent upon their help in developing your successor's business and leadership skills.

When you are ready to name the family member as your successor, make a formal public announcement. You may also want to release a statement to the press. The key to making the transition work is to tout your successor's qualifications so no one thinks you've anointed a second-rate player. Be sure to play up educational credentials, outside work experience and success within your business so that everyone is convinced that you are promoting a talented, competent family member to leadership of the organization.

Equally important, you must make sure that working family members respect nonfamily employees and are sympathetic to the fears that undoubtedly will arise when a change of leadership is planned.

Accept the fact that there may be some turnover and fallout. Your successor may have his own people to bring in when the time for his ascension draws closer. However, he should respect the dignity and past contributions of those he chooses to replace. Make provisions for early retirement of managers or provide outplacement services as appropriate. Develop a consistent company policy to ease the transition to new management so that there will be some continuity of objectives, planning, products, dividend policies and compensation.

If you don't do this right, here is what can happen. One company founder brought his son into the company without proper qualifications, education or training. The son came in and immediately replaced the chief financial officer and, even worse, demanded special treatment despite the fact that he came to work late and left early every day. There was tremendous resentment toward him by all employees. In addition, the son used profanity in e-mails and yelled at employees in the hallways if he didn't get his way. Soon key people who had been with the company for years started to leave. Morale suffered and threatened the survival of the firm.

Reality Check: Regardless of how well you plan for an entering family member or for the ultimate succession of management, your key managers and other employees will feel unsettled. It's only natural. Prepare them far in advance. Seek their help and support, making it clear why it is in their best interests to provide it. Make a formal public announcement verbally and in writing only after discussion with affected employees. Accept the fact that there may be turnover. You can provide some early retirement incentives or outplacement services if they decide it's better to leave than stay. Make sure that your successor is adequately trained, particularly as it relates to handling the sensitive personnel issues associated with taking over a leadership role.

61. How does the family business leader attract (and keep) good professional nonfamily managers and employees who most likely will never "run" or "own" the business?

CEO Paul Holt, 37, of GroupComm Systems (a Holt Company) in Waltham, Ma., a toy and software, school furniture and audio visual equipment distributor, made drastic changes in the second-generation family firm started by his parents in 1979. Once he came into the firm full-time in 1984, after receiving a business degree from the University of Massachusetts in Amherst, he knew it was time to take the company to another level and enter the digital age. However, Holt wasn't sure how the then 40 employees would react and whether they'd want to stay on during the transition from a Mom-and-Pop company to web retailer. Holt had a brainstorm to keep everyone happy and in the loop. He decided to retrain key managers as well as employees at all levels and give them the skills and technical proficiency they needed to go from paper to computer electronics. That, he felt, might encourage them to stay. He instituted a four-month retraining program taught by a consultant who offered both technical and teamwork skills. Little did Holt know at the time that retraining was a wonderful way to keep valuable employees from getting stale or burned out in their jobs. "In fact, we gave them skills that, if they ever were to leave, would make them much more worthwhile in the workforce." Another key to retaining nonfamily key managers and good employees, Holt realizes, is to continue to keep the workforce pumped up by finding new challenges. "It's also a matter of communication and giving each employee a say. I'm constantly stopping by employees' desks and asking how they are doing, taking them to lunch, giving them little cards that say 'you're doing a good job,' sending e-mails saying 'thank you' and offering a profit-sharing program that's very active," says Holt, who now works with 50 employees and four other family members.

Serving in senior management of a family firm can be a thankless job if you're not family. Why work for an organization that will not allow you to advance unless you have the proper genes? Why not work for a public company where there are no constraints on your advancement other than your own abilities? Surely that's better than family businesses' way of nurturing nepotism and all the ills associated with family and business overlapping?

Well, there is potential to get to the top of a family business. The *Arthur Andersen/MassMutual American Family Business Survey '97* showed that 12 percent of the 3,000-plus respondents have had nonfamily CEOs. Some 52 percent of those with nonfamily CEOs rated the experience as "very" or "extremely" successful. But attracting and providing advancement for nonfamily managers were reported to be the greatest employee-related challenge, according to the survey. The survey also identified major concerns with compensation, training, retaining and providing outplacement for exiting nonfamily managers.

There are many top-notch employees who prefer working in a closely held environment where key managers have a direct pipeline to the top. Some other reasons include:

- Those who like family firms prefer the genre's long-term approach versus the short-term profit orientation of public companies.

- There are less bureaucracy and politics, and often greater nimbleness.
- It's a different (often more paternalistic) culture that certain types fit into better.
- Many family businesses have professional managers in key management slots and give them significant autonomy and authority.
- Key managers can become objective, trusted participants who keep an eye on what's best for the company. They also are typically well compensated, secure in their positions and have a sense of who they are. They can become highly visible in their companies and communities.

Family firms that restrict stock ownership to family members have a disadvantage compared to public companies that offer stock options. However, percentage bonuses, phantom stock, stock appreciation rights and other creative incentive programs can be equally as effective at rewarding employees.

Many of the smaller family firms have an edge over large, more layered public corporations in their ability to offer creative lifestyle perks that win over and keep nonfamily managers. In today's tight labor market, family firms have to be creative to offer nonfamily members reasons to stay, beyond just financial compensation.

There's a veritable buffet of possibilities. Some companies offer training or retraining, a well-stocked refrigerator at work, flexible work weeks, longer vacation times, lower employee contributions for medical insurance, biannual rather than annual review times for raises, vacation time that accrues the first month of employment instead of waiting the de rigueur one year, flexibility in lunch schedules, and on-site day care. Many family businesses also provide country club memberships, holiday presents or use of the family's vacation homes.

It's crucial that you talk with key nonfamily managers and prospects. Map out with them their goals and objectives. Be direct so they'll be honest. Competent people look for more than just a great compensation package. Find ways to provide new challenges and opportunities. If the family expresses and acts on their concern for employees' well being, you can create an incredibly attractive work environment.

There are other questions to grapple with when dealing with valuable nonfamily employees and candidates:

- Should you pay nonfamily more than market rates to keep them? Generally not. However, in determining compensation, you must look at all benefits, not just salary, to determine whether you are offering a competitive package.
- Do your family members really understand the value of nonfamily managers? Will the nonfamily managers have a job when the successor takes over and the CEO leaves or retires?
- Can you include nonfamily managers in special task forces or high-level decision-making? Do you truly treat your key managers as members of your management team or just as order takers? Is there room for nonfamily managers to be rotated or promoted? Can they aspire to lead a division or other major operation?
- Are there challenges on a continuous basis such as special projects, marketing strategies, new areas of growth?

Reality Check: Some highly qualified nonfamily managers who have worked for public companies prefer the intimacy of privately held family firms with long- versus short-range planning and objectives. These firms offer interaction with employees at all levels and a chance to advance faster toward the top, albeit very few nonfamily members will ever have the top job. Keeping your nonfamily management content involves monetary as well as creative compensation, a sense of responsibility and autonomy. Psychologically, these "second fiddles" must be made to feel special and be challenged constantly.

62. How do you attract young people today to middle management positions when so many want to work on their own for the freedom?

If you think competition in the NFL is intense, look at what a small family business must do to attract good talent. Some businesses have trouble finding good middle management talent and keeping them. Others have such a good reputation that good talent finds them. This is the case with Printer's Row Restaurant in Chicago, an anomaly in the restaurant industry where turnover is traditionally high. Michael Foley, 46, founder of the eatery in 1981, reforged a partnership with his father Robert in 1987 to continue in Printer's Row and start other ventures. Both report that their turnover is perhaps two or three employees a year. Sure they pay at or a bit above market, and give bonus packages to certain people at the end of the year; however that's not what attracts or keeps their young talent. It helps, too, that the restaurant has built a reputation known for quality and strong sales, which hit almost $2 million last year.

Robert Foley, who's in his 70s, offers his point of view. "I think talented people want to be among other talented people. We provide a good training format for them so they can deepen their skills and knowledge of the profession they're in. We prepare them for a future. We don't expect them to give us their life. We look for four or five years, more if possible, and sometimes less. And they have a future with our organization whenever possible. Another prime ingredient is that they're working in a family-oriented environment where there is no corporate hassle."

In addition, says Michael, the staff is cross-trained. "Our employees must be able to be a busboy or a captain; they learn it all. Every year each of our eight captains has to spend a week retraining in one of the other positions. They have to convey an attitude to the other staff that they know all jobs completely and thoroughly. The kitchen staff also cross-rains on stations so that everybody can perform each job. We do hire people for a specific position but cross-train them in order that they know the complete kitchen. We also look for a staff with an entrepreneurial spirit and those who understand that working here is a team effort."

Printer's Row is a comfortable well-priced high–quality American eatery featuring classic and contemporary cooking such as a ragout of mushrooms with Madeira and cream, duck with corn crepes, all types of wild game as well as a full complement of meats, fish and vegetable-grain based dishes. The restaurant has molded itself to enter the next Millennium in terms of its dress code and attitude, says Michael. He knows this business well for he and his father represent the second and third generations to enter the restaurant business. Their ability to change with the times, has also helped attract top-notch talent. "The early days of the restaurant business were more formal. Service was stiffer to meet the demands of the market. Slowly we moved from stiff fine dining to a more comfortable service level. We became more casual to broaden our market and to deal with sociological trends." At the same time, customer expectations are high. They expect the staff to be very knowledgeable. "The staff meets four times a year to re-identify itself," says Michael. "Everyone goes through a training program until we consider them ready and then they're verbally and mechanically tested. Anyone who works nightly is briefed and tested weekly."

Michael knows Printer's Row is a good training ground and is quick to tick off all the people he's mentored from waitstaff, chefs to general managers who have gone on and started their own restaurants. "At least 10 of our former staff have opened up continuously successful places in and around

Chicago and another 10 in other cities." When young people work at Printer's Row," says Foley, "we give a boost to their entrepreneurial instincts."

There was a time when company loyalty was like a badge of courage and leaving a company of one's volition was as rare as getting fired. However, today leaving a company has lost its taint. Young people want jobs that will be a jumping off point for them to fuel their own careers.

So how do you recruit and keep good talented people? You should try to find those who want to be part of a family culture. They should view the family business environment as a place where they will fit in because they're valued long-term for their contributions, which some larger public corporations may no longer do.

You may not be willing or able to offer your middle management staff expensive perks, and in many cases that's not what they want. However, you can offer them compensation competitive with non-family firms as well as some softer benefits that larger companies don't provide. Among the possibilities are: trips to special places as incentives for hard work or attaining a certain level of sales, tuition reimbursement for courses that relate to their current job, flexible hours, computer and other technological training, a telecommuting, a periodic sabbatical for whatever length of time your company can allow time off, the freedom to build a department or division.

In addition, you must listen better to your staff's needs. Ask for feedback, act on useful suggestions, nurture your employees and keep finding ways to reward them to stay. The two things that employees have expressed that they want more than anything else today is challenging work and time off when they need it to care for a spouse, child or elderly parent.

Try not to take resignations personally and do not assume those who resign are disloyal. Don't be surprised if some of your best and brightest eventually depart for greener pastures. Many will leave to work for other businesses, maybe even the competition, or start their own venture. The latter in particular is understandable since entrepreneurship and control of one's destiny is very much in the business wind today. You can't worry about it or prevent it from happening. What you can do is operate a good, collegial family business where the energy level is high and where new recruits will constantly want to come to fill the pipeline.

Reality Check: It may be difficult to recruit and keep talented middle management in a family firm, but you have many pluses on your side. First of all, sell your culture as friendly and non-bureaucratic. It is a place where ideas will be listened to and work will be new and exciting. Perhaps you cannot pay high salaries, give cars or other types of perks, but softer perks such as freedom to leave work when necessary, the opportunity to build a new skill set or take on more challenging work may be even more appealing.

63. Should a nonfamily employee have a contract?

J. Bernard Haviland of Haviland Enterprises, a Grand Rapids, Mi. chemical distribution and manufacturing business, died suddenly in 1982 without a succession plan. Three of his children were in the business at the time. However, the business was not doing well. The family had sold a major division that was one-third of the business, and it was hard to get overhead reduced in line with the downsizing.

In 1991, the family board decided to bring in an outside CEO. After an extensive nationwide search, they gave the nod to Dick Garner, who was handed a six-month contract as a consultant. "We decided to live together before we got married," he says. During the negotiations for salary, perks and benefits, Dick, now 64, gave considerable thought to the amount of micromanagement he might have to endure. What would happen when the company began performing better? "I came in thinking in two or three years, if I turned the company around, they might decide they didn't need an outsider and revert to family management," he says. After six months, an employment contract was drafted that was good for three years.

Dick didn't seek equity but owns a tiny portion of stock through an ESOP. "I don't see the value in being a minority shareholder in a family-owned business. The Havilands provided me with a better salary than in my previous job where I worked 35 years for a publicly held chemical company." He also was given a car and a membership to a business club. "I didn't have a country club membership. How could I? When I came on board, I eliminated all country club memberships."

Dick also was supposed to mentor the three children in the business at the time, E. Bernard (Bernie), who is president of both operating subsidiaries, Haviland Products and Haviland Consumer Products; Marie, who serves as assistant to the president and wears many hats spending most of her time as credit manager; and Michael, who has a Ph.D. and later left the company to teach. Dick also added an independent board and took the company from an entrepreneurial to a more professional participative style of management. He's pleased to say that the family never showed any resentment toward him, although he was reticent about taking on the job with a family firm at first. "I've always viewed myself as a professional doing a job on behalf of the family shareholders."

Dick says he's ready to retire and has made a public announcement that he'll leave at the end of 1999. Bernie, who is in his mid-40s and is the youngest of J. Bernard's 12 children, waits in the wings. "He's definitely a possibility to take over some day, but right now he likes his life and not having the top position."

Dick adds that he's had more fun working for a family business than for a public company. "I like the cultural nature of family business; it's a little kinder and gentler." But, before coming on board, Dick set the boundaries. "I made an overt decision to become part of the business, but not become part of the family."

If you're considering bringing in an outsider for a top position at your company, be sure you know what you want in a nonfamily leader. You probably want a person with a proven track record to manage, communicate, understand today's technology and think strategically. Perhaps you desire someone with product development and marketing talent who will make your company more aggressive by rolling out new lines. Or maybe you need someone with a global vision as you expand internationally.

Once you've found this nonfamily superstar, you have to do what you can to keep him. As the national employment pool shrinks, seasoned top managers are a hot commodity. You don't want snafus down the line. To protect yourself and your nonfamily manager's security, you may decide to have him sign a contract, which offers pluses for each side. But is it really necessary?

There is no hard-and-fast rule except to be consistent in your choice. It depends on the business and the parties involved. Contracts make some owners uneasy because they feel they're having their hands tied, losing control and giving up flexibility if the economy changes. If you, as the owner, are a good communicator, can sit down and state your expectations up front, and are known as someone who sticks by your promises, you probably don't need a piece of paper to make your case. Verbally tick off the person's title, duties, salary, perks, what's ahead and reasons you might be dissatisfied. Certainly it's wise to put the job requirements and expectations in writing, but not necessarily in a binding contract that provides little flexibility to either side.

However, if you have been burned in the past by nonfamily hirees who didn't perform well but whom you rewarded richly by your calculations, you may prefer to put their responsibilities and remuneration in writing. A word of caution: Don't single out one person who must sign a contract. It should be an across-the-board-or-nothing rule for all top management. A good, detailed contract also should include a noncompete clause for a set amount of time, intellectual property provisions to safeguard corporate secrets, reasons for termination and what the severance package would include. Typical contracts run for three to five years.

If the tables are turned and you're the nonfamily manager contemplating the advantages or disadvantages of a contract, you might want one as a guarantee of control and autonomy or because either of the following two situations exist:

- The owner doesn't communicate well or the firm is volatile. Perhaps the company has had three presidents within a short period of time. You may want the security of a contract.
- You're starting at the top. Experts say the need for a contract depends on your level of commitment, your position, how important the job is to the company, and the state of the economy in terms of whether people think they're at risk of being out of a job or downsized in a short time frame.

Whether you, as a potential nonfamily employee of a family-owned firm, are asked to sign a contract or request it on your own, you should know that many of the nitty-gritty issues that need to be addressed between you and the family leadership never work their way into a piece of paper. For example, the nonfamily manager needs to be compatible with key family members, communicate to all what he's doing, mentor others, problem solve, manage employees who don't do their jobs efficiently, and agree to stay out of family disputes. These are issues that can't be easily drafted in words, but can be best determined by prior work experiences and your gut instincts.

Reality Check: Whether a nonfamily employee should have a contract depends on the individual family and business situation. Whatever the owner or family decides should represent an across-the-board policy decision. Either your company has or doesn't have employment contracts for its top leaders. In some firms where there's been high turnover, contracts may be more appropriate for job security or retention. If you decide to have one, keep it simple and stipulate salary, perks, terms of termination and general job expectations. For the most part, contracts are unnecessary, however, and a better tack is to discuss the particulars up front and make sure everyone understands expectations.

64. Should nonfamily employees expect equity? What are other options?

When a company has 1,500 employees, many key nonfamily senior managers, and 46 family members active in a fifth-generation firm (two members of the second generation serve as board members emeritus), it's important to keep them content. That's why Hatfield Quality Meats, a 103-year-old pork processing firm in Philadelphia, offers family as well as nonfamily employees a bundle of benefits.

Nonfamily perks include the opportunity for top management to buy stock through a stock option plan. Also, other employees have stock by participating in a profit-sharing plan instituted in 1951. "Along with family, nonfamily members helped to build the company and deserve the perks of ownership," says CEO and president Philip A. Clemens, 49, the youngest member of the third generation who was voted to his post three years ago by an advisory board of eight—three outsiders and five family members. "We tend to treat employees and their extended families like family," he said.

This firm takes a holistic approach. Other benefits for nonfamily include day-care and fitness centers on site. The company also offers a 24-hour chaplaincy service for weddings, funerals, counseling, hospital or home visits. "Our employees have more needs than just a paycheck. For example, so far, employees have contacted chaplains more than 1,000 times in less than two years," says Philip, a distant relative of author Mark Twain a.k.a. Samuel Clemens.

He adds that the company is managed much like a public firm. There are 182 family shareholders plus an additional 75 nonfamily shareholders. One hundred percent of the voting stock and 80 percent of the nonvoting stock is held by the family; the remaining 20 percent is in the hands of nonfamily employees and management. The largest block of nonvoting stock is held by the profit-sharing plan. Four family voting trusts contain all the family's voting stock. "It came about from the four brothers of the second generation who worked in the firm started by their father John C. Clemens," says Philip. The firm also pays dividends and holds annual shareholders' meetings.

As a rule, benefits given to reward valuable nonfamily employees in a family firm include salary, bonuses, commissions and perks. Family firms rarely offer equity as remuneration to nonfamily employees. It can cause headaches and havoc when differences arise or when they decide to leave the firm. But exceptions abound. Some nonfamily employees come to closely resemble family because of their commitment and longevity with the company. An owner may also have no heir-apparent and the nonfamily employees help fill that vacuum.

If you award stock to nonfamily employees, you absolutely should have a buy–sell agreement to set forth the rules under which the stock must be returned if the employee leaves the company.

Some companies offer an Employee Stock Ownership Plan (ESOP). These plans offer a tax-advantaged way for family members to gain liquidity and provide ownership incentives to employees. They must cover a wide range of employees and cannot discriminate in favor of your top management. Employees may feel a greater kinship once they own a piece of the pie and may be inclined to work harder. However, many businesses that provide these plans are not convinced that they gain the desired result because many employees do not believe that their individual efforts have much impact on stock value.

The prime advantage of an ESOP to the family is that it provides family members with liquidity. If it is properly structured, family members may sell their stock and defer capital gain taxation by reinvesting in marketable securities. The company can get an income tax deduction for stock that it purchases and places in the ESOP.

An ESOP is not effective in all situations and can trip up some families because it takes shares out of family hands. If your goal is to keep the firm squarely in the family, this may not be a good tack. There are additional headaches. With an ESOP, the company becomes almost like a public operation with employees owning pieces. Suddenly, you are accountable to them. They can look over your shoulder and question what the firm is doing. They have a right to financial information and the company's stock must be appraised periodically. Plus, the company may experience unexpected capital demands since it may be required to buy back stock as employees leave the firm.

Some family businesses implement a phantom stock plan to attract and retain top managers. A phantom stock plan is a contractual agreement with selected employees that gives them a right to future compensation based upon future increases in the company's stock value. Since they do not receive actual stock ownership, they are not entitled to vote and there is less potential for problems upon their departure.

Another alternative to equity ownership is a bonus plan based upon measures that are important to the business. For example, a manager may be entitled to a percentage bonus calculated by reference to increased sales or net income.

There are other ways to keep nonfamily employees happy and boost their morale. Examples include use of vacation homes, sabbaticals, time off for good attendance and performance, holiday gifts, lunch or dinner with the boss, a chance to sit in on strategy meetings, new challenges and projects, and healthy raises.

Reality Check: Nonfamily employees rarely should expect equity in a family firm. Most families cherish family ownership too much to allow stock, even a minority interest, to pass to nonfamily members. There are numerous alternatives, including phantom stock plans and incentive bonuses based upon company or job performance. Other more tangible and personal ways should be considered to recognize the worth of nonfamily managers. Often, a "thank you" and a pat on the back can go a long way to instill loyalty.

65. Should nonfamily employees avoid socializing with family members outside the company? How can nonfamily employees avoid taking sides in family squabbles?

Michael Boland, 48, now president and CEO of Performance Technology in Dayton Oh., a consulting and training firm, always wanted a sales job after he finished college. So, after a stint with a large public company, he went to work for a family-owned construction supply company where he worked his way up to national sales manager. But with the job came the responsibility of mentoring the owner's four sons, whom he considered not terribly qualified for their positions. Michael quickly learned to keep his distance as a nonfamily member in a family business, including not socializing with the family or getting embroiled in family squabbles. He was constantly covering up for the owner's sons. One day, the owner called Michael into his office and asked him how the boys were doing. Michael tried to be magnanimous. "Rather than getting in the middle of their struggles, I tried to be forthright with the owner and to find ways to present concerns," he says. Instead of getting caught in an untenable situation, Michael threw the question back to his boss: "What kind of feedback are you getting, Mr. President, from the dealers and from the clients? Go talk to the customers if you want to know how your sons are performing."

How much you interact away from the office with a boss or employee should reflect a lesson your parents probably taught you: Don't get too chummy and cross the invisible boundary between employer and employee. You may regret it later. When you mix business and friendship, it makes it terribly difficult for you to be a boss and owner, issue directives, be honest, criticize, and demote or terminate someone who may have outlived his usefulness to the company.

In turn, an employee with whom you socialize may take advantage of his position, expect special privileges and perks, make you feel guilty if you aren't forthcoming with benefits, and use friendship as leverage to hold on to a job or advance.

It's tempting to befriend someone who works with you—you probably share many similar interests, know similar people, frequent the same events and have the same long-term objectives. You also understand what each other does for a living, which represents a large chunk of the way you spend each day. But it's far better to make your nonfamily employees feel special in other ways that stop short of an intimate friendship.

The reasons have less to do with the risk of personal fallouts than with the potential to cause problems for the business. For example, if siblings in a firm who don't get along each befriend different nonfamily employees, it will appear that everyone is taking sides. This can impede everyone's ability to function and make rational decisions.

Obviously, in certain instances friendship can work. But it is critical that you try to avoid talking about business away from the office. Avoid discussing your investments and personal matters such as troubles with your spouse or other family members. You may regret such conversations later when bits and pieces make their way through the office grapevine or around the office water cooler. Instead, find some other common ground so that the relationships do not interfere with your ability to function at the office.

For nonfamily employees, steering clear of family often requires great restraint on your part. It's tempting to go to dinner with the boss and his spouse. Being invited to an employer's club to play golf also may be tough to turn down. It's fine to go ahead and accept occasionally, but try to set boundaries. Do not ingratiate yourself by accepting too often, and remember you are not a "member of the family." As a nonfamily member, you may initially think socializing with the boss is critical to your career. However, it is far better to prove yourself through your hard work and ideas rather than by the number of times you play gold with the boss.

It's also vital for nonfamily employees to avoid getting trapped in the middle of family battles. If an owner complains to a nonfamily manager that he thinks his successor is doing a terrible job and should be fired, don't offer to be the henchman. That's the job of the owner, CEO or board. If you don't feel comfortable getting involved in such sticky situations, say to the owner,"Please don't put me in the middle. I'll offer an objective opinion, but not be the final say."

Reality Check: As a rule, try to avoid mixing friendship and business whether you're the boss eager to extend the invitation or the employee on the receiving end. It's fine to socialize occasionally with nonfamily employees, particularly to open communications. The danger becomes that the friendship may start to supersede the business. If the friendship falters, so, too, can the business relationships.

66. How can nonfamily employees help a successor grow professionally?

When Edsel Ford died suddenly at an early age, his father Henry Ford, the founder of Ford Motor Company, reentered the family business. He was 80. A struggle for control ensued and he finally handed the reins over to his grandson, Henry Ford II, 28. Henry II was aware of his shortcomings and recruited executive Ernest Breech to serve as his mentor and interim manager. Before Henry II was comfortable in his role, he credited Breech with making the company's major operating decisions. At the same time, Breech taught Henry II all he knew. Once Henry II was ready to take full control, he removed Breech, who bowed out gracefully in a symbolic gesture that signaled that the young Ford heir was now in full command.

A seasoned nonfamily manager has resources and experience that can be invaluable to share with a neophyte family member coming into your business. He also may be the most objective person to mentor your heir.

This is not a new idea. The concept of mentoring has its roots in ancient Greece. In Homer's *Odyssey*, Mentor is the loyal friend and sage counselor to Odysseus. When Odysseus goes to fight the Trojan War, Mentor plays guardian to Telemachus, Odysseus's son.

A more well-known example portrayed in literature is *Pygmalion's* Henry Higgins. Professor Higgins takes on the mentoring of street urchin Eliza Doolittle. He is determined to transform her into a lady who can mingle and converse in proper British society.

In the business world, Katharine Graham, chairwoman of the Washington Post Co., alludes in her best-selling autobiography, *Personal History* (Albert A. Knopf, 1997) to her mentor Warren Buffet. William Dillard Sr., head of Dillard's Department Stores in Little Rock, Ar., proudly gives credit to his right-hand man, Ray Kemp, in developing the retail chain and acting as a bridge between the generations, which include five Dillard children now in the business.

When an older, more experienced person takes a younger, less seasoned one under his wing to counsel and advise, that's part of mentoring. Today, the concept has gained wide acceptance among family business owners who want a successor mentored before power is transitioned to the younger generation and the older member steps away from the business.

Whether the process takes months or years, a scion grows in his mentor's shadow. If the nonfamily employee agrees to take over the assignment, he should have some say in setting parameters that include the successor's qualifications and what he needs to learn to run the business and keep up with the global economy. Among the questions he must consider are: Does the successor understand the business and its industry? Should he first work in another firm before coming to work for the family? Can he handle leadership duties, draft a business plan, handle strategic planning and make decisions?

The heir-apparent's advisor will offer insight into handling office politics and understanding the company culture, strategy, policies and hierarchy. He also will teach intangibles of successfully dealing with the styles and quirks of different clients, suppliers and key accounts by making calls and attending meetings together. By working in tandem, the mentor will transmit the owner's expectations to the successor and enable the scion to ease into his new position more seamlessly.

A mentor may also:

- Help the successor build a personal development and career plan by setting goals. The mentor will have the successor decide where he sees himself in the company and whether he hopes to become CEO. The mentor can help the family member determine the need for additional credentials and experience by working outside the company, going back to school or taking courses, attending seminars, or participating in workshops on business and family business.

- Serve as the owner's eyes and ears. The mentor keeps the owner apprised of the successor's progress through regular calls and written reports.
- Act as the heir-apparent's advocate to the owner and other employees. The mentor relays what his charge has learned, what he still wants to learn, how his goals have changed, and where he feels his talents are maximized or underutilized.

One nonfamily COO in a $15 million manufacturing company helped with the development of two potential successors. He was instrumental in mentoring the owner's son, who headed the company's international operation, and the owner's nephew, who had taken over the electronic data processing function. The hope was that one of the two would head the firm some day. The nonfamily manager had prior experience mentoring successors in another firm, and was known for his integrity, good credentials and objectivity. He was skilled at not meddling in family problems or taking sides, two critical characteristics. The mentor provided educational direction as well. In doing so, he created two separate career development plans. The mentor's input was crucial in helping the owner tap the right successor. This mentoring lasted more than seven years. Part of the process included mentoring the owner, who was CEO, to convince him to empower and give responsibility to the potential successors rather than make all decisions for them.

Reality Check: Often, a nonfamily manager who does not have an emotional tie to the successor is asked to step in and mentor him or her. If the nonfamily employee is called upon to assume this responsibility, he should have some input into the successor's qualifications and career path. The mentor must show the heir-apparent the proper ways to conduct business within and outside the firm, handle social responsibilities and deal with sticky matters such as office politics and morale. He also should evaluate the successor's performance and offer ways to improve. He can serve as a crucial link with the owner and other employees in initially bringing the heir-apparent into the firm, ensuring a successful transition and setting the candidate up for a long-term leadership role. Mentoring is a critical job to be offered only to your most trusted employees, who should be recognized appropriately for taking on such an important responsibility.

67. It doesn't seem fair that some siblings don't work in the business but are paid salaries or dividends, or are given stock. What can be done to rectify this inequality?

Siblings Bill, Sally and John (not their real names) all worked for the family business. Bill and Sally were the true "leaders" and had a marvelous relationship. John never got along with his two siblings and lost interest. Over time, their parents engineered a buy-back of John's stock and John left the company. The parents continued their "policy" of paying Bill and Sally equally and instituted a small bonus program for them of a few percent of business income. That enabled them to take more money out of the company on a tax-deductible basis. Later, the parents passed away and divided their remaining stock one-third to each child's family line, with John's share going in trust for his children.

Over the next decade, the company grew like topsy thanks to Bill's and Sally's leadership. The little bonus plan grew to paying Bill and Sally $1 million annually. Bill decided that he wanted to work less and brought in some capable nonfamily managers to help. Sally, who continued working long days, started questioning whether Bill should still receive the bonus. Bill felt that a continuation of the bonus plan was appropriate because that was the "deal" that was made. Besides he had worked many of the early years at low pay and felt the current larger bonus made up for prior sacrifices. Plus, he still contributed to the company at a high level. John appeared on the scene, as the representative of his children, and asserted that both his siblings were overpaid to the detriment of the company and his family's interest in it. You can imagine what ensued.

Besides succession, probably no issue divides family members more than whether and how much to pay family members who don't work in the business. This tough problem inevitably comes from Mom and Dad's position. As the children grow up, parents discover that there can be income tax benefits from putting their children on the payroll (although the IRS will disagree if the pay exceeds the value of their contribution). Then, wearing their parent "hat," they decide to continue the lifelong mantra of equal love for children by making sure that all the children are paid the same, regardless of their position or job. Finally, they split the stock equally among their children. After all, you can't expect a parent to disinherit some of the children from the family's primary source of wealth. The children grow up in this environment and develop expectations accordingly.

Whether or not you have compensation issues in your family, it is helpful to envision the ideal scenario:

- Family member compensation (salaries, bonuses, perks, etc.) is determined based on the job performed. Ideally, each family member is compensated the same as an unrelated employee in that position and at the same level of contribution.
- Family compensation is determined with input from unbiased parties, like outside advisors or a board of independent directors.

  Working family members understand that they have responsibilities toward all shareholders, that their efforts are rewarded through compensation, and that stock appreciation is a reward for capital ownership, not the services they render. Just like good public company management, working family members recognize the distinction between shareholders' capital rights and their own compensation rights.
- Stockholders receive a reasonable current return on capital, meaning dividends, and recognize that they are not entitled to salary or other perks. They are investors who benefit from ownership through appreciation and dividends.
- Stockholders recognize that they received their stock because their parents chose to give it to them, just like anything else that they were fortunate to receive, or because they invested capital.
- Stockholders are sufficiently educated in basic business issues to understand the trade-off between distributing all earnings to shareholders and retaining capital to invest for growth.
- Stockholders undertake periodic personal financial planning and recognize the perils of building lifestyles based on the dividends they receive.
- Unbiased people, like outside advisors and a board of independent directors, are tapped for their knowledge and are involved in analyzing potential major capital expenditures that may cause a reduction in dividends.

How do you get from where you are today to Nirvana described above? It can be easy if you start early enough to educate family members and avoid tax-motivated actions that can trip up your family in the future. But what if the bed has already been made? Money is probably the most addictive narcotic of all. If parents have disguised gifts of cash by calling it compensation, and the children have built their lifestyles accordingly, it can be devastating to suggest a cold-turkey "withdrawal." The family may need a crash course in reality if the business is suffering or relationships are near the breaking point. Perhaps, once the family understands the issues, a gradual solution and better compensation system may be worked out. Outside advice and family meeting facilitation may be required. Unfortunately, left too long, the patient may be DOA, dead on arrival. Sometimes, the only solution is either to buy out some shareholders or sell the company.

Reality Check: Despite some children's expectations, you have no obligation to bequeath to them any sort of financial package, whether through company stock, dividends, salary or outright cash gifts. However, if you don't tell them what you are doing and why, you leave yourself open to hostilities or your children may turn on each other. Be courageous and bold. Make a decision based on your standard of fairness and what you think is best for the company and your children's well being. Think about the precedents you set. Explain them while you're alive. If family members can't accept the decision, drastic actions such as stock buyouts or even a sale of the business may be necessary to preserve family harmony and the business itself. The efforts you make to deal with these toughest of issues are some of the best, or worst, legacies you can leave to your family.

CHAPTER IX
SIGNS OF A HEALTHY FIRM

68. Experts advise that there should be clear procedures and expectations for how family members participate in the business. What are they?

The most difficult part of bringing a son (or daughter) into your firm, John Dutra, 62, learned, is allowing him to make mistakes and live with the consequences. However, Dutra and his son Dominic "Dom," 36, worked out the kinks. Dom was well positioned to take over the reins of Dutra Realty Enterprises this year. The company, founded by John and his wife Bernadine in 1972 on a shoestring, $15,000 in savings, is today a six-branch northern California residential real estate and brokerage firm with 270 associates and annual sales just shy of $1 billion.

John Dutra's careful choice of a successor is even more understandable with a look into his past. His success in business is a classic tale of the American dream. He was one of five children who grew up without a father in a family on welfare. John went through college on the G.I. Bill while supporting his own family, eventually earning BS and MBA degrees. It was his dream to pass on the business he and his wife founded. Their youngest son and fourth child, Dom, seemed to be the most suited and interested. Not only were father and son simpatico, but Dom was the first of his siblings to go to college and the only one to receive an MBA. However, John didn't intend to hand Dom the company. Don had to earn his spot.

After Dom received his MBA, John and a friend traded sons, so to speak, to give each an opportunity to work for someone else. Dom went to France in 1988 to work in construction, and the friend's son went to work for the Dutras. It was an exchange program that proved to be effective. One year later, Dom was back home, ready and willing to work with his father.

John laid out a plan. He needed some assurance that Dom was serious about staying in the company and keeping it going for the long haul. "He wanted to know that I would be here for more than one year and not say, 'I'm tired of this' or 'it's too hard.' So I made a five-year commitment." And it took every bit of five years to learn how to work together, Dom adds. "The ability to earn a mutual level of respect for each other took time and lots of patience and confidence on each of our parts. On the flip side, a family business owner has to have a son who can take stern criticism about the way he's doing something and say to himself, 'Hey, this isn't personal. I realize this criticism is best for me. Dad knows what he's talking about and he loves me.'"

Slowly and progressively, as Dom earned the respect of others in the company, most of whom were older than he, his father parceled out more operational control. In 1994, Dom was named president. One year later, when the company started a mortgage subsidiary, he was made CEO.

This year, John stepped aside completely and anointed his son CEO of the entire firm. The actual transition took almost 10 months, which allowed everyone to get used to the idea, says Dom. At that point, his father gradually stepped back, showing up occasionally for a meeting but always leaving early. "Once he gave up control, he was gone. Dad is essentially out of the business, having turned to a new career as a state assemblyman." Dom is quick to add that he and his father speak weekly. "He remains and will always be an incredible mentor and he's actually one of my best friends."

Like a scrimmage before a game, family firms must prepare a strategy for battles they face. One of the most important game plans is to have a set of clear standards and expectations for those family members who want to get into the game as well as for nonfamily managers already on the team.

When people in your company know what's expected of them, the result will be a workforce of family and nonfamily who are in a perpetual state of readiness. They don't second-guess. They're part of a healthy culture that encourages sound planning.

Assuming they are businesslike, a clear set of procedures and expectations lets those inside and outside the firm know that the business is not meant to coddle family—or nonfamily. The company is not a parent, but a place of work. Family members, like everybody else, must prove their worth.

Following are some expectations that should be clarified relating to family employees:

EDUCATION AND EXPERIENCE. What education and prior work experience are required for entry into the company? These may vary by type of business and probably should vary depending upon entry position.

RESPONSIBILITIES. Some owners expect family members to move quickly into the firm's upper echelons; others think it wise for them to float among different areas to learn all aspects of the business. The best practice is to require meaningful experience in many critical areas of the company, not just a few months' exposure to each. Promote family members and increase their responsibility only as they earn it. Family members also need appropriate titles, a challenging length for their workday, reasonable pay scales and a code of behavior.

CHAIN OF COMMAND. It is best if a family member not report directly to a parent or other family member, at least until later in his career. Try to place the family member under a nonfamily supervisor, especially during the early years. Make it clear to both sides that you will not interfere in their relationship and they should not try to put you in an awkward position of refereeing.

MOTIVATION. This is terribly difficult to define, but you need to try to specify the company's culture and work ethic. Yours may be a hard-charging business that demands long hours and results. Family members typically should exceed expectations for nonfamily employees in comparable positions.

THE ROLE OF NONFAMILY TO THE FAMILY MEMBER. Set expectations for nonfamily employees regarding the family member. Prepare your executives in advance for relatives entering the firm. Communicate to them that you want the business to continue indefinitely and that the family member may become your successor, if that is the case. It's in your managers' best interest to do what they can to prepare and teach family members to be good workers and leaders. The better prepared they are the better the succession process will go and the less resentment will fester.

OUT-OF-THE-OFFICE ACTIVITIES. The successor needs to know your expectations for travel and for calling on suppliers and customers.

SUCCESSION PLAN. An heir-apparent needs to be told whether you've fleshed out a succession plan and whether he may be a contender. If you don't know and want to wait and see about his performance, be honest and say so. If you expect to name a nonfamily manager in the interim, state that, too. Not knowing is more anxiety-producing than knowing. If you have a set age at which you plan to retire or if you never plan to step away, convey those sentiments.

SELL, GO PUBLIC OR KEEP THE BUSINESS IN FAMILY HANDS. You may not yet have made a decision, but again honesty is the best policy. Keep your heir apprised of any thoughts you have, which will affect his work plans as well.

In addition to the communication of expectations, there is another sign of a healthy firm: family members receive the same treatment as other employees. They should have written job descriptions. Their salaries should be commensurate with their qualifications, position and performance. Overpaying or underpaying is bad practice and creates bad morale.

Family members need to understand that they may have a harder time than nonfamily empoyees in the business. They usually have to work harder to prove themselves since they're often judged more harshly. It's only human that others in the firm may have a built-in bias against them. Good deeds and hard work can help dispel those impressions over time.

Your company should have policies and procedures for dealing with family members who do not live up to expectations.

One father who was going to fire his son invited him into his study one morning at home. With a deep sigh, he conveyed the sad news: "As your boss, I'm sorry to tell you that you'll have to leave the business." Then, with a more consoling look, he added, "As your father, I heard you just lost your job. What can I do to help?" An owner is in the best position to talk to his scion about why he needs to find other employment and to help him get over the lost opportunity.

Reality Check: Healthy firms spell out expectations clearly and treat family and nonfamily employees equally. If expectations are defined and a family member defies them, a process should exist to deal with the problem. When people understand policies that are spelled out before an issue arises, they are more likely to accept and support them, even if they don't like them.

69. Strategic planning, mission statements, business plans? How do these concepts apply to a family business?

One way to do strategic planning, draft a mission statement and a business plan is to institute an independent board of directors to help you do so. A Midwest grain company, founded right after World War II, installed an independent board in the late 1940s. This company was clearly ahead of its time. The founder's son, Robert (not his real name), one of the successors, attributes the company's dazzling success to its board that professionalized the company. "It's one of the reasons we grew so quickly in our industry. Since the board's inception, our family in the business, along with our management team, have presented plans to the board to seek its input and judgment." The board has been instrumental also in helping the family deal with succession. Robert was the first sibling to come into the almost 1,000-employee firm. Soon after, his sister Marcy (not her real name) followed in his footsteps. Robert ran one division and Marcy the other with their father still at the helm. But Robert and Marcy didn't see eye-to-eye on most issues. For almost seven years, the two siblings battled while, at the same time, urging their father to give up control. They went through the usual family business consultants, therapists, everyone conceivable who, as Robert says, tried to help them pull a rabbit out of the hat. Clearly, there was not room for two leaders. Fortuitously, with the board's nod, the company diversified into chemicals. Now the company was clearly divisible. In 1992, Marcy bought into one company with her father, and Robert took control of the other. Their father agreed to step down and is in a totally different career. Robert, as head of his own company, knew he'd have to start doing some savvy planning. Almost immediately, he installed an independent board of five outsiders and four insiders. The board meets four times a year for a half day and lunch. "One of the biggest advantages of such a board is that it forces goal setting," says Robert.

Most first-generation entrepreneurs build businesses from the hip and eke out a living by the seat of their pants, at least initially. Those who are successful work hard and were lucky to be in the right place at the right time. Many family businesses, particularly those in the first generation of management, rarely do formal business planning or strategizing. They don't have enough time, have a bias against it because they don't understand its importance, think their businesses are too small, or they simply have to focus on immediate issues and crises.

Today, business is changing faster than you can say, "smart planning." To make it in the current economy, you have to take time to plan on multiple fronts. Not to do so is risky business. The market and competition will get ahead of you before you know it. You have to be nimble, and that requires taking time occasionally to reflect on the state of your business and industry. Get some of your key people involved. That translates into the basics of strategic and business planning.

No doubt, many family business owners have plans in their heads, but few put their plans in writing. Less than one-third of the 3,000-plus respondents to the *Arthur Andersen/MassMutual American Family Business Survey '97* reported having a written strategic plan. Many of those companies do not adequately communicate their plans to management or their families. Interestingly, the family businesses reporting that they do strategic planning engage in other types of planning as well. For example, they are more likely to have buy–sell agreements, a formal redemption plan and formal valuations of company stock. They hold board of directors meetings more frequently and rate the contribution of their boards more positively. They also tend to have qualification policies for employing family members, are more likely to have selected a successor, and often have higher sales revenues and greater international sales.

Perhaps the most important part of planning is the process. Getting family involved can help to align individual expectations with business objectives and demands. Involving employees can assure their support and commitment to reach your goals. Planning can be daunting, but taking a "baby" step-by-step approach can break the process into manageable parts.

Don't spend a lot of time wordsmithing because the concepts are more important than the way the plans are written. Too many companies spend all their energy on getting the plan to read like a classic novel and then lose interest. Get the main thoughts down on paper and get everyone to execute the plan.

THE MISSION STATEMENT

The mission statement is your *raison d'être,* the heart and soul of your business. It says why you are in business, and helps keep you, your managers and employees focused on your business' purpose. Again, the mission statement should be short and succinct, perhaps several sentences to a few paragraphs.

When drafting a mission statement, take a long-term view, with a philosophical outlook. The statement should sum up why your company was founded, what it's all about, what it wants to achieve in a broad sense and how it wants to be viewed in its industry. Many companies go to great lengths to communicate their mission statement both verbally and in writing to employees, suppliers, customers and others. It can explain the essence of the company's purpose and objectives, and it can also help keep you focused.

In your statement, don't forget family. Ideally, there should be significant connections between your business' mission and your family's values. The mission statement should make family members proud to be associated with the business. If not, the family is unlikely to support the company over the long term. Some families supplement the business' mission statement with a family values statement. The latter describes in more detail the ways the family intends to interact with the business world and community, as well as how family members will treat each other.

THE STRATEGIC AND BUSINESS PLANS

Conceptually, a strategic plan is relatively long-range and contains objectives and general notions of how the company expects to reach those objectives. These days, strategies tend to last three to five years, so the plan typically would have that time frame in mind. It should address new products, expansion of current product lines, geographic expansion, major human resource and technological objectives, expected changes in industry conditions, potential new competitive threats, acquisition possibilities and other major issues.

To kick off the strategic planning process, try to envision where you would like the company to be five years from now. After this, consider what obstacles stand in the way of accomplishing that vision and then what strengths your business has to help it overcome those obstacles. The planning process next shifts toward developing strategies that use your strengths to accomplish your objectives.

A business plan often is more detailed and tactical than a strategic plan. It spells out specifically how your company is going to accomplish its strategies. The plan will probably cover the next year or two and set forth detailed action steps and measurements to use to assess progress toward meeting objectives. Your management team should be involved in developing strategic and business plans. These groups can provide excellent input. Equally important, their involvement will increase the chances that they will buy in and support the plan, rather than just view it as another document sent down from on high and destined for a file cabinet.

Your board of independent directors, if you have one, should have a significant role in the planning process. You and your management team should present the plans to your board and seek their experienced judgment. Then fine tune it based upon their suggestions. As the business owner, you have to keep the plan alive and make it part of the work-a-day routine. Plans that lie unopened in file drawers or sit buried on a computer file are ineffective. Business owners and management should make appropriate portions of the plan visible (put it in a memo or publish it in a company bulletin). Communicate its contents to staff and new recruits, use it to guide the company's direction, and periodically revise it to reflect company, industry and overall economic changes.

Why do all of these tasks take so much time and energy and often foster debates and arguments? The reasons are simple. First, and perhaps foremost, if you want your family and employees to support the business in the long term, you have to make them feel a part of it. Allowing them input into the driving motivations and strategies that will be important to its success will increase the odds that they will commit the effort necessary to help accomplish that success. Second, you'll be amazed at how helpful and perceptive your family and management can be in anticipating problems and competitive threats, along with devising clever ways to deal with them.

Consider developing a reward system in which you peg compensation of your staff to better business planning and accomplishment of plan goals. If employees and management strategize and develop solutions, then perform particularly well, you can reward them verbally and financially with incentives and raises. The motto can be: Everyone participates, everybody benefits.

Reality Check: A company that wants to survive beyond the current generation in today's fast-churning economy needs to have a mission statement, good short- and long-term business plans, and a well-developed strategic plan. The owner, managers and board of directors should all be involved in developing these plans. Employee performance can be measured against the plan and incentives created for accomplishing objectives. The plans need to be communicated to everyone in the organization rather than stuck in a desk drawer or on a computer file for posterity. The future belongs to family businesses that take the time to anticipate and respond. Planning is the best way to meet challenges and overcome problems.

70. Are there some positive benefits to a dispute among family members? What are the best methods of conflict resolution?

Morris Housen, 34, grew up thinking he'd work side-by-side with his father in the family paper firm, Erving Industries of Erving, Ma., a manufacturer of high-quality paper products. Although Morris and his father Charles, 67, loved and respected each other, they didn't work well together. They had a difference in management styles, says Morris. Morris considers himself a professional manager and has credentials to support it—a degree in managerial/applied economics from Carnegie Mellon and an MBA from the Stern School at New York University. His father, he says, is more of an entrepreneur. "My Dad's vision for me and the company was different from mine. He is a powerful administrator and a fast decision-maker with a good track record. I'm slower and deliberate when I make decisions. College trained me in logic and cognitive decision-making. I list all the alternatives, weigh them, do the math, and only then do I add a bit of emotion and feeling. Dad tends to operate more on gut feeling."

After graduate school, Morris entered the business. He was placed in a high-level staff position, but longed for the true bottom line, profit and loss responsibility in order to prove himself. Morris and his father had limitations when communicating with one another. "We couldn't have an argument and then come up with a sensible solution or consensus based on each other's point of view," says Morris, who admits that some outside assistance would have been helpful.

In May 1996, Morris purchased three divisions of Erving Industries, Inc. and incorporated them as a new company, Birch Point Paper Products, Inc. "I used some cash and my father loaned me the rest." This gave Morris the autonomy and bottom-line responsibility he was looking for, but he grieved a bit. He says he missed the camaraderie and interaction with his father.

In the meantime, there was still a need to resolve the future of the family business and by chance, the two men were invited to appear before their peers at a family business forum to confide their concerns. It prompted a discussion of how the Housens could get past their impasse and plan for the future of their firm. A year later, Charles and Morris have discussed the situation and have come to an agreement. Morris will be moving back to his father's company. His father will remain chairman and president for about a year while Morris serves as executive vice president. "We'll have a full year of working together and eventually I expect his love for golf will occupy his entire week. At that point, I should be able to take the reins. Yes, we've had some conflict, but it turned out to be a positive experience that didn't undermine our relationship."

Have you ever talked to a married couple who claims they don't fight? "Oh sure," you think to yourself. As surprising as it may seem, disputes can be healthy and a positive way to build better relationships. It's one way to communicate. What's most important is not always what's said but rather that you fight and keep communicating rather than slam doors and never speak—or even yell—again.

What's so healthy about fighting? Conflict can lead to change and be a catalyst for building a better family business future, as long as family members know how to turn around and resolve their differences. There are three primary benefits that can result from discussion of sensitive issues, even at the risk of initially creating conflict:

- As part of many discussions, family members should state their priorities and their concerns. To avoid sparking any controversy, some members are reluctant to speak out and list their true beliefs. They think everybody is content, and they fear being the one loose cannon. Disputes, however, help to get the adrenaline and conversation flowing. You can't resolve underlying issues unless they are brought to the table for everyone to debate.
- Shared family disputes allow members to avoid stewing in private. They can vent their grievances and arguments in a group, which saves time and energy. If problems are kept under covers, they tend to get worse. As a result of airing disagreements, everyone works as a team to resolve them and find common ground.
- Trying to develop a vision for the future often leads to strong disputes, but the drive for a strategic plan can lead to an in-depth look at the company's strengths and weaknesses and to a shared outlook and reinvention of the company. Although potentially contentious, these discussions can lead to agreement on issues like how the company should spend its capital, whether to provide dividends to nonworking family members, and who should next run the company.

Each family needs to decide in advance whether to bring in an outside facilitator to help resolve a dispute. If your family decides it prefers to do so on its own, ask all participants to answer the following questions as a way to initiate a dialogue:

- What factual information is presently available to me regarding the business and family and what additional information do I need? All participants need a common base of information.
- Why is the business important to me? Participants in a dispute need to state why, which affects the degree to which they'll become vested in resolving the dispute. Use "I" messages.
- What business issues does the company face? A business has value only if it competes effectively in its market. The business issues that confront a company daily must be addressed in a way that's consistent with the goals and objectives of participants.
- What knowledge or expertise do I need to evaluate the dispute correctly? The answer depends in part on the true reason for the dispute. If it revolves around succession, you will need to understand estate tax laws, capital expenditure needs, buy-sell agreements and valuation formulas, to name a few. If it hinges on fairness—like whether your nonworking sibling is entitled to a paycheck—you may need to take a deeper look at your attitudes about fair versus equal and any long-simmering rivalry between you and a sibling.
- Are there issues on which the parties involved in the dispute agree? Often participants are more in agreement than in disagreement. They should start discussions by identifying areas where they agree, which helps them to develop a strong common bond. For example, even if you resent your nonworking sibling sharing in the company growth, you may have to alter your view if that's what your parent who started the company wished. Perhaps there is some other asset that person can receive; perhaps there isn't, and you can be rewarded in some additional way.

Set some ground rules for the discussion. Examples include:

- Set a date and time acceptable to all.
- Hold the meeting away from the business to reduce distractions and potential gossip among employees.

- Have an agenda.
- Agree that each person will be allowed to speak without interruption.
- Encourage everyone to express views as constructively as possible and insist that others listen carefully to what each person says.
- Try to make sure that everyone understands the points raised by each participant.
- When facts are unclear, get them clarified as objectively as possible. Use advisors as needed for this purpose as well as to address legal, tax and other issues.
- Encourage participants to focus on the future, rather than on past grievances. Don't turn meetings into whining sessions.
- Urge everyone to try to see issues from all angles, not to feel defensive and to recognize that compromise often is necessary.
- If necessary, use a facilitator to help settle a dispute. Consider taking business-related issues to your board of independent directors, if you have one.

Probably you and your family members will need to improve a number of skills and develop a better understanding of personalities. Some suggestions include:

- Take courses or attend seminars in communication, negotiation and problem-solving skills.
- Talk to a therapist, advisors or even other family business owners about how they've resolved conflict.
- Take a Myers–Briggs personality test and have other family members do so, too. Then have a therapist interpret the results.
- Read self-help books on how to negotiate effectively.
- Attend family business seminars that will help family members better understand issues and ways to deal successfully with them.

If you can learn to argue effectively, you'll establish trust. Most important, if you can communicate, listen and purge your anger constructively, you'll have more energy to produce for the firm and family.

Reality Check: Disagreements among family members are inevitable, but it's how you argue that's key. There may be conflict about any number of issues from pay, to responsibilities, titles and succession. The first and most basic method of conflict resolution is to address the issue openly with the whole family. If done on a formal and regular basis, in a family meeting and often with a facilitator, it will lessen conflict. Hot issues often can be hashed out over time with repeated discussion. There are ways to learn how to argue—courses, self-help books, consultants and therapists. The bottom line is that conflict won't disappear. However, if it is left to simmer, it will only worsen. The best way to deal with it is to get it out on the table and work constructively to address and resolve it.

71. What are the distinctions between the roles of the board of directors, advisors and managers with participatory roles?

Chiles & Sons Funeral Homes in Lima, Oh., is run by a family that believes in getting help when needed to resolve business and family issues. "But the company does not have an outside board," says Jim Chiles, 58, third-generation president and CEO. Rather, the firm's inside board is comprised of three family members (all cousins) and two nonfamily employees, all licensed employees of the funeral home as dictated in the bylaws. "Our board was originally set up this way when the business was incorporated in the late 50s," says Jim. The board makes policy decisions and controls the affairs and actions of the officers. According to Jim, it's not a board that gets involved in day-to-day operations. However it does maintain a close watch. "We meet twice a year, but oftentimes call meetings when there are bigger decisions to be made such as an acquisition," he adds. The business, founded by Jim Chiles' grandfather in 1928, handles 450 funerals a year in three locations. "I have no objections to outsiders serving on the board, but I'd probably look more strongly at someone who has a relationship with the operation, such as the firm's corporate accountant or attorney." As long as business is brisk, the family doesn't see the need for an outside board at this point.

Some family business owners are skittish about hiring an outsider to help. According to Craig E. Aronoff and John L. Ward, authors of *How to Choose and Use Advisors: Getting the Best Professional Family Business*

Advice (Business Owner Resources, 1994), here are some examples of owners' skewed thinking:

- "Professional advisors should be used only as a last resort; an outsider could never understand my business;
- high-powered experts wouldn't be interested in my business;
- an advisor will raise issues I don't have time to bother with right now;
- I don't want to share information with an outsider; professional advisors cost too much;
- our long-time attorney is a family friend and knows us best and we don't need anyone else;
- I'm unsure how relationships with professional advisors work."

Some business owners also do not seek input from their management, at least in any organized way. They view managers and employees as order takers or restrict them to narrow limited roles. Perhaps these owners view restricting employee involvement as a way to retain control and reduce the risk of errors or misunderstandings. Or, perhaps these owners simply aren't good at delegating and team building.

So, many business owners rely on instinct and, perhaps, some input from trade or similar associations. Unfortunately, these resources often are not enough to avoid being too insular. The Swiss watch industry never recognized the threat of electronics because it was focused on doing its own "thing" and doing it in the best possible way. Outside input helps you to see situations in a different light. Objective input can help you to make difficult decisions when the advice from internal resources might seem limited or suspect.

What makes an owner take that first step to seek counsel from managers, advisors or other outsiders? One expert said, "Family business owners will turn to outside resources when they find their business is in trouble and it's not growing." Long-term success requires new ideas and searching for new paradigms. With the rapid change in business today, "long-term" may be just a matter of a few years. Waiting until there are problems may be too late.

The best resources for advice are advisors, managers and your board of directors. However, they have to have the right attributes and you must use them correctly to get the most benefit from them. Furthermore, you must understand their differing roles.

Advisors—lawyer, accountant, banker, insurance agent—are, or at least, should be experts in their field who are paid for their professional services. Certainly, they should be called in as appropriate when there is a problem or issue. Better yet, they should be consulted periodically even if you have no known need. They often can identify opportunities when you don't know enough to ask a question. They can help take you through the paces of defining priorities, solving problems, working out a business plan or other types of strategies that affect the family and business. Moreover, they should be used collaboratively. Their advice will be more complete this way. Don't shop around among advisors until you get the answer you want. You'll get more confused because they will give you differing answers based upon their individual perspectives or because you define the issues differently in separate discussions.

Don't measure the cost of professional advice solely by the amount of the advisor's invoice. Measure it in terms of opportunity. The best advisors can give you many options and help you understand and quantify the risks and rewards. Although their fees may be less, incompetent advisors can be costlier due to lost opportunities and bad advice.

Advisors come with various areas of expertise. Some specialize in family business, taxes, estate planning or some aspect of your business. They should be good communicators, have a clear picture of your family and your business, understand the interrelationships between family and business, offer advice that works for both the family and the business, hold regular meetings for update and review, share information, spot contacts and opportunities for the owner, work with heirs, discuss the future, and above all, be honest, according to *How to Choose & Use Advisors.*

Managers help run the business. They should be used to operate the business, help develop and execute business and strategic plans, and train successors. No surprise there, but many business owners don't take full advantage of them. Periodically, perhaps even weekly, you should hold organized management meetings. The objectives are to make sure that all your managers work toward common objectives, develop a clear understanding of the interactions between their and other managers' areas of responsibility, and contribute their ideas for identifying and capitalizing on business opportunities. To accomplish these objectives, the business owner must share and bare full information about the business and financial performance.

A board of directors can be the only real source of true, objective feedback and guidance in a family firm. But you will not gain this important advantage if the board is filled with family members, advisors and employees. The board is not there to manage the day-to-day affairs of the business, become involved in short-term planning or train successors. It's there to represent the best interests of all shareholders and provide them with the assurance of high-level oversight of both family and nonfamily management. The board's function is to look at long-term strategy and major transactions like acquisitions and significant investments. It can provide deep insight and guidance for the owner–manager.

Why don't many family firms have boards of independent directors? There are so many reasons and excuses. For example, some owners simply don't understand the concept or the benefits. Others are afraid that they will lose control or do not want to be answerable to anyone. Some are secretive and fear loss of privacy or trade information. Still others are afraid of the potential embarrassment of high-powered businessmen questioning out-of-date methods. Some simply don't believe that outsiders can understand the peculiarities of their unique businesses or don't want to take on the additional time, energy and expense of properly using a board.

Yet, virtually every family business that creates and properly uses a board of independent directors says that it is one of the best decisions they ever made. That should make you wonder what you're missing. Is it luck to have a good team of advisors, key managers and independent directors backing you up? This isn't about luck. It's about finding and using these resources correctly.

Reality Check: There is, or at least should be, a definite difference between the roles played by a board, advisors and key managers. The best type of board of directors consists of a group of objective, non-self-interested, successful businesspeople who help management and shareholders with major decisions, strategy, succession issues, evaluation of management and other long-term planning. Advisors are people whom you pay to help you solve problems and identify opportunities within their areas of professional expertise. Managers help map out short-term strategies and execute business plans based on strategies approved by the board. All three groups should interface at various times, but their roles are distinct and should not be confused.

72. How should the company institute guidelines and a plan for succession and continuity? How should they link with the long-range plan?

Stefan Pollack, now 32, did something few sons would do. After finishing college, he marched into his mother's office and asked if he could have a job in her public relations and marketing firm, The Pollack PR Marketing Group, in Century City, Ca. At first Noemi Pollack said, "What would you do? You're not a PR person. I don't really need a 22-year-old with a business degree."

Stefan wasn't about to give up. He had been a finance major and a graduate of the entrepreneurship program at the University of Southern California. He told his mother that she needed someone with business credentials to beef up the client roster. Noemi made a deal with her son. If he'd draft a strategic plan for the firm showing that there was indeed a place for him, she'd put him on staff.

This was right up his alley. "I structured a position for myself, justified a salary and offered a long- and short-range plan to grab new business," says Stefan. Stefan's plan lit a fire under his mother and that fire has been burning for 10 years, he says. Business has increased some 400 percent and the agency now employs eight professionals plus a support staff.

Two years ago the agency incorporated and Noemi started some strategic and succession planning by giving her son voting shares. She also says she's stepping back and giving Stefan more control. "I'm planning for the long-term," she says. She plans to give him shares annually. "We're also in the process of drawing up a buy–sell agreement." Although it's understood that Stefan will take over when his mother retires some day, their succession plan is still a work in progress.

Even if your business is doing well, and the good times have never been better, common wisdom says that you ought to be making the most of the situation and looking to the future. Now is the time to consider the long term; to grow your company and build its net worth; to figure out how you'll fund that growth; and to focus on crucial issues such as the future of your firm and whether to keep it in the family.

You may cringe at the suggestion and believe that you have no time to plan for the long term while you're building a business and trying to increase sales in the short term. But all owners of growing family businesses who intend to stay in business and transfer the firm to the next generation need to draft a long-term succession and a strategic plan. All family businesses, regardless of size, would be well served by taking the time to develop these plans. They need not be particularly formal, but a business and family that fail to think about the future do so at great peril.

Perhaps a firm can exist without these plans in an industry that doesn't experience major change. An example would be a company that manufactures brake linings for tractors. It has a niche. The firm tinkers with the product, improving it incrementally, but never really changes the core product. Unfortunately, those situations are relatively few and the rapidly changing business environment can sneak up on you. For example, this niche manufacturer may be blindsided if its primary customer decides to take the brake lining manufacturing in-house. In addition, even if your business does not change, your family situation will.

Retailers have seen tremendous turmoil in recent years due to superstores and industry consolidation. Those retailers most affected are the smaller independent office products businesses, grocery stores, bookstores, stationery shops, hardware and home improvement stores, pet shops and pharmacies. Those that have survived this industry trend have done so by foreseeing the changes and developing strategies to distinguish themselves from the new wave of competitors. Your chances of success in that regard are improved if you take the time to address thoughtfully the issues and experiment with alternatives for dealing with them. That is a major purpose of planning. The earlier you address future challenges, the more likely you will have the time to identify and implement approaches to dealing with them.

A long-term strategic plan for a family business should address not only how the business will compete in a changing marketplace, but also how it will deal with issues where the family and business intersect. What resources, both personnel and financial, are required to accomplish the business' objectives? Which family members are best suited for various family and business leadership roles? What skill sets are missing to accomplish long-term plans? Is the family supportive of the business' objectives? What demands might the family place on the business to fund shareholder buyouts, estate taxes and living needs?

A succession plan should be a subset of the strategic plan. This is an advance disclosure of how the owner plans to turn over the reins to the next generation. It includes whether the family wants to continue the business and will commit to passing on ownership to the next generation, sell or go public. It also may address company values, rules for company employment, dividend policies, need for a family council and what its goals will be, ownership versus management, and estate planning. Has the senior generation determined what its activities will be after retirement and are retirement financial needs fully addressed? Will there be a board of independent directors? Are the firm's advisors and consultants up to the challenge of assisting in the transition?

Most businesses need some type of planning, but a family business has needs that are distinct to this type of operation. For example, most businesses need capital to grow, but a family-owned business needs capital not only to grow but also to pay estate taxes or to buy out departing shareholders. Where will these funds come from? Will capital continue to be sufficient as the business' value grows and as more family members come onto the scene?

Once these plans are drafted, the results must be communicated to the family members and to key managers. If you keep the results to yourself or on your hard drive, it's not too likely the family and key employees will support and buy into the concepts. Absent that support and a full buy-in, you'll fail to implement and achieve the plan's objectives.

Reality Check: Many entrepreneurs don't want to take the time to sit down and think about long-term planning because they are too busy fighting fires every day. Who has the time or the energy to think about the future? Also, it's tough to deal with mortality and your business surviving without you. Even if you do take the time to initiate long-term planning, doing so in a vacuum is shortsighted. You need to sit down with family and plot out objectives and how to implement them while you're alive, well and interested in seeing your business continue.

73. Is it a good idea to spend time together away from the business? Can you ever really have a separation between family and business?

Sometimes work and home intersect. Two years ago Christopher Malter started his own full-service public relations and marketing firm specializing in health care and high technology services, Integrated Marketing Communications in Weston, Fl. When he brought his work home, he decided to bring his wife Sonia into the firm to help out with administrative tasks and research on a part-time basis. The two had met when Chris worked for Ruder Finn (a public relations firm) in New York City as a senior account executive in the health care department. Sonia had been an administrative assistant to the president of his division.

Chris knew that if he and his wife worked together, they'd have to work on their marriage and try to keep the business and personal sides separate. They set boundaries, allotting time for work, time for themselves, and time for their two teenage daughters.

Their solution? When they have a meeting about business, they get together outside their home to avoid interruptions. When they work, they're strategic-oriented because that's the environment in which they trained. They sit down, look at the next two or three months and plan.

Similarly at home, they try to leave the business and beeper behind and avoid talking about work, particularly in front of their daughters. "Last night we took the time to sit outside and talk about ourselves. Sometimes it must be more planned. We may do a picnic, take a walk in the morning, read the paper together," Chris says.

Yet, even in spite of their objectives, they find it hard to separate family and business. The prime advantage, they agree: They both know and understand the public relations business. "We talk the same language and the same shorthand. The key is knowing when to stop talking business and have fun," Chris says.

One day George came into the office looking happier than he had in a long time. He was in a great mood. He had just spent a long weekend with his extended family at the lake. Everyone could tell he had had a wonderful, relaxing time. He was especially pleased with himself since he had planned the whole event, and it turned out as splendidly as he had hoped. Family unity among second-and third-generation family shareholders was stronger than ever. But more important, the ups and downs George had experienced with his three sons in the business were straightened out that weekend . . . at least for the time being.

You've heard the atavistic adage: The family that plays together, stays together. The same is true of the family that's in business together. The family firm represents serious business, and members tend to lose their sense of humor if they're tense and angry with each other or disagree about the company direction or even one specific problem.

Having fun together as a family unit is one conduit to maintain healthy family business and familial relationships, and it's a low-risk way to achieve those goals. Whatever the terms of the gathering, and wherever it's held, the emphasis should be on building relationships for the long term. Goodwill usually emanates from this type of gathering.

Family get-togethers purely for social reasons are also the first concerted step to providing some space between family and business, which represents an extremely healthy tack. The separation needs to start at the top with the business owner whose responsibility it is to see that everyone participates and that family fun time doesn't digress into a business meeting. The time away is strictly for family togetherness. Here are four ways to achieve these goals:

- Don't make business the topic of first or last resort. How do you not do so? In small families, specific times should be set aside for business. If that's dinner, then business discussions should cease after dessert so that you can relax together as a family after the business discussions. For larger families, family meetings can be regularly scheduled to discuss business topics. That way, family members begin to understand that there are specific times for those discussions. There should be an agenda with appropriate business-related topics. Separately, social gatherings should be scheduled without business topics. The two can be combined, but only if the agenda delineates clear lines between the two. Whatever approach you use, make sure that all family members understand the rules.
- Get away from home or have a vacation for the family in a nice location. There's a high correlation between a healthy business and a healthy family when families go on vacation together, even if only once a year. Getting away from the distractions of business and your home town and spending time together will also make the gathering more memorable.
- Activities need not be terribly extravagant. Organize them around recreational activities, whether they are sporting or cultural events, concerts, treasure hunts, dinners or barbecues.
- If a family fun gathering continually digresses into a whining session, know that it may be appropriate next time to call in a facilitator. Your family may also need to establish a more specific agenda of events.

Reality Check: Fun family gatherings without an emphasis on business issues will build goodwill among family members, including those who rarely get together. These gatherings will improve camaraderie within and across generational lines. The get-togethers need not take place at a luxurious resort thousands of miles away, but can be held close to home and represent an inexpensive, safe and almost foolproof way to bolster relationships and create a good, healthy vehicle for separating the family and the business.

74. When you and your sibling are contemplating joining the family business, what should you, your sibling and your parents have in mind concerning sibling relationships and roles?

To ensure harmony when siblings work together requires careful planning. Like the finest diamond, which depends on the four "Cs" of cut, clarity, color and carat to make it worthy, the jewelry business Erwin Pearl founded has been lovingly and carefully built. It incorporates all the essential facets to guarantee family unity, if any of his four daughters expressed interest in joining. Pearl started his New York-based business, Erwin Pearl, more than 40 years ago, designing and manufacturing precious jewels. Since 1977, he has focused exclusively on more affordable "fashion" jewelry, which he felt reflected a wider market. The first facet for his success has been its ability to be different from the rest of its market in its designs and consistent high quality. "People came back because they found new items in our stores, the workmanship was always good, and the perceived value always reflected the best price," he said. The business has also always been financially stable, reflecting Erwin's desire to be conservative regarding growth. It has expanded to include a large manufacturing facility in the Providence, R.I., area, which sells to other manufacturers and wholesalers, a large wholesale distribution network, and an expanding retail division of 16 jewelry stores, which are expected to number 20 by year's end. The second facet he developed has been an expanding and capable management team of nonfamily employees. Altogether his company employs 450 throughout its locations.

Equally important, two of his four daughters were eager to join, rather than pushed, helping to keep the business in family hands. "We had a dialogue going on within the family between the parents and children, and all had a choice (to join) if they were interested," Erwin says. Two were. Fortunately, each had different strengths to offer, and he knew it was critical to keep "reinventing" the jewelry wheel, so to speak. "You have to keep reinvesting profits to add new machinery, do enough research and development, and offer new products if you want to continue," he says. His daughter, Suzanne, he says, has a great ability to understand business as a whole and shows good acumen in building new divisions and creating new sales. His daughter, Deborah, has wonderful people skills, shows tremendous energy and is able to excite and motivate others. In addition to having varied talents and focusing on different areas of the company, they share a secret ingredient: an ability to get along and respect each other, which Erwin says his wife Bettina is primarily responsible for instilling. "She raised all the children with enormous love and gave them a love of one another. She also encouraged them to support each other. The sisters get along well and are protective of one another," he says. "There's always a certain amount of rivalry with children, but it can become beneficial rather than detrimental."

To avoid conflicts between them or any of his other daughters if they were to join, he decided that none of his four sons-in-law could work in the business. He's delighted the prospects for a second generation are healthy, though he has no immediate plans to retire. "I intend not to be as active and to turn over more responsibility to my daughters and nonfamily management, but working keeps me young and vital," says Erwin.

Harmony is never a given and can't be guaranteed. A lot will depend on the siblings' relationship in years past, whether there was intense competition between them and whether they still have love and mutual respect. Harmony among family members also can be a function of expectations and understandings created as they come into the business.

Even when relationships seem amazingly healthy, giving siblings some distance by letting them work in separate areas of the company, or at least on different accounts, can go a long way, particularly as they mature, both mentally and in business skills. You can create additional buffers by assigning different supervisors and mentors. At some point, either because of your company's size or the children's advancement, they will have to have contact and overlapping responsibilities.

Now comes the rub. Either they will figure out how to work together, or not. The senior generation can play a crucial role, especially if it addresses this issue early in the children's careers. First, it must realistically assess the situation. If the children can't work together, the ultimate solution, as tough as it sounds, is for one to leave or at least agree to take a backseat in management decision-making.

If the children exhibit the ability to work together, the older generation must help to set the stage. Competition for the top job is okay. However, the children must understand that uncivilized competition will not be tolerated. They must be taught that appropriate behavior toward other family members will be mandatory in assessing leadership potential. A leader who fails to respect other family members, whether active or inactive, will destroy the company, the family or both.

The siblings should sit down and discuss the potential for problems when a second or third one joins the company. By recognizing the possibility that conflicts may arise, the siblings can go a long way toward alleviating them. They can discuss and even write down how they want to resolve problems and jealousies. Possible approaches include involving key nonfamily managers in assessing business issues, use of outside advisors, and the creation of a board of independent directors.

They also can learn how to disagree and fight fair, without bringing up past baggage such as "Mom always liked you better" or hauling Mom and Dad into the current-day fray as the perceived peacemakers. Siblings should take a course together on building teamwork, along with negotiation and communication skills. They should learn to assess objectively issues from both their own and other family members' perspectives. Facts and figures are a good antidote to vague assumptions.

Finally, siblings need to keep in perspective why they're working together. The ideal family business scenario should be to pursue meaningful work and make their company the most successful it can be so that it can be perpetuated long into the future. Their reasons should not be to beat out a brother or sister. If that is the direction they take, they are the only ones who can be held accountable to their heirs for leaving a potential legacy of hate, or worse, the destruction of the business.

Reality Check: It's tough to eliminate old rivalries and it's hard to stop new ones from developing when one sibling earns more, gets a fancier title and has the parents' ear because he has worked at the company longer or is perceived as favored. It's critical to be aware of potential squabbles and to stop them early if siblings are going to work together. Rather than dragging Mom or Dad in to mediate, siblings should learn to rely on an impartial person or group, such as a board of independent directors, to help with the analysis and resolution of disagreements. Ultimately, it is the siblings' responsibility to work together; however, the parents must anticipate potential problems and avoid putting their children in an impossible situation.

CHAPTER X
HEADING OFF TROUBLE IN YOUR FAMILY BUSINESS

75. Why is a succession plan necessary? What can be done if there isn't one?

Alexandra Lebenthal, 34, president and CEO of her family's now full-service New York brokerage firm, didn't aspire to enter the family business. However, after graduating from Princeton University and working two years on Wall Street, she decided to come into Lebenthal & Co., then a municipal bond brokerage firm that her grandparents founded in 1925. "It was always understood that anyone in the family could take part in the business if he or she wanted to," says Alexandra. "Qualified? We're all qualified so that was never stipulated," she adds. Alexandra started as a salesperson/broker. At that time, her father was chairman and a nonfamily member was president. Her grandmother Sayra Lebenthal, who at 91 years of age still worked in the business, needed someone to start taking over her accounts. Alexandra was tapped. The two shared an office so Alexandra could learn by example.

"I knew that I needed to go back and do sales in a way I knew I could and really devote full time to that activity," says Alexandra. After one year, at age 26, she was back in sales. Then 18 months later, the nonfamily president promoted her to head of the mutual fund department. "I didn't want to leave sales, but I knew I'd have to if I were ever going to enter management. So I grabbed the opportunity."

Alexandra and her father James hadn't discussed succession until the nonfamily president left the company. He said he wanted to keep the slot open. However, a couple of months later in June 1995, he came to Alexandra and asked her to become president and CEO. Her father, now 70, is still chairman. He oversees advertising and marketing and she's in charge of day-to-day management.

Alexandra owns some stock in the company through a trust set up by her grandparents and on her own purchased some stock through a bonus program offered to senior managers. Her siblings, who are not active in the business, also own shares through the trust.

Alexandra says the succession has worked because she is qualified and has the support and guidance of her father. Under Alexandra's leadership, the firm has registered a profit each year.

Nobody disputes the fact that it takes a long time to train a successor so he has the experience and wisdom to run the firm. Most owners are willing to bring their heirs on board. But how do you get an owner to sit down and draft an actual succession plan so people know where they stand, where the business stands and what the future holds? This is the key question. Most family business heads don't have a succession plan. Yet, it's irresponsible not to. For starters, this can endanger the future of your company and family. If you say you're too busy or can't make a decision, you're simply delaying or trying to rationalize your inaction. If your company has a board of independent directors, you're in luck. You can work miracles if the recommendation to draft a succession plan comes from the board. As part of the company's strategic and long-term plan, the board can hold you accountable for succession. A push from the board can both motivate you and help by sharing some of the heat.

What if there is no board? Try family business workshops and seminars, newsletters, books, consultants, advisors or whatever it takes and whoever it takes to grab a parent's attention.

If that doesn't work, scare tactics might. If a parent or other relative dies suddenly without a plan for a successor, the owner's spouse, who may know nothing about the business, will inherit the problem. Most aren't prepared to manage an inherited business, especially one in financial trouble. Right after the death of a spouse or parent is a horrible time to have to learn how to run a business. One woman talks about how her father passed away without leaving behind a plan for his clothing store in Pennsylvania. When he died, her mother stepped in. She had to pay off his debts because he had been ill a long time. She had to develop relationships with customers and suppliers. In short order, she had to develop business skills and understandings that took her husband a lifetime to learn. Fortuitously, her mother was able to turn the store around and make it profitable enough to sell. Most families are not that fortunate.

There are other ramifications of a lack of a succession plan. The biggest risk is losing employees and customers who lack confidence in the business' prospects for surviving the transition. Key employees may exit because to them it appears that no one is guiding the ship. A lack of a succession plan is also something that competitors can seize as an opportunity to take over your market share by creating uncertainty in the minds of customers. Will this firm continue to be a reliable source during the period when there is no leadership? Competitors may convince your customers and suppliers that the answer is a decided "no."

Add to this the fact that there may be queasiness on the part of lenders who now see a company with question marks after its name. Will your trusted bank continue to provide financing on the same basis and for the same amount? Lack of a succession plan is an irresponsible act that puts everything important to the company at risk—capital, customers, suppliers and employees.

There is no canned recipe for your succession plan and what it should contain, and there will be no right or wrong answers for those who execute any succession plan once you're gone. So much depends on your specific company, its needs, values and idiosyncrasies. However, one approach is to put your ideas on paper. Do a skeletal outline and circulate it to other knowledgeable people who are familiar with your firm such as key managers, the company lawyer, your accountant. Ask them to edit your outline and add their thoughts. Look for consensus. Choose an opportune time to bring the family into the discussion. Discuss the required attributes for a candidate to be considered for the leadership role.

Will the business succeed to family or nonfamily? The key point is to consider identifying more than one person who can fill your job. Have a backup plan as well. Perhaps choose two already working in the firm and indicate the pros and cons of each. State that you have to know which person can fill the job three years from now or you'll be forced to fill the position with someone from outside the firm. Start thinking about who those outside people could be.

Other considerations to include in your plan:

- Family members' acceptance of your chosen successor and steps to take if they do not agree to your choice.

- Whether to give equal shares to family members or how to equalize assets for those who are not in the firm.
- Tax consequences of selling or transferring the firm.
- Interests and reactions of managers, employees, customers, suppliers, creditors, shareholders and investors.

Reality Check: Most family business heads don't have a succession plan and that's why only about one-third of these firms make it to the next generation. If you want your business to survive, you might consider starting succession planning now. Begin a process for selecting a successor, decide how you'll divide your estate between your active and inactive heirs, and consider tax consequences and future management of the firm. Your business is at risk if you don't plan for the future. With the right type of plan, you have a good chance of passing the business on to the next generation and maximizing the value of it for your family, employees and other interested parties.

76. What about planning for income and emotional needs in retirement?

After Raymond Olesen took over the O & H Danish Bakery in Racine, Wi., founded by his father the late Christian Olesen in 1949, his dream was to have his three sons run the business some day. The full-line bakery is best known for Kringle, a flat oval-shaped Danish coffeecake.

Ray, 65, planned properly. Four years ago, he enacted a retirement plan, stuck to it and left the family business in the capable hands of his three sons: Eric, 38, administrative manager; Michael, 42, production manager; and Dale, 46, purchasing manager, all of whom now run the company jointly. The transition of power went smoothly because Ray had informed his sons of his plan in advance, the very same way his father had. He divided the firm by responsibility and ownership, did essential estate planning and then stepped aside.

A major reason for the successful transition is that the brothers were allowed to make their own career decisions. Although the three boys had grown up working in the business, each went his separate way initially, but came back into the business. "Our parents' plan, from the time we were little, was to develop a relationship among the three of us so that first and foremost the family would survive and the business would survive as part of the family," says Eric. Ray launched his retirement and succession process soon after it was clear all three sons were interested in running the firm. He enacted it in stages.

By 1990, Ray had developed a formal succession plan, and by 1995, the boys were ready to take over as equal partners. The transition was as smooth as the batters whipped up by the firm's bakers. It was also a boon that the three brothers shared the same vision and goals. Although Ray and his wife Myrna retain the majority of shares, the rest of the stock is divided equally among the three sons. "We are being gifted stock and purchasing it as well over a 10-year-period using our income to buy it," says Eric.

Eric adds that the family's goal for the firm is to grow, but to continue to maintain quality. The boys started a mail-order business. Today almost 3,000 Kringle coffeecakes are sold through the mail weekly. During the Christmas season, tens of thousands are shipped weekly. "We realize we must continue to expand so that we develop a foundation for the seven children we have among us, should any be interested in pursuing this as a career," adds Eric.

You've always worked. You delivered newspapers as a teenager, had a part-time job during college, and joined the Navy. You spotted an opportunity to buy a small business and you grabbed it. Running your own firm has been your work and your play. It provides the structure in your day, a place to go. The bulk of your friends, or at least those you feel comfortable with, are business associates.

You have few outside interests. You have a bad back so you never took up golf. You never learned how to play tennis. You loath cards, so you never became consumed with bridge. In your mind, retirement was akin to a gigantic punishment, or the next closest thing to euthanasia. However, you know it's time to think about retiring or at least stepping back, particularly since you have several qualified successors chomping at the bit to take over. What do you do?

Like a David Letterman list, here are The Top 10 Reasons "Why Not to Retire" from *The Family Business Succession Handbook,* (Family Business Publishing Company, 1997), compiled by Mike Cohn and Ernest A. Doud Jr. and the editors of *Family Business* magazine. Be aware that they should be read somewhat tongue-in-cheek:

10. Too many people I know have died soon after they retired.
9. Without me, the business is nothing.
8. Without the business, I'm nothing.
7. I hate gardening and get sunburned if I play too much golf or tennis.
6. I need someplace to go.

5. The kids want to change the way the business is run.
4. I have several capable kids and don't want to have to choose one to succeed me.
3. The business is my major source of income. I have to stay active to protect it.
2. Nobody can run the business as well as I can.
1. Somebody may run the business better than I do.

Some retirement planning ideas are outlined in *Family Business Succession: The Final Test of Greatness* by Craig E. Aronoff and John L. Ward (Business Owner Resources, 1992). First orders of business are to draft a strategic business plan, develop a personal financial plan for the founder, write a family mission statement and craft an estate plan. Next, name a successor, agree to groom him, come up with a date to retire and do so.

You should not view retirement as a mysterious, scary event. If you plan for it now, you can greatly influence your own future and leave a wonderful legacy to your family and staff. Everybody needs a strategy. Too many just wander mindlessly through the retirement process without a vision for themselves of where they want to go, what they want to be, what they want to do and what they want to leave behind. Instead, they think only in terms of one or two days ahead.

FINANCIAL SECURITY AFTER RETIREMENT

Yet, the good news is that there is life after retirement, and here's how a plan can be put in place. Remember, you can shape the future to be as good if not better than the past. First and foremost, it's absolutely crucial to succession that you believe you have financial security. So, a key to any succession plan involves financial planning for your retirement. Without it, you may be reluctant to transfer leadership to the next generation. The worst-case scenarios are parents who are beholden to their children for income to maintain their lifestyle.

There are numerous options to ensure your income. You'll probably need to use a variety of techniques, some dependent upon the business and others not dependent on it. Unless you are very confident in your successor management, the key is to build enough capital and income not dependent upon the future success of the business, while not placing stress on the business' operations and capital needs. Otherwise, you are not likely to shift sufficient authority to your successor. That may take time and it does take planning. This is another reason to start early and use competent tax and financial advisors. Here are some examples of techniques:

- Engage in personal financial planning to determine your retirement cash-flow needs. Structure a savings and investment plan to build the required capital outside the business. Perhaps you'll need to forego some current lifestyle needs, but isn't that true for most people working towards retirement?
- With competent tax advice, consider alternatives to take cash flow out of the business, such as renting business-related property to the company, consulting fees, director's fees and the like.
- Transfer ownership to the next generation through a buyout plan that occurs over multiple years so that the company can fund that buyout.
- Put into place a preferred stock recapitalization. By doing so, you will be the owner of a different classification of stock known as preferred stock and will transfer common stock to your heirs. It freezes the value of your estate for tax purposes and it gives you a preferential right to dividends and capital. (Note that Subchapter S corporations may not use this strategy.)

LIFE AFTER RETIREMENT

Business leaders also must find something to occupy their time in their retirement years. Otherwise, they will go into the office and confuse the employees as to who is in charge. Without intending to do so, you may usurp your successor's authority and hurt his ability to lead the business.

It's tough to find something to occupy your time, especially if you have not developed outside interests. Most entrepreneurs will not find satisfaction in retirement just by traveling, golfing or participating in some other leisure activity. If that's true for you, you need to find something that is as equally productive, challenging and rewarding as running your business. That will take time to find, so you need to start looking early in the retirement process. There are numerous alternatives. Examples from real life experience include:

- Trade association leadership.
- Politics or lobbying related to your business' needs.
- Consulting with other family businesses.
- Serving on other family business boards.
- Starting a new business that complements the family's business or is totally different.
- Existing hobbies.
- Studies and activities in a new field that has always been of interest to you.
- Volunteering your business skills to charitable or civic organizations.

Enlist your spouse's help and input. After all, he or she may have reservations about your spending your entire day puttering around the house and being home for lunch!

Reality Check: A successful succession cannot be accomplished without a retirement plan that includes both financial security and continued productive activity. There are numerous ways to ensure cash-flow needs so that you are taken care of by the company and independent of the company. But, you need to start planning now, just like other people who have to plan for retirement. You also have to plan for what you will do with your time after you retire so that you won't return to the office and intentionally or unintentionally interfere with your successor management. Only entrepreneurs who truly retire and turn over authority can experience the joy of seeing their successor's success. And that joy is worth the price of planning for both your financial and emotional needs in retirement.

77. If trouble brews, should you seek outside help? And from whom?

For years, Bennett Truck Equipment rolled along a fairly smooth path. The full-line Orlando, Fl.-based truck equipment distribution, manufacturing and retail sales company, founded by Randle L. "Ray" Bennett Sr. and his wife

Hazel in 1953, finally hit an enormous bump. At age 66, Ray passed away. Fortunately the firm was not rudderless. Beginning in the early 1970s, all four of Ray's children started coming into the firm. The two who remained, Randy Jr. and Glenn, suddenly found themselves in charge.

For the next few years, the brothers experienced a significant test of their relationship. The two had to learn how to work together as business partners and equal shareholders (they were gifted shares from their mother Hazel and began buying the rest). For a while, the brothers had no one to turn to for help when they faced a crisis or disagreed. At times, the two were more like rivals than business partners. Although Randy, now 45, had worked more years in the firm than his younger brother, the two flipped a coin to see who would be president. Glenn, 43, won the toss. He became president and sales manager. Randy was named corporate secretary and general manager. The two decided to take home similar salaries. "A title is just a title," Randy says.

The brothers knew they needed help to continue to get along and work better together. They hired an outside consultant. He taught them how to disagree gracefully and then reach a decision. The two began to consult each other before either spent money or made a change. The consultant also helped the company make internal changes. He zeroed in on profitability, job descriptions, cash flow, management and more. The consultant more than paid for himself. Last year, the company reached an all-time high in annual sales of $6 million.

The brothers' two other siblings—a sister and older brother—own no shares. Randy says, "They had the same opportunities we did. My sister got married. My older brother wanted to do things his own way. So he went out on his own."

The two brothers have six children among them who may want to come into the business some day. They've done no formal succession planning, but Randy is quick to say, "One thing for sure, we won't give out equal shares. Someone has to have the majority and the final say."

Business owners: Here's a wake-up call that's too important to ignore. There is help out there, if you need it and if you are willing to ferret it out. Begin by recognizing a hard reality: Sometimes you cannot count on yourself, your family or your staff to solve all your problems.

One easy way to seek help is to attend a workshop or seminar or join some type of family firm membership group or forum. This is a safe uncontroversial interim step. You start with an educational forum where you learn what others face. You tune into those who are dealing with similar situations, not unlike a parenting or grief support group. As you learn how they've approached a problem, solutions for your particular issues may become clearer. In doing this, you may also learn how severe the consequences can be if you ignore action and fail to get help. Don't expect a miracle cure, however. Such gatherings represent a starting point. Most family members leave knowing they have more work to do on their own, with a facilitator present or with some other advisor.

Another place to turn is peer groups. Experts say that CEOs tend to take a lot more stock in what their peers say and do than in what advisors, employees or family members suggest. Of the various types of peer-support groups, consider the Young Presidents Organization or trade organization groups. Know, however, that a lot of CEO groups don't deal exclusively with family business issues. These types of meetings can be better suited for picking up business tips.

Secrecy is a big issue among family business owners who don't want to air their dirty laundry in front of people they know. If you can't open up with people or peers whom you know, consider a seminar or peer group in another location where you are anonymous.

Another alternative is a university-based family business forum, where you can learn from other family businesses that have experienced similar problems. Forums are a good place to meet and talk with family business professionals.

Still another option is family business consultants who may be associated with a university or a professional firm and specialize in family business matters. Many have additional expertise in law, accounting, tax or psychology. It's best to deal with a consultant who has a track record of working with other family firms and the institution of family business. He should understand your family and its dynamics, plus the relevant financial and tax issues.

What makes family business owners or successors take the initial step to seek help? A variety of factors from simple curiosity to desperation. And sometimes the desire to get help can be piqued just by being in a certain place at a certain time. For example, you may be attending a trade show where the attendees are mainly thinking about sales, marketing and improving the business. There's one session on business issues that segue into family business. You feel comfortable in a room full of others who have had similar experiences. It's not so bad, you think, as you consume information. You go up after the session to talk to the facilitator–speaker and ask more questions. He gives you his card. You may or may not call him, but at least you're thinking about getting more input.

Other safe ways to find some answers to family business problems are to subscribe to family business newsletters. These tend to cover key issues and what others have done to be successful. Or go to your local library and take out any of the narrative or "how-to" books on the subject. There are magazines and journals that feature family business news sections. *The Wall Street Journal* and *BusinessWeek* regularly now cover entrepreneurism. And even non-business publications such as *Town & Country* monthly magazine periodically focus on family business issues since the topic is so pervasive and interesting to nonfamily business members as well. Also turn to the Internet where you will find hundreds of family business websites.

Reality Check: Like someone who refuses to ask directions and then gets lost, many family business owners are leery of getting help with unresolved issues, only to find themselves headed down the wrong path. If you are skittish about bringing in an expert, consider attending a peer group, family business forum, workshop or seminar, or a session on family business at your next trade show or convention. If you want to maintain anonymity, attend a seminar out of town. There is also a plethora of books, articles, newsletters and websites. (Some of these are listed in Chapter XI.) Knowledge is power in this case. With that knowledge, you can determine the best course to find solutions to the issues you face.

78. What can be done if the founder or owner fails to heed outside advice that may jeopardize his position or the future of the business? How can he be encouraged to listen to someone else?

Sheer luck is pretty much the way succession has worked for W. A. Bean & Sons in Bangor, Me. and one of Maine's oldest independent meat packers, now in its fifth generation with 20 employees. Succession has been a serendipitous affair. Fourth-generation brothers, Albert and Frederick Bean, who hold all voting stock, are still in the business but consider themselves semi-retired. "They come and go as they please," says Albert's daughter, Elizabeth Trommer, treasurer. Elizabeth, 50, and her brother David, 41, are co-heads. David is production and general plant manager. There are two other siblings in the firm, Albert in shipping, and Judith, who works part-time in the packing department.

Sooner rather than later is the time this family should start planning for the next generation to step into the company. Yet, no formal plan has been enforced, which Elizabeth thinks is "insane." They have attended seminars at the Husson Center for Family Business in Bangor on the importance of succession planning, the psychological issues of working in a family business and marketing. But the only changes made after attending were in marketing, Elizabeth says. When the two brothers pass the baton and the stock on to the next generation, Elizabeth believes that only she and her brother will receive shares. The family hasn't considered the tax ramifications of such a transaction.

"David is the male heir, so he would receive the majority. It is a family mindset that the men will primarily run the company, and Albert and Fred think it is important to give a controlling interest to one person," says Elizabeth. "I gave up worrying about their thinking in this regard years ago because I love the firm and I like being involved in a family business," she adds.

Anyone running a business can stumble, tripped by intense competition, falling prices, other countries' financial crises, the lack of a succession plan, poor leadership or management and the absence of a clear vision. A consultant can help if the leader is unsure where to turn to rev up the company after a year of sluggish growth or is uncertain how to develop a succession plan when a company appears rudderless. But stories of bullheadedness on the part of owners to call in someone for help can result in more of a downturn, additional problems, frustrated successors and a weakened infrastructure.

Owners tend to refuse to deal with issues that are painful but often stare them right in the face. This may include getting on with a retirement plan or dealing with disruptive family members who work in the business. Not taking action or trying to fix the situation without knowing how allows problems to fester. Resentment may grow like a fungus.

You want to maintain that fine yet precarious balance. You don't want to rock the boat of personal relationships by naming a successor and risking alienation of someone who doesn't get chosen or worse, the wrath of your spouse if you upset your children. So, you think about bringing in an objective third party, a consultant, to help you with your decision.

But you resist. You're reluctant to give up control to someone else. You're not receptive to others' advice, and you frankly don't want to spend the money. You don't want to retire because you love the business. Finally, you rationalize you don't have the time to sit and listen to an outsider's latest pop psychology.

Family members can help unwilling participants to be part of the process, or they can hinder it. Somehow, those who seek change must convince those who want the status quo to consider alternatives. Sometimes, that can be facilitated through reading appropriate articles or attending seminars on the subject under contention. The concept is to get recalcitrant family members to recognize that a problem exists through a non-threatening mechanism. Sometimes, the process can be aided by eliciting the help of a spouse, another more senior family member, a trusted advisor or a friend. The best family business consultants may be able to help initiate the process through preliminary discussions with the family.

No one can force you to resolve problems that are growing within the business and family. An advisor or consultant can't make you or anyone else follow recommendations. Yet, you should think through what will happen if you don't address them. Your dreams for yourself, your family and your business might be shattered if you allow problems to grow unresolved.

Finding the right consultant can make all the difference in the world, as countless family businesses have discovered. Your process of selecting an advisor must be sufficiently thorough so that you and your family will respect and trust the advice you are given. Otherwise, you will undertake an exercise in futility. A skilled family business expert will emphasize the need to talk things through, to work at being honest, to find creative ways for you and your family members to communicate and to solve problems. Once you're certain that you're looking for outside help for the right reasons, make sure everyone in the family is in the loop on your goals. You need consensus and enthusiasm when you outline your problems to consultants.

Once you've decided that you can set aside the time and pay the fees, find whom you want to work with. Then, plan to listen and take action. Make sure you're on the same wavelength with the consultant. Don't allow him to make more of the assignment than it is. Nail down the goals and the scope of the project—whether you're tackling one issue or many—but don't restrict his ability to pursue issues that are important to you or other family members.

The consultant should build rapport and trusted relationships with the family members and others involved. Make sure that he's independent and looking for the best long-term solutions that address both the family and business ramifications of the issue. More important, make sure that all family members recognize the advisor's independence. If he's perceived as your or another family member's spear carrier, the process won't work.

It's possible that taking the consultant's advice will be difficult for you or other family members. You must help family members swallow potentially bitter medicine. A good advisor, like a good doctor, can help you and your family understand the risks and rewards of what he prescribes. Keep in mind that what he suggests is given in good faith.

Reality Check: Founders or owners often fail to look to outside help when they most need it. If you're stuck and not sure where to turn, hiring a consultant to custom-design a solution for your company is a smart way to shore up your family firm both from a business and family standpoint. Most owners avoid doing so, saying they don't have the time, don't want to spend the money, or don't believe that a consultant can understand their industry. But why allow problems to fester? They'll likely only get worse. Find a consultant who is objective and commands your respect and the respect of your family members. Then, work with the consultant to find the solution.

79. What red flags may arise as senior-generation family members begin to transfer their stock to the children?

Oh, what a tangled web they could have woven. After brothers Paul and Bendros Sharian took control of Sharian Inc., the 67-year-old two-store carpet cleaning business their parents started in Atlanta, Ga., they knew they'd have to give planning some time and attention before bringing four of their six children into the business. There was no succession plan when the two of them came into the firm after their mother died and their father retired to Florida.

Twelve years ago, they started the planning process by calling in two key advisors, their attorney and a financial consultant. The brothers felt there would be a smoother transition if they turned over management while they were still alive and active. Their plan was to provide equal ownership to all third-generation members in management positions. Those who were not in the firm would own no shares. When all was said and done, Bendros' daughter, Ruth Sharian Garner, 42, who had run one of the stores since 1983, was tapped to be chairman. Son Ritchie, in his late 30s, took over for Paul as president, and Bendros III, 44, was elected secretary and treasurer. Paul's daughter, Lydia, in her late 30s, was elected vice president. Once their children were placed, the brothers wanted to start to give them shares.

There was only one problem—how much ownership would Lydia get? Should Lydia, Paul's only child in the business, end up with 50 percent while the other children would have to divvy up Bendros' 50 percent? To even out the pot and avert any internecine squabbling, the brothers drafted a cross-purchase agreement. Both agreed to distribute a certain amount of stock to all children each year. In the event of Paul's death, 75 percent of his stock would be sold to Bendros' three children and one-fourth would go to Lydia. They agreed to make annual gifts and adjust the buy–sell agreement annually so there would never be any more, or less, given to Lydia or the other three children. In addition, the four children with ownership drafted a buy–sell agreement. This would allow them to purchase stock from one another, should one die or leave the business.

Your advisors are urging you to start shifting stock to the next generation to take advantage of planning techniques that are available to you while you're alive, but are unavailable at your death. Your business is chugging away vigorously in its 45th year. It's growing and your children are entering one by one. You foresee significant future growth opportunities. Now is the time to give stock to the children before the share value rises.

Can you merely grab the stock certificates and start assigning them? Unfortunately, nothing is that simple. There are numerous factors that can throw you a curve. Here are some thoughts to ponder with just a sampling of creative ways to deal with the issues:

RETIREMENT FINANCIAL NEEDS. You must arrange your affairs to provide for your and your spouse's financial support when you retire. Ideally, you should accomplish this feat by building wealth outside the business so that you transfer all the stock to your successors during your lifetime. Building that financial base may mean that you should sell, rather than give, some stock to the children. They can finance the purchase from future business income, and you can stockpile the proceeds for the future.

CONTROL. You probably want to retain voting control until you are 100 percent confident of your successors' business savvy and your financial security. However, retaining control need not mean that you can only transfer 49 percent of the stock to the children. Consider a recapitalization of the corporation. Turn virtually all the stock into nonvoting stock, with just a few shares remaining as voting. That will allow you to transfer virtually all the equity, while retaining only the small percentage that represents voting control.

UNCERTAIN MATURITY AND INVOLVEMENT. You might resist transferring any stock until your children are old enough to demonstrate that they can cooperate as owners and handle the responsibility appropriately. You also may decide to give stock only to those working in the business. That will tempt you to delay your estate planning until they're 30 or 40 years old by which time you will have lost many opportunities to reduce your estate tax. Rather than delay, consider the benefits of transferring stock sooner. But, be sure to have a buy–sell agreement in place to create the ability to buy out stock from any children you ultimately determine to be inappropriate owners. You also could consider making gifts in trust to delay your younger heirs' receipt of shares.

UNBORN CHILDREN. If you make stock gifts to your two children each year and then a third bouncing baby turns up in the future, the later-born baby starts out behind the eight ball. He'll own less stock than his siblings simply because he happened to be the last to come on the scene. Of course, you can equalize this inequality by transferring extra shares to the late arrival. Alternatively, you could avoid the problem from the start by making gifts into a single trust that benefits all your current and future children. That trust will divide equally among your children after your child-bearing years.

Second- and later-generation family firms face an additional issue. Suppose that you and your sister each inherited 50 percent of the stock from your parents. You have five children and your sister has only one. In the normal course of affairs, your children each will wind up owning 10 percent (one-fifth of your 50 percent), while your sister's child will own 50 percent. Your children may see a real inequity here, especially if they work in the business, while their cousin does not. Your parents might have altered this scheme if they had made equal gifts of stock directly to their grandchildren, rather than or in addition to gifts to you and your sister.

There's no easy, fair answer to the vagaries of ownership caused by varying gift strategies and family sizes. However, there are a couple of points to keep in mind. First, parents must realize that they cannot forever treat their children equally from a wealth or stock ownership standpoint. Your children's different skills, objectives, spending patterns and simple good luck will still make them different even after you equalize them. It's a fact of life and the longer you try to force equality, the harder it will be for them to accept inequality when that reality hits.

Second, it is important for the family to realize that ownership is not a birthright or entitlement that somehow ensures that each family member will own the "right" amount of stock. Furthermore, ownership and employment need not be synonymous. You can own stock in General Motors without working there. Having said that, General Motors' management deserves fair compensation for their services to the company, but not the right to own all its stock.

As the family grows, stock ownership may be spread among an increasing number of people. At some point, no identifiable family line has control. Family line jealousies and desires for board representation diminish. The business becomes more like a quasi-public company. The management learns to operate with openness similar to that practiced by their public counterparts. These businesses, which typically are in the fourth or later generation of family ownership, have made an important transition. They have adopted and practiced policies that reduce family frictions, provide for the involvement of a board of independent directors, and better separate family issues from business operations.

If the family members believe that they have rights to demand employment or cash from the company, and if the company is not large enough to satisfy those demands and still grow, the company is doomed. At that point, either the business should be sold or a small group of family members should buy out the interests of other members. Pruning dissenters and other unwilling shareholders from the ranks can rejuvenate the family and business, so that the process can start anew.

Reality Check: It's a big mistake to delay transferring stock to the next generation. Situations will change. Before you know it, your estate tax problems may become unmanageable. Uncertainty about the future need not stymie good planning. Through the use of trusts and shareholder agreements, combined with open communication and ongoing education, you can foster relationships that can adapt to changing circumstances.

80. How does the founder deal with a lack of competence or commitment in the next generation? What are the options?

Fred (not his real name) built a muffler business that was doing well. The business was predicated on the idea of superior service and convenience to customers. Even though people didn't make appointments, few had to wait. Business was booming and Fred needed to add more employees to his staff of 20. He brought his son Bobby (not his real name) into the business and agreed to pay him a salary pegged to what another trainee in the industry would make. However, shortly after coming into the business, Bobby started slacking off. He took long lunches and the company lost customers who were driving in at noon and not getting the service they expected. Over time, Fred started to see profit margins dwindling. He started to cut staff. Employee morale was at an all-time low, and they complained about Bobby. But Fred wouldn't budge. He wanted to give his son every opportunity to succeed. As an incentive, he offered Bobby company stock if he managed to work longer hours and improve service to customers for at least a year. Otherwise, his father threatened, Bobby would be asked to leave the business until he could get his act together, which meant going back to college to get his degree. Bobby chose to leave and now is a self-employed mechanic.

Your successor will need more than just bloodlines to become a leader in your firm. He needs credentials, determination and a good work ethic. How does he achieve this when there are no instructions in the family business manual on how a parent can breed competent children and motivate them to enter the business? It's even more difficult to instill good business values if your children have been reared in the lap of luxury and have no sense of responsibility. Children who haven't been told "no," who haven't had to work for success and possessions, or who never experienced failure because their parents were always there to catch them before a fall are being bred for disappointment and incompetence in business—and in life.

Chances are they won't make good candidates to enter, stay in or do well in your firm, or keep it going once you're gone. They won't be able to identify opportunities for growth and new products, move the business forward, and attract and retain dedicated employees.

Avoid the trap in the first place by knowing that your business and employees are too valuable to sacrifice to unprepared successors.

You must rear your children with a proper appreciation of the business and its importance to employees, family and community.

Objectivity should be key when you decide whether to hire a relative, including your children, who, you hope, will benefit your company. If you're uncertain what to do or don't want to be the bad guy, bring in an expert to help decide. If you have a board of independent directors, tap their expertise and judgment. Seek input from advisors. Don't try to make the decision completely on your own.

Don't bring incompetent successors into your firm out of guilt or because there's nowhere else for them to find a job. Don't consider them easy hires when the pickings are slim. Don't bring in indulged heirs, who don't want to do what it takes to work or run the company one day. Don't think you can change their mindset. In many cases, you don't have much influence over your children's motivation or work ethic once they reach a certain age and maturity. You also need to realize that, as a parent, you may have had the power to tell your children how to do things a certain way at home, but the rules change when they're grown and have become your business partners.

So how do you handle an heir who may be a problem, but wants to join the business, or who already works there, but is doing a less-than-stellar job? Be compassionate, but firm. Sit down with the person in private and explain the problem. Be as specific as possible about shortcomings. Set specific expectations for improvements and develop ways for him to gain additional training if needed. Let the family member express concerns and feelings. Reach agreement on a specific time frame over which improvement must be demonstrated. Develop a mutual understanding of yardsticks to be used during this period. Explain the consequences of failing to meet your expectations. Provide periodic performance reviews during the probationary period. If possible, have a nonfamily mentor assume responsibility for the performance reviews. Stick with the agreement.

A successor must demonstrate a proper work ethic and commitment or be told as compassionately as possible to pursue other options. Explain to your heirs that they are not the only inheritors. Others in the firm are affected if the goose doesn't continue to lay the golden eggs. Employees, suppliers, customers and even communities depend on your business running successfully. Make it clear that you will find the right person to succeed you, even if it means bringing in a nonfamily member or promoting another employee. No one ever said this sort of detachment is easy. In fact, it probably will be emotionally difficult for you to rise to the occasion. If it doesn't work out, you both can feel comfortable that every effort has been made to remedy the situation. You have a reasonably good chance of a friendly parting of the ways, if that is necessary.

If your successor is proving to be totally worthless and you cannot communicate your expectations, encourage him to leave. He's probably not very happy anyway. If necessary, fire him. He's only costing your company money and breeding resentment among hard-working, successful employees. The best thing for everyone involved is for your heir to find another pursuit that he loves and is good at and for you to hand the reins to a more competent nonfamily member as an interim or permanent solution.

This worked well for one Midwestern conglomerate, which named a nonfamily member president because none of the heirs-apparent held the necessary leadership capabilities. Yet, all work in the business in some capacity. For example, one is in charge of real estate transactions, a specific area that doesn't interface with the rest of the business. He likes to ski and takes time off to pursue this avocation. He receives compensation pegged to his job responsibilities. The family business generates enough of a profit to pay dividends to all family stockholders who find time to pursue their passions.

Reality Check: If you cannot separate yourself from your incompetent successor, you are likely to transform a good firm into a shaky one. You are setting yourself, business and heir up for failure. You can piggyback incompetent successors with competent nonfamily, give them big salaries, and try to get them to work, but you make it difficult for hardworking employees to stay loyal and stay on. Putting up with incompetent family members in your business is risky. If you cannot turn your incompetent successor around in a year or two, you must take more dramatic action to remedy the situation. And, you must take that action before it's too late.

81. What can be done when family members' skills and talents are underutilized?

John T. (not his real name) allowed all four sons to enter his Cleveland-based construction supply company that manufactured and distributed its own products. Three of his sons were clearly unqualified for their management positions and were less than enthusiastic about working there.

The youngest son, Don (not his real name), on the other hand, who was working his way through school, seemed to have the greatest potential. However, he was stuck in a menial job because he was the "baby." He could have contributed the most. Don tried to talk to his father about giving him more responsibility. He enlisted the support of a key nonfamily manager to plead his case and he suggested holding family meetings or truth sessions where the responsibilities and goals of each brother could be fleshed out. He wasn't able to convince his father to make changes. Bored and burned out, Don eventually left the firm.

In retrospect, John knows that he should have handled things differently, but didn't know how. He should have been precise about the jobs for his sons, known and accepted the competencies of each, regardless of who was the eldest, and tested those abilities. Today the three eldest sons are still in the business, but the firm has shed its manufacturing and distribution arms and only provides contracting services.

The flip side of the incompetent heir-apparent is the one who is talented and underutilized. This can cause just as many problems. Out of frustration or sheer boredom, the successor may act inappropriately or shut down completely. He may be an asset, but quit before he's given a chance to prove himself.

If you're, the heir-apparent, you need an ally in the firm, someone who will be your advocate. The ideal person is a senior manager or an advisor, someone whom Mom or Dad trusts and with whom they have a good personal relationship. Your mentor–advisor needs to understand your goals and expectations, the contributions you think you can make to the business and your qualifications and skills. Here are some questions that you, as the successor, need to ask yourself before you can address the larger issues at hand:

- Why do you want to work in the family business? What are your personal, career and financial expectations?
- What are the roadblocks to achieving job satisfaction? Do you see them as solvable?
- Is there a culture clash between you and your father, mother, siblings, and/or other family members? Is the clash over differences between your and your family members' views on how the business should be run or some other relationship issue?

- How well do you think you can serve the business and in what capacity? Do your views differ from those of your parents and key managers and, if so, how?
- What's the best way to communicate your frustrations to your parents and maintain a professional relationship?
- What else is hindering your advancement and contributing to your being underutilized? Are you really not up to handling the job to which you think you're entitled?
- If you don't get your way, your parent doesn't realize your worthiness or the job doesn't work out, are you prepared to find a new job?

Be specific. Plead your own case. Say to your Dad or Mom, "Here's what I'm doing. If you were to give me responsibility for XYZ operation—say the technology services division—here's what I can commit to and what I can deliver."

Work extra hard at what you do. If need be, make your case again, then again over a reasonable period of time. If nothing happens, or your father undermines everything you do or still calls you junior at age 45, you, the successor, need to give the ultimatum. Realize you may have made a huge mistake in hindsight, then leave. Many of us spend too much time at work to be demoralized. Assuming you have skills and self-esteem, go someplace where you can use your talents and have your contribution recognized and rewarded.

Always remember that the family business is only one option for most hardworking, intelligent people. Worry about what you can control and your own personal destiny. Don't bother attempting to control (or change) the founder. Always try to leave the door ajar since situations change.

Reality Check: If you are being pushed around, underutilized or discounted in the family firm, you need an advocate, someone whom your parents trust. A company manager, advisor or independent board member can help plead your cause. But you must ask yourself a number of questions before you begin your campaign to get ahead. You must realistically assess your skills and abilities. You must develop the credibility and qualifications to go after what you want and what you think you're worth. If you don't achieve those goals over a reasonable period of time, explore other options, possibly outside the firm.

82. How should family members' compensation be set so it doesn't initiate conflict?

Cousins Randy Schoedinger, 30, and Michael, 31, sixth-generation co-executive vice presidents of their family's 100-employee funeral business, Schoedinger Funeral Service in Columbus, Oh., are paid fair market value wages for what they do. This family business, which conducts 2,400 funerals a year, is run by a family that doesn't believe in paying itself outrageous salaries or taking fancy perks. Family members in the business receive what nonfamily employees would receive at their same level.

Michael entered the firm first, after receiving a degree in business management from Miami University in Ohio. Randy received his degree in finance from the University of Colorado and first went to work for a bank in Columbus. More than two years later, he decided to enter the family firm.

Both had to interview with the personnel director before joining. They had to be qualified and were given salaries equivalent to what they would receive in the public market for their level of responsibility. Both joined as apprentice funeral embalmers and directors and earned equivalent starting salaries.

Although Michael came into the firm first, the cousins today earn the same salaries and own the same number of shares of voting stock. Their fathers David, chairman, and Jay, president, are still active in the firm and own the majority shares. Their grandfather and uncle, both in their 80s, also work in the business but just recently sold their shares in completion of the firm's succession plan. Do the cousins mind being paid the same? In response, Michael quotes his wife: "You're lucky to have Randy, and he's lucky to have you because you have different personalities and don't think alike but get along so well." Randy concurs and adds, "If you're equal partners, you have to be able to trust the other person with the business. Whether or not I agree with a decision Michael makes, I know that what he's doing is best for the business, rather than for any individual person."

Compensation is one way an employee gauges his worth, but how does a parent put a pricetag on a son's or daughter's talents and contributions? It's one of the stickiest issues debated within family firms, especially if the expectation is that the son or daughter should have the same lifestyle as the parents or other siblings in the firm.

Some family businesses overcompensate family members relative to what nonfamily employees would receive in the same position and for the same or even less performance. There are many pros and cons to overcompensating family member employees.

Arguments for overcompensating family members:

- Attracts family members into the business and retains them.
- Gives children a better lifestyle.
- Controls children by hooking them into the business, since they can't earn as much elsewhere.
- Provides favorable income tax consequences relative to other approaches for putting money into their hands.
- Allows all working family members to be paid the same amount (regardless of differing contributions) consistent with family views on equal love and equal treatment.
- Buys peace within a family, at least for the immediate future.

Arguments against overcompensating family members:

- Unfair to those heirs who contribute more than others.
- Creates a welfare system within the family and business.
- Sets a bad example for the next generation.
- Corrupts the heirs' views of their self-worth.
- Creates improper expectations.
- Places financial strain on the business.
- Traps the successors because they cannot support their resulting lifestyles elsewhere if necessary.
- Creates friction with inactive owners who will come to believe that the working family members are taking advantage of their positions.

Conversely, there are many pros and cons to undercompensating family members, a practice in place at other family firms. There are at least two sides to each pro and con.

Arguments for undercompensating family members:

- Builds character.
- Requires them to "pay their dues."
- Provides strong dose of humility.
- Provides cheap labor for the business.
- Prevents the family members from developing "lavish" lifestyles.

- Avoids potential conflict with inactive owners over appropriateness of compensation.

Arguments against undercompensating family members:

- Discourages family members from joining the business or encourages them to quit for greener pastures.
- Poses unfair disadvantage to those whose talents could generate better rewards elsewhere.
- Sends signal that family members are not "worth it" or that their contributions are not appreciated.
- Damages morale.

Experience shows that neither over- nor undercompensating family employees works over the long term. What does work is a system that pays employees fairly for their positions and performance, whether family or nonfamily. Too often, parents confuse compensation with other objectives. It is not a substitute for gifts or inheritance, which have nothing to do with job performance. Compensation also is not a substitute for return on invested capital, despite the fact that the income tax law favors compensation over dividends. Compensation also is not an appropriate way for a parent to control an adult child's lifestyle. Despite good intentions, confusing compensation with these other objectives sets the stage for problems in the future. Just reread the previously cited pros and cons and you'll understand why.

The best approach to compensating family employees is to provide a package similar to what you would provide for a nonfamily employee in the same job. Future raises and perks should be based upon performance, not blood relationships.

Compensation of family members doesn't have to become an issue if handled rationally and with forethought. Here are some steps you can take to ensure that it is addressed in a professional and equitable manner:

- Establish a compensation policy for family members. Set policies for all types of remuneration, including bonuses, cost-of-living raises, perks and other benefits. If possible, make your policies clear before your family members enter the business.
- Be consistent with family and nonfamily employees in setting compensation levels and raises.

- Set guidelines for performance reviews.
- Incorporate some form of incentive or performance-based compensation that rewards employees, both family and nonfamily, for achieving goals.
- Establish a special group to resolve compensation issues. This group could include owners, directors and managers. Your board of independent directors can play a pivotal role.

If you have trouble determining what is fair compensation for different positions in your business, given your industry and size, look to consumer and trade publications in your industry. Contact your trade organization or other business groups, research the Internet, and talk to others in your industry. Also consider consulting experts who are skilled in surveying compensation practices and designing appropriate packages. Many factors should be considered for you to determine "fair" compensation: company size in terms of sales and revenues, number of employees, cost of living in your company's location, number of people supervised, hours worked, educational requirements, experience, contacts, performance and degree of specialization.

PITFALLS TO AVOID

Pitfalls to avoid in setting compensation for successors are addressed by Craig E. Aronoff and John L. Ward in *Family Business Compensation* (Business Owner Resources, 1993), which is part of the Family Business Leadership series. Some common ones to watch out for:

- Using pay to keep your children dependent. You shouldn't trap them in their present jobs because you pay so much that they can't leave if they're unhappy or want to do something else.
- Using pay to mitigate guilt. Perhaps you didn't spend time with them as children or failed to provide them with certain benefits such as an adequate education. Don't overpay them now to compensate.
- Using pay to take the relationship for granted. A wrong tactic is to think that you can pay them more and avoid mentoring or advising them.

- Using salary substitutes such as fancy perks instead of a decent annual wage.
- Adjusting family members' compensation to address the ups and downs of business cycles.
- Using pay to punish family members. You don't like some of their lifestyle choices so you lower their earnings. Perhaps you don't approve of your son's or daughter's spouse. Conversely, perhaps a new grandchild comes along, so you increase your child's pay to help cover new family-raising expenses. Remember your children are grown and allowed to make independent decisions. Anyway what does this have to do with their business acumen or contribution? Probably nothing.

Reality Check: As a rule, you should pay fair market value for any position in your company, whether a family or nonfamily member holds it. It is extremely important to develop compensation policies relating to working family members and to make sure that everyone understands them. Don't confuse everyone by setting compensation and perks in nonbusinesslike ways. You should pay working family members based on their contribution to the business, not because of love. Separately, and when appropriate based upon business performance, owners should receive dividends or other returns on their invested capital.

83. Should advisors be or become personal friends?

Erwin B. (not his real name) stands in his art gallery in Rhode Island, dwarfed by some of his prized works. Advisors crowd around him, watching his every move, as he experiments with different frames and juxtapositions of art on his walls. They toss out advice. Erwin thrives on going against expectations. He is not bothered by contradictions, and, in fact, is motivated by them. Although Erwin has made his mark as an art impresario, he gives credit for his success to his advisors. However, speculation about who will inherit his position fuels hours of gossip in the gallery. Along the way, he used advisors but never broke one rule of thumb: he never befriended one. He consulted them, listened to them and adapted what they said to fit his needs. He may have depended on them and even had close relationships with them, but always maintained his distance and objectivity. He learned the hard way after confiding in his corporate controller one year that sales were poor, which leaked out and caused some artists to pull out of the gallery. When you cross that boundary into friendship, it's hard to remain impartial.

A friend listens to what you have to say and tries to accept it unconditionally, offering advice when it's critical or when you've asked. Friendship implies trust, confidentiality and respect. Certainly you also should trust and respect your advisors who should, in turn, maintain total confidentiality about their knowledge of you, your family and business. But there are important distinctions between friends and advisors that you disregard at your own peril.

Unlike a friend, an advisor is someone who you pay for your relationship, a hired gun. While you should have a respectful, friendly relationship, it should be on a professional rather than social level. An advisor should have your best interests at heart, but should not be a pal. You admire and listen because an advisor understands you, your business, objectives and vision, not because you share the same interests, laugh at the same jokes or like to eat at the same restaurants. Getting together should not be a time to schmooze about aches and pains or problems with your spouse (unless of course it relates to the business). You both need to focus on issues.

If you cross the line into personal friendship, your advisors may lose one of the most important attributes of their role—the impartiality for which they were originally hired. Friends have difficulty risking the relationship with advice that you may not like. Advisors have enough trouble not holding their punches to protect their revenue stream. Don't make it even more difficult by making them risk friendship as well.

Developing a social relationship with advisors can keep you from being objective in assessing their capabilities and contributions. Loyalty towards friends and advisors is admirable. In a friendship, that loyalty means that you can overlook a friend's shortcomings. But you must not feel compelled to retain an advisor whose skills fail to meet your or your business' needs.

As your family members mature, they also need to develop respect for your advisors. If they perceive that they have crossed the bounds and become personal friends, they will question whether the advisors' recommendations are impartial and in the overall family's and business' best interests. Advisors are simply what their name implies—they are there to advise you, not be your buddy. Maintaining a reasonable level of professionalism avoids confusion for you, your family, employees and clients.

Reality Check: Advisors are hired to offer expertise. Cross the boundary into friendship, and they may shed their impartiality. It's fine for an advisor to develop a close, respectful and friendly relationship with you and to care about what you do in your business, as well as care for your family, but that's as far as you should allow the relationship to go. Of course, exceptions occur and over time you may find that a caring, even loving, relationship develops. Just be careful that impartiality is not lost in the transition.

84. Has the family set unrealistic family and business goals, such as all family members must come into or run the business?

Many family business owners put a premium on being equal. They equate equal with fair so they allow all their children into the business and don't set boundaries. While their hearts are in the right place, this often proves to be an unrealistic expectation. In some cases, power struggles surface and once-thriving businesses can become another casualty as siblings fight for their share of power.

This is similar to the scenario faced by the MacDonald family (not their real names). John and Mary MacDonald, who founded their $5-million computer services firm on the East Coast in 1973, wanted to retire and leave the business to all three children who were already working in the firm. However, there was no delineation of responsibilities. The siblings were left to divide them up. The message was: You run it. It's yours now. It's up to you to figure out who does what. The expectation was that all would do the same thing—sell their computer services—and they'd live happily ever after. Wrong!

Says Ann, 38, who has been in the business since 1989, "This was a totally unrealistic expectation. Although my parents did very precise financial, tax and estate planning, they sidestepped family issues."

Ann, who has a degree in engineering and is president, works with her two brothers. Art, 36, who is executive vice president, has been in the business since 1983. Stan, 37, who has a degree in communications, worked with a government contractor for nine years before entering in 1995. "My parents' goals were unrealistic. How do you serve as equals in a family business? It depends on what you mean by equal. We're going through the process right now to figure out what the expectations are and what equal means, what each of us wants to contribute and how we want to be involved. Each of us has different wants and needs in the business and in our lives outside the business. And we all have different levels of knowledge and experience. We're trying to assess all that by working it out with a family business consultant," says Ann.

The MacDonald children understand why their father and mother planned the way they did. "My father came from a partnership that wasn't equal and that's what framed his mindset. He felt he was treated unfairly and that caused problems. He believed that if he swung in the opposite direction with us, there wouldn't be the same problems he faced. You can argue both ways. Ultimately, you cannot mandate either way. There have to be discussions and agreement," says Ann.

Another wrench in this arrangement is that at times it becomes two against one. Ann says that she and Art get along well because they think alike. "Also, Art and I have been working together for a long time. However, now that Stan's here, he adds another point of view. We are still learning about each other." It's also important, Ann has found, to keep each other informed. She says that information flow seems to be one of the biggest issues from a power standpoint.

Advice from Ann: "In an ideal world, everyone would be equal and get along perfectly well. However, the reality is that everyone in a family business needs to have a role, responsibilities and accountability defined specifically. I wish our parents had done that."•

You only need to hear anecdotes like this to gain a clear picture of why you and your company may be moving down the wrong path. If your goal is that every single family member work in or own your family's business, whether or not he wants to or is qualified, you're possibly in for a rude awakening and trouble. Alternatively, you may have assumed that some family members who happen to work in the business are qualified, while others are not or lack interest.

Try to paint a hypothetical picture of someone who wants to be a scientist, his goal in life is to do this, and he needs the necessary credentials. Obviously, the scientist would be out of place and unproductive in the family business, unless there is a need for someone with his skills and interests. In the same vein, you cannot suddenly motivate someone to work hard, particularly in a line of work they don't love or even like. You can't instill passion; it has to be there. The central concern is obvious: the successor might be a fish out of water who needs to splash around in a different pond.

The problem is that parents tend not to talk openly enough with their children, don't realistically assess their abilities and interests, and don't admit their deficiencies. Try to open your eyes to the potential hazards of what you're doing. Here are some positive alternatives:

- Find examples of successors in other family firms who have first gained experience outside the family firm. This will illustrate how that's been helpful and healthy for their transition into the family firm.
- Attend business and family business seminars so you can talk to others in the same boat.
- Read books, magazines and newsletters that are chock full of stories about succession successes and failures. Share appropriate examples with family members as a way to start conversation.
- Have a backup plan if your dream of working together as a family or other unrealistic expectations don't work out.
- Give any disgruntled family member who doesn't want to be at the firm some special projects to work on away from the rest of the family.
- Never turn your home into another office.
- Do something social and fun together as a family to build rapport. Don't let the business be a substitute for social time together or a chance to vanquish the guilt you may have because you didn't spend enough time with your children growing up.
- Attend trade shows together so your successor can see you in action and meet contacts, both of which may spark interest in your family business.
- Help the family member find his niche. Listen to what each member wants. Perhaps he really wants to meet with customers and attend major trade shows. Or maybe he wants to play a larger role in mapping the company's future and making major financial decisions. Perhaps he wants to be a supervisor of the warehouse. If the family member doesn't want to stay, let him off the hook graciously. Again, the key is communication.

Involve others in assessing your family members' abilities and performance. Your advisors can give tremendous insights into the skills and objectives of family members, while your board of independent directors can provide objective insight into working family members' abilities and shortfalls. You need to constantly readdress policies toward family members and assure that they are understood. Perhaps more important, you should be realistic in your expectations.

Reality Check: A parent's fantasy is that the family that works together stays together. Not always true. If your dream isn't the same as everyone else's, don't impose your ideas on them. Give family members autonomy to pursue their own dreams, not yours. A son or daughter who is unmotivated and unqualified probably cannot be taught motivation. If the successor isn't made of the right stuff to run your firm, accept that fact and allow him to take a different role where he's comfortable and happy, even if it's outside the family business. In fact, a parent's greatest reward should be happy and productive children who successfully follow their own dreams.

85. Can power struggles between siblings and other family factions create a bad business climate? How can such struggles be defused so they don't undermine the business?

The struggle between Terri Swain-Leaver, 36, and her half-brother was the apotheosis of what can ensue if siblings cannot get along in a family that works together. Terri, a CPA who had worked for one of the international accounting firms and subsequently for Colgate–Palmolive Corp. in New York as a financial analyst, went into her family's 103-year-old business serendipitously. She took a leave from Colgate in 1994 to help out her half-sister, Vicki, 43, a New York attorney, who also owns a restaurant in the family's quaint and historic hometown, Cape May, N.J., an enclave of 4,500 residents year-round and 30,000 in the summer.

While working in the restaurant, Terri also started helping out in the family store, Swain's Hardware, a fourth-generation family firm founded by Terri's great-grandfather Charles A. Swain and his wife, Margaret. Terri's father Charles "Bud" Swain, 68, became dependent on Terri to relieve him of the day-to-day accounting and office duties. "I wanted to retire and spend more time with my (second) wife Eivor," he said. "I have been in the business 42 years. Terri is a CPA and I felt she was capable of doing all the finances and taxes." There was one glitch. Terri's half-brother, who came into the business in 1982, was less than thrilled to have his sister on board. He wanted to be the boss. "However, he didn't have the ability to run the office," says Bud. "He was more of a salesperson. He would write schedules for the employees and handle defective merchandise. Terri could handle the very complicated paperwork." Bud reasoned they could serve as co-managers.

However, tension between Terri and her half-brother was palpable. He wanted to run the show, says Terri. "Dad wanted me to interact with him more because as time went on I became involved in more areas my brother was responsible for. We tried to draft a business plan that would enable us to work together. It was difficult because I had different training and background than he did. I like to oversee a project from beginning to end. He didn't develop this style. Serving as co-managers was a disaster. We couldn't reach a meeting of minds. I suppose it was also the mindset of a man who is 10 years older than a sister coming in and taking over his turf. He didn't want it to look like I knew more than he did," Terri adds. Bud interjects. "I told them I wanted them to get together and decide, on their own, how to get along and who would do what: develop a plan—segregating responsibilities to effectively co-manage the daily operations without my assistance—and not to bother me." Apparently, this was a pipe dream.

Finally, Terri's half-brother requested incentive to leave the family business in order to pursue self-employment. A severance package was put together to accommodate his needs. "It wasn't hard to do because I felt like I tried for two years to help them get along. Also, we were part of the True-Value hardware buying co-op, now called Tru-Serve after the merger of hardware chains True Value and Service Star, whose members said we couldn't have two bosses running the business. I said, 'My kids can do it.' But they couldn't. For the sake of the business, I had to have one boss in charge." Bud says that if he had kept Terri's half-brother on staff, it would have ruined the operation. "You need strong family support to expand and succeed. There was too much friction between them. Some sided with him; others sided with Terri. There were too many bad feelings and lots of undertones among employees as well as those in the community. In a small town like this gossip and rumors can run rampant."

Bud's decision proved to be prescient in an industry where many independents are being squeezed out by superstores. Fortuitously, this has not been the case with Swain's which needed Terri's deft financial mind to run the 25-employee store. The store has maintained and improved its sales levels and margins with gross sales last year of $2.8 million. "We've become more efficient in the past few years and we've expanded. Most important of all, there's a lot less waste," Terri says.

A CEO and COO get together for a management meeting to discuss the introduction of a new product. Should they start to advertise and market the product? The CEO tells the COO to put the project on hold. There's no money in the budget. The COO is disgusted. Every time he needs to make a decision he needs an okay from his superior. Sounds typical, right? However, in this case, the COO tends to take the "no" personally. That's because the CEO is his sibling.

Their main common bond is a desire to grow the company. They know they must be honest and communicate to reach a consensus on issues. But their honesty with each other is clouded by their years of sibling rivalry and competitiveness. Their father unwittingly created an even worse situation. He put them in their positions in the firm before he passed away, and now they are pitted directly against each other in making management decisions, with one sibling having power over the other. The possibility of a big blow-up seems a matter of time. The fallout may result in business problems, low morale among employees and other family members, and the need for one to leave.

Sometimes when two siblings work together, their leadership styles and philosophies never gel. Both may be intense, but in different ways. One may need his independence and be unable to take orders from the other, especially a younger sibling. Said one older sibling who works with his younger sister, "I am independent, and I like to have things done my way. Perhaps as the eldest child, I'm used to getting my way."

Sometimes sibling rivalry can be friendly and sometimes it becomes ugly. Perhaps the siblings compete; they cross the same turf—both manage the same types of accounts and present similar sales pitches to the same clients. Perhaps they don't go head-to-head on a personal level, but they battle for the same business or accounts.

Here's how some companies have helped siblings to work together in a healthy way, while giving each enough autonomy to reduce the risk of conflict:

- Create two separate divisions. Allow each sibling substantial authority over his respective division's operations.
- Give each sibling responsibility over a different location, possibly in different cities or states. If they have to work together, perhaps they only need to do so on an administrative level. For example, cousins Barry and Matthew Forman each run one of their family-owned wine and liquor wholesale distributorships. One branch

is in Washington D.C., and the other in Virginia. They share administrative and technical services staff and resources.

- Segregate responsibilities based upon individual talents. Figure out a niche for each. One may excel at customer relations and work in sales, while another has organizational talents best suited to managing warehouse operations.

As your children progress with the firm, their roles undoubtedly must overlap more and more. The child running purchasing must interface with a sibling in charge of sales, or the whole operation gets hurt by products not meeting the demands of the marketplace. Perhaps they will develop greater maturity as they get older. Regardless, it will be important to create mechanisms for enhancing communication and resolving disputes. A board of independent directors, plus meaningful involvement of nonfamily key managers, can be instrumental.

In addition, you should begin developing policies to deal with issues that may arise in the future. For example, your guidance in developing policies concerning appropriate levels of investment versus dividend payouts, family employment, compensation and evaluation standards, and the like, can help avoid or deal with future disagreements.

Ultimately, siblings and other family members working in the business must be able to put rivalries and disagreements behind them. If they can't, there must be mechanisms in place, like buy–sell agreements, to allow them to separate gracefully and fairly.

Reality Check: Siblings who grow up without too much rivalry and have a history of getting along can probably work together in the family firm, but it's rarely a great idea to have one working for the other. If there had been rivalry growing up, you should expect it to intensify if they work together. The best solution, if you are unable to choose which sibling to name as successor, is to divide the turf. Best case: separate them geographically, and if not, at least by divisions. Institute mechanisms, like a board of independent directors, to help resolve disagreements and instill professionalism into the relationship. Create ground rules for a friendly "divorce" if future business pressures and disagreements make it impossible for them to work together. Make sure that they understand that they must agree to separate before they let a bad relationship destroy the business and family.

86. How do you handle theft or substance abuse in a family business?

It's no fun being backed up against the wall, but that's how Jane and Larry (not their real names), co-owners of a retail shoe franchise, felt when they agreed to enter Larry's family's firm. The couple came in when the operations manager became ill. All of Larry's brothers had worked in the store on and off, but no one wanted anything to do with the business on a full-time basis. Jane and Larry were between jobs and agreed to help. They came, they saw and they ended up staying.

When the franchise agreement was up, it was time to decide whether to liquidate, merge or keep the store in the family. Jane says her mother-in-law wanted to keep the business going. Seven years ago, Jane and Larry agreed to run it. They moved the shop to tonier quarters, brought in some imports they had seen in Italy and renamed the operation. Larry's father pumped some cash into the new store on the condition they employ Larry's older brother, Jim (not his real name), who they knew was incompetent. No one wanted to be responsible for him, so Jane and Larry took on the task of babysitting. "He'd sleep all day and party all night. He drank and took drugs. He'd come into work hung over and disheveled, which was unacceptable in a high-end retail shop. In addition, he made almost as much as Larry and for doing nothing," Jane said.

Jane and Larry didn't want to tattletale. They tried to reason with Jim. At the same time, the business encountered problems. The couple discovered that the company accountant hadn't paid the firm's property taxes so they faced an enormous tax liability. Adds Jane, "Here was this crisis and my brother-in-law was behaving inappropriately. He'd spend his paycheck before he'd get home and then claim my husband didn't pay him. For seven months he went on strike and refused to work. We were delighted, but I was *persona non grata* in the family. It was affecting my relationship with my husband. The business also became the family cookie jar. Family members would come in and help themselves to whatever they wanted. We became the policemen of the store. We struggled to pay bills and wanted to keep the inventory to sell."

The last straw, according to Jane, was the day Jim grabbed a bunch of checks out of the check box to pay for his honeymoon. Jane fired him, then had to deal with repercussions from the family. In retrospect, Jane says, she should never have agreed to let Jim work in the store in the first place. The good news is that the business is now thriving with better-quality inventory and only two family members in the firm—Jane and Larry. Others outside the company recognize its success. The business recently received a trade association award.

Business is stressful enough, but a family business with dishonest or drug-abusing family employees is simply intolerable. A spoiled heir waltzing into the business and contributing nothing but aggravation, while taking healthy paychecks and perks, is a disaster in the making.

Some family members may turn to alcohol or drugs to mask anger, frustration, insecurity and other uncomfortable feelings. They may steal or commit other illegal acts. They may feel underutilized, underpaid, discounted and pushed around. Each family member may be so caught up in his own needs, that listening, communication, love and healing are tossed out the window. This is when managing a family business may become unbearable.

The head of one family firm was the sixth oldest of eight children, five of whom were in the family business. He did a phenomenal job running the firm. He tripled revenues in five years, dramatically increased profits and acquired a competitor in a shrewd deal. Unfortunately, he was an alcoholic. While going through a nasty divorce, he developed other substance abuse problems in addition to his drinking. It began to show in his behavior at the office. The other family owners intervened, quickly taking their brother out of his role and doing everything in their power to get him help. They read him the riot act: Dry out or don't come back. He went to drug rehab, but escaped from the program. The family business board, comprised only of family, voted him out of the firm. They put another family member in charge who didn't want to be president, wished his younger brother would get back on his feet and return to the company. The rest of the family agreed that they'd take back the errant sibling as soon as he cleaned up his act and was willing to earn back his position.

Every family should determine in advance how it would handle any fraud, substance abuse or other undesirable behavior by family members. Should the family fire the offender, ostracize him from family events, turn him in to the police? Will a second chance be given to a family member when it would not be provided to a nonfamily employee? In one manufacturing business, the eldest brother was found taking products from the warehouse, reselling them and making money on the side. Ultimately, he got caught and was fired on the spot. The family didn't press charges, but insisted they be able to buy out his shares. Why had he been so dishonest? He said that he had lost his motivation to work in the firm and wanted out.

What can a family do to avoid such problems in the first place and maintain family relationships? Experts suggest that every family create an environment of nurturing, caring and competence to encourage talking, responsibility and commitment to the business. Avoid trouble before it begins. Don't feel obliged to hire incompetent relatives who may be potential troublemakers and don't settle for an in-law or sibling who isn't willing to work his share. No other business would hire an inept or dishonest employee. Why should you? You can take some of the sting out of a refusal to hire unqualified family members if you have stated rules requiring minimum qualifications for employment.

In addition, set rules for what will and won't be tolerated as an employee of the family business and enforce them. Create a clear understanding about rules for business loans, personal use of company products and supplies, using company credit cards, making long-distance calls and using other company resources. Ideally, unless these benefits are provided to nonfamily employees, they should be prohibited for family employees.

Decide the punishment in light of the crime. If the person is taking monies from petty cash, you can make them aware you're cognizant of their behavior and watch their reports more carefully. If the person is repeatedly making two-hour calls to a foreign country, a form of stealing, point out that the calls are being made on company time and are costing the business. If, however, they're falsifying records or checks and taking kickbacks, there should be no second chance. Some families may want to keep embezzlement quiet and remove the responsible family employee. Others may offer the person a second chance. But the latter course can prove disastrous. It creates a terrible precedent. Accepting such behavior sends a bad signal to other employees and could lead to poor morale companywide.

If a family member is abusing drugs or stealing, consult a professional psychologist or other advisor who is experienced with these problems. Counseling may be necessary for the offender and for other family members. However, if you are unable to get the offender to face up to and deal with the problem, even with the help of a professional, then the best answer is to fire him. Sometimes the best love is tough love.

Reality Check: If you're considering bringing a family member into your business, make sure you have policies regarding rules of behavior, payment, expenses, vacations, benefits and perks. If you know a family member has a substance abuse problem, is incompetent or a troublemaker, don't assume he'll change or that he'll suddenly become a rocket scientist when he enters the business. Furthermore, he'll probably never win your trust. You must be able to count on family to be hard-working and honest. Personal problems cannot be allowed to interfere. If you already have a troublesome family member working in the business, it's even tougher. Don't hide from the issue, because it likely won't get better on its own. Seek professional help and strongly encourage the offending family member to address the issue. Don't just tolerate the status quo. If the offense is severe, the punishment must be as well.

CHAPTER XI

WAYS TO STRENGTHEN YOUR FAMILY BUSINESS AND ITS CULTURE:

Seminars, Consultants, Boards, Councils and Retreats

87. You need outside help, but where do you turn?

Challenger, Gray & Christmas is one of the country's leading outplacement firms, routinely quoted in business publications to get a pulse on hiring trends. Founded by James Challenger, 70, the Chicago-based company has resisted setting up a board of outside advisors for several very typical reasons: to do so would be an intrusion into the privately held family business, might take away control from family members and would cost money. Yet second-generation executive vice president John, 43, says he and his younger brother and brother-in-law, who are all active in the firm, might do so when they take over the business some day. "Family businesses go through different stages, and we're beginning to bridge the gulf between the first and second stages," John said. "When we're in the second generation, we very well might need some neutral, equitable sources to help resolve issues where family and business systems do not coincide and the values are different. That's where outside directors and advisors might prove helpful." For now, however, the family remains steadfast in retaining and managing exclusive control.

You're tired of flying solo. It's easy to feel intimidated if you're a family business owner who's alone at the top. It can seem as if all the other businesses out there must know more about what they're doing than you. Even informed or educated business owners may be guessing about the answers to tough business issues and how to position themselves strategically in a complex world. You need the assistance of someone who knows more than you do. It doesn't matter how well educated you are, how many books you read, how many courses you take, what branch of accounting or law you've specialized in or how many companies you've observed. Sometimes, the first-time entrepreneur simply needs to get hit on the head before he'll seek advice and counsel from the people best qualified to give it.

If you read or attend meetings or seminars having to do with family business, you find that there are many different types and groups of people available to you. The terminology is confusing and the differing roles of these people and groups may seem unclear. Here's the scoop.

ADVISORS

Most business owners are familiar with advisors. Advisors are professionals in their respective fields who earn their living by, yes, giving advice. Lawyers, accountants, insurance brokers and bankers are obvious examples. Advisors often have specialties within their professions. For example, not all accountants or lawyers are particularly familiar with the tax law. Those who are familiar with the tax law may not be particularly experienced in estate tax planning. So, you need to be careful to pick advisors whose knowledge and experience meet your company's and family's specific needs.

The best use of advisors is to periodically bring them together as a group or a "council of advisors." Sometimes, people refer to a council of advisors as a "board of advisors," but that confuses this group with the board of directors. If you bring the best advisors together, tell them the same facts, and let them combine their expertise, they will craft the best solutions for you. The idea is that you will get better advice, whether about a specific issue or just looking for opportunities.

DIRECTORS

Another potential source of assistance is your "board of directors." Most states' corporate laws require this body, yet most family businesses ignore it by electing family members, employees and advisors who never meet. Shareholders should seriously consider electing independent people to the board of directors. If you do so, you have created a "board of independent directors," which often is called a "board of outside directors" or an "outside board." We prefer the use of the term "independent" because it is more descriptive of the characteristics and role, while "outsider" sounds unnecessarily threatening and even strange.

The qualities and roles of independent directors are different from those of your professional advisors. Independent directors do not serve in that capacity as a profession or to put food on their tables. They should lack any real or perceived conflict of interest. They should have been successful in the business world and have actually made and lived with the results of major decisions, unlike advisors who only give advice and then leave the decision to someone else. Properly chosen and used, a board of independent directors can provide assurance to the shareholders that the business is being run in the interests of all owners. It also can provide a tremendous source of confidence and inspiration to company management as it tackles thorny challenges.

ADVISORY BOARD

Some consultants use the term "advisory board," although such a group typically would not have professional advisors as members. Instead, common parlance says that an advisory board is a group of people who act like a board of directors, but lack legal authority. They are informally appointed, not elected by the shareholders and therefore lack any legal standing under corporate law. Business owners typically choose to create an advisory board rather than a legally elected board of directors because:

- They lack the necessary commitment to submit themselves to the review of a true board of independent directors;
- They are unable to get shareholder approval to elect "outsiders" to the board but still want to avail themselves of many advantages that arise from the involvement of independent people; or
- They or the directors are uncomfortable with the legal liability exposure inherent in serving on the legal board.

A good executive is only as good as the people around him, some wise person once said. You'll never survive if you're narrow minded in how you view your company. Family business owners potentially have tremendous resources available to them to help resolve their unique issues. It's up to you to make the effort to find, create and use them properly.

Reality Check: You may be very smart about running your business every day, but you, your family members and closest advisors may have become a bit narrow in your thinking. You need some fresh expertise and a different mode for getting advice and analyzing tough issues. Once you understand the differences between advisors and directors and explore how to use them, you'll be amazed at how they can help you and your business.

88. How do you find the best family business consultant for what you think your family business needs, even if you aren't facing a crisis?

Azteca Foods Inc. in Chicago has undergone several incarnations. Founded in 1970, it is finally once again 100-percent family owned by founders Art and Joanne Velasquez. Art is chairman, president and CEO. Joanne is vice president.

The couple had sold the Mexican food producer, which now does about $30 million a year in revenue, to Pillsbury in 1984. Five years later, they and a partner bought it back. In 1996, the couple bought out the partner. With more family members, including children, their spouses and Joanne's brother in the business, the founders are determined to do all they can to help the business grow and succeed now and after the next generation takes over. Many of the family members have taken courses and participated in seminars at Loyola University Family Business Center in Chicago, and the couple is seeking two advisors. One would counsel family and nonfamily on organizational development issues such as improving teamwork, communications and managerial skills, and the other would help with more personal family issues. "We're considering people we've met through Loyola and asking friends in other family businesses," says Art.

It's far better to consult with an advisor before a crisis, sometimes simply as a way to test the pulse of your business, the relationships among family members and your family's support of your business' strategies. If you care about your health, you visit a doctor at least once a year for a check-up, even if you're not ill. If you become ill, you go more often. The same should hold true for a family business. It may need an outsider's periodic review to check its health. If problems arise, it may need more frequent attention.

How do you find the right family business consultant for you and your family? What characteristics should you look for in an advisor who can play a crucial role in accomplishing your dream of maintaining a successful family-owned business? How do you distinguish between a charlatan, a well-intentioned incompetent and someone who can help you accomplish your objectives?

There's no sure-fire way. However, there are a number of things you can do to increase your odds of finding the best consultant. First, don't assume that a person is competent simply because he is active on the speaking circuit or is quoted from time-to-time in the press. Frankly, good public speaking skills and the patience to court reporters do not an expert make.

Determine whether your family's issues are purely personal (e.g., drug problems, long-term interpersonal relationship problems), purely business (e.g., cash flow, tax, competitive problems, legal), or a blend of family and business issues. That may give you a clue as to whether you need a psychologist at one extreme or a lawyer or accountant at the other.

If your issues fall in that middle area where family and business overlap, you need special help. Before you settle on a specific person or firm, try to zero in on your family and business goals. Many consultants purport to be family business advisors, but they have a diverse range of qualifications and experience. There are lawyers and accountants, who may focus primarily on the financial or legal aspects of family business ownership; psychologists, who work on the family and relationship challenges; mediators, who are trained in dispute resolution; academics, who may not bring practical experience to the situation but have a good general perspective; insurance salesmen, who may care about and understand your issues, but believe their product is the way to solve all problems; and numerous others.

Look for integrity, multidisciplinary competence, experience, compassion, empathy and independence. Ask tough questions. Are they selling something else, like another product or service? Might they have a vested interest in whether you take their advice? Do they have practical experience, or have they recently hung out their family business consultant shingle to supplement their primary occupation?

Family and business issues intertwine, and resolving them requires assistance from someone who understands both. The best advisors are knowledgeable in family and business dynamics. Many advisors work in tandem with colleagues for an interdisciplinary approach, whether they work in the same office or refer clients to someone else when the need demands. Some family members may resist this approach out of fear that the more advisors they tap the longer the process to get help will be, the larger the bill and the less chance of confidentiality. Although interdisciplinary teams can work, and your family business consultant must collaborate with your other advisors, be skeptical when a consultant insists that you engage multiple professionals. Don't compensate for one consultant's deficiencies by hiring others.

You should also ask other family business owners for recommendations. Ask your accountant, lawyer or other trusted advisors for recommendations. As previously stated, don't hire someone simply because they are often quoted in the press. You should find someone whose views and principles are appropriate for your family. Their written and spoken thoughts provide some evidence to assess their appropriateness, if not their skills. In addition, as you interview candidates, ask them for their recommendations about alternative consultants. The best advisors in any profession tend to know each other due to professional relationships, common clients and the like. If one or two names often pop up in your searches, you should check them more closely.

Also ask yourself whether you want a facilitator or an active advisor. Some facilitators view their primary role as a conductor, meaning that everyone gets an equal chance to speak and that no one jumps over the table and hits someone else. That accomplished, the meeting is deemed successful whether or not the conclusion makes good business or family sense. The best advisors go a step further. They provide active guidance based upon their training and experience. They try to motivate family members and others to accept the advice they give.

After identifying several candidates, call each one. Describe your issues and ask how the candidate proposes to proceed with your situation. Does he want to meet with family members individually or together? Who does he think is relevant to the issue and is he right? What you want to determine in this initial discussion is whether the person appears to be especially perceptive about your specific family and business.

Ultimately, the chemistry that the advisor can build with you, your family, key managers and others will be critical to successfully helping your business and family succeed and prosper. Your entire family leadership should agree on the choice, which is sometimes easier said than done.

If one or more members represent stumbling blocks in the decision process, get together as a family and, without pointing fingers, find out why anybody resists the choice that everyone else favors. Perhaps some family members are nervous about sharing personal family history and inside business information. Those are legitimate concerns. Take that sensitivity back to your potential advisor and ask what safeguards can be offered regarding confidentiality. If the concern relates more to the consultant's experience, ask the consultant for references, types of issues on which he or she has advised and the outcomes, whether considered successful or not.

Once you have made a decision, see if the chemistry gels between your family members and the advisor. In general, sharing your problems, dreams and goals can help your family deal with specific issues and long-term strategies. It can uncover underlying issues you may not know existed and, if you choose the right family business consultant for your family, doing so can help create and preserve long-term business success and family harmony. You may be able to determine that over the phone, but an initial meeting likely will be necessary for that purpose.

Reality Check: A growing legion of consultants from many different disciplines is available to help address your family and business issues. Check recommendations carefully and ask a sufficient number of questions in advance—how they work, charge, follow up. Confer with family members so everybody's in agreement on the choice, which will spur cooperation. If you don't think you're getting sound advice or results after your sessions, speak up and try someone else. You're allowed a second opinion.

89. How do you find and select a family business forum or other organization? What are the right questions to ask and what should you expect? If you don't have the money for these types of groups, are there other options?

Although, The Cleveland Group Inc. in Atlanta, Ga., had survived into its fourth generation, president James R. Cleveland Jr., 60, a third-generation member, was concerned. At one time, the company, which originally offered electric motor repairs and later added distribution and electrical and mechanical construction, had 25 family stockholders. Twenty of these did not work in the business. James came into the business in 1963 after serving in the Navy. He believed that for the business founded by his grandfather to continue the active members needed to buy out the others. Those remaining in the business needed to professionalize operations.

How would he convince other relatives of what he felt was necessary? A mailer about a forum from a well-respected family business consultant caught his eye. He asked colleagues who had attended whether it was useful. The answer was yes. He consequently joined the forum, which included participants from other family businesses and the presence of the consultant as facilitator. The meetings were similar to group therapy. Typically, a member gave a presentation of his or her real-life problem or issue with the understanding that the information was to remain confidential. "Right away you understand you are not alone in the issues you deal with, and you hear good and bad solutions, some of which are helpful. Everybody asks a lot of questions. Nobody does any criticizing," says James.

After being suitably impressed with what he was taking away from the sessions, he convinced his elders to attend a single meeting. They were also pleased and with their blessing the family hired a consultant. The subsequent changes the family made at the company have been significant and productive. The company sold its motor repair business which required large fixed assets. It instituted rules that require family members now joining to first work elsewhere. Two senior members retired, as did one older third-generation member.

One big remaining task: the remaining active family in the fourth generation needs to name a successor. "I don't think that it's necessary at this time," says James. "There are five very capable fourth-generation members. They get along well. Each has different talents, and I hope they can decide and tell me some day who will be the next president."

James no longer attends the sessions of a forum. "Over a period of several years, the stories may have had a different twist, but the issues were basically the same and became a bit repetitious. I found them very helpful, but it was time to stop." The company, which employs between 700 and 800, does about $150 million in annual revenues. It now seems destined for a long, healthy future.

Family business forums offer an ideal way for family business members to exchange ideas and learn about issues and solutions in a controlled, non-threatening setting. There are close to 100 organized forums throughout the United States, with increasing numbers in countries around the world. Chances are there is one near you.

The typical forum is a membership organization led by a university professor or other professional with substantial interest in family business issues. The leader signs up sponsors, usually an accounting firm, law firm, insurance company and/or bank, that provide core financial support and expertise. The leader and sponsors seek family businesses to join, with membership fees ranging from a few hundred dollars to $2,000 or so per business.

The leader and sponsors develop the program, which typically consists of periodic meetings and seminars, each with speakers covering a variety of family business-related topics from estate tax planning to team building to strategy development. Speakers often come from the sponsor firms and there is a "speakers' circuit" of out-of-town experts who probably will be brought in periodically. Some forums publish quarterly newsletters or coordinate additional programs.

The university professor (or other leader) and the sponsors also are usually available for personalized consulting or other services for additional fees. Some programs, like LEADS—Learning Environments for the Assessment and Development of Systems—sponsored by Wharton's Family-Controlled Corporation Program, perform leading-edge research and provide personalized feedback, specifically designed to create new methods to improve family business performance.

The primary advantage of these forums lies in the meetings and seminars. They offer an invaluable opportunity for family members to discuss touchy issues in a "safe" environment, according to Sharon Nelton, editor of the former *Nation's Business* magazine. In such settings, trained professionals can help family business members really understand one another and avoid the usual family patterns that may lead to anger and frustration, notes Nelton. In such intimate gatherings, founders can complain about their children, children can vent frustrations about Mom and Dad, and everyone can trade war stories, which can help turn their family businesses into happy, healthy ones. You gain an opportunity to hear how other families have dealt with issues and profit from both their successes and failures.

Some of the longest-running university-based programs are associated with Loyola University-Chicago; Kennesaw State University's Family Business Forum in Marietta, Ga.; the University of Pennsylvania's Wharton Family-Controlled Corporation Program in Philadelphia; Oregon State University's Family Business Program in Corvallis; Baylor University's Family Business Institute in Waco, Tex.;

the University of Cincinnati's Goering Center for Family and Private Business; and the George Rothman Institute of Entrepreneurial Studies at Fairleigh Dickinson University in Madison, N.J.

You can locate a forum near you by contacting the Arthur Andersen Center for Family Business at 800-924-2770 or consulting *The Directory*, edited by Randel S. Carlock and sponsored by MassMutual—The Blue Chip Company. The Boston-based Family Firm Institute (FFI), an interdisciplinary organization consisting primarily of advisors, offers a free directory of programs affiliated with universities and colleges. FFI also has a free directory of speakers and consultants in print and at its World Wide Web site (www.ffi.org). The listings are paid for by consultants, who include therapists, accountants, lawyers and others, so be sure to check them out on your own. For a written list call FFI at 617-789-4200 or write to it at 221 N. Beacon St., Boston, Ma. 02135.

If there's no university in your area and no existing forum, you can start one by gathering together entrepreneurs and family business members. You will need a facilitator who can serve as an executive director. This person must be an aggressive organizer with good administrative skills because getting a forum up and running and keeping it going are not easy. Perhaps a local college or university can be enlisted to provide assistance.

If a forum is unavailable, or you do not want to make a membership commitment, consider attending one of the recurring family business seminars. For example, the Arthur Andersen Center for Family Business offers twice a year its two-and-a-half day seminar "Managing Succession without Conflict," which was started by Dr. Léon A. Danco over 25 years ago. There also are numerous "one-shot" seminars, mostly offered by one or more professional advisory firms. Unfortunately, these seminars often are disguised sales pitches for the sponsoring firm's products or services. If the admission fee is free or cheap, you'll probably get what you pay for. However, you sometimes can pick up something useful from each, so attend but be wary.

No matter the program, you should seriously consider having all or as many family members attend as possible. It's critical that everyone hear the same information at the same time. The programs create a common understanding, which then forms the basis for additional constructive discussion within the family. It is extremely unlikely that a seminar and discussion led by dispassionate experts will create or increase rancor within the family. Quite the contrary, you'll most likely be pleasantly surprised how this type of activity can elevate the quality of the family's discussions.

Some accounting and law firms also provide symposia and seminars on business issues facing small and emerging companies. Trade associations are another resource for help and information.

Whichever route you take, some key questions to ask before you sign up, organize or participate in any program are:

- Will there be a limit on membership?
- What types and sizes of businesses will participate?
- How often will we meet?
- Where will we meet?
- How long will meetings last?
- How much will membership cost?
- Will there always be a leader and a pre-scheduled format?
- Will meetings address specific or general questions?
- Will the members have a say in the direction of the discussions?
- Should family members come alone or with relatives?

You should expect results and concrete help from family business forums, but don't expect dramatic change overnight. Maximize the advantage by scheduling follow-up family meetings to discuss and plan to use what you experience at the formal sessions. The most immediate advantages include understanding issues you should address, discovering others' experiences, learning up-to-date estate planning and compensation techniques, and finding that there are ways that you can talk about important issues openly and without hostility.

Reality Check: Family business forums and seminars offer an ideal, non-threatening way for family members to understand current and future issues, discuss concerns and seek resolutions. Through sharing experiences with other similarly situated families, and with guidance and input from professional advisors, you can start to address and eventually resolve many family and business issues.

90. What are the different types of company cultures that can exist in a family business and does it matter for family harmony and good business? What can you do to emphasize more the culture's good points and change its negative ones?

You may never have heard of Belfonte's ice cream; it has yet to invade the entire country and is limited mostly to western Missouri, parts of Kansas and Oklahoma. Compared with some companies in the ice cream industry, it's a pipsqueak. However, it's a $40 million family enterprise started by Sal Belfonte, now 64, president and CEO of Belfonte Dairy Foods Co. and Belfonte Ice Cream (started 12 years ago), both in Kansas City, Mo.

Belfonte started out as a milkman. He parlayed the values he learned in that profession—treating customers with respect and offering good service—into the dairy distribution business he started in 1967. Since its inception, the firm's culture has remained constant: to convey a "hometown" focus that puts quality before size. "We are very much customer-oriented," says Sal, who built the company to 170 employees. He's determined to continue this culture into the next generation with his sons, John, 40, heir-apparent; twins David and Henry, 36; and son-in-law Ernie Stewart, 41. One reason the founder believes he will be able to do so is that the 22-member closely knit family is still very much a part of what goes on in the business, even if they don't work in it any longer. Belfonte's wife and daughter were in the firm at one time. The family is often used as guinea pigs to taste-test, even though matriarch Lillian Belfonte has final say.

The reason the firm's culture has worked, Sal says, is because it doesn't have a bottom-line mentality. It's a friendly paternalistic culture. "I have passed this down to my children. All the children worked with me when they were young. John, the eldest, began when he was a senior in high school delivering milk to schools. And he got used to my way of working. I let all the children take over literally a little at a time by teaching them all I know, a little at a time. And they have picked up my habits. Our goal is still to do things better and work on making a better product," adds Sal.

Stable. Flexible. Determined. Secretive. Generous. Congenial. Paternalistic. Greedy. Any of these characteristics may mark the culture of your family business, just as any nonfamily business reflects different personalities. But there's a difference with family businesses because most are likely to reflect the values, traditions and ethnic roots of the founder, possibly for many generations. Long-time family businesses typically change operational styles over time, but still cling to core values that emanated from the founder and are viewed as contributing to both business and family success.

Different business cultures translate into different operations, specifically when it comes to setting goals, resolving conflicts, disclosing information, separating work and fun, and employing spouses, children and other relatives. Some put family first and business second. Family needs and objectives take priority. Family members defer to one another with great sensitivity to family issues and roles. Other families make business the Bible, with family needs playing second fiddle to what's viewed as important from a business standpoint.

Balance and acceptance probably are the keys to long-term family harmony and business success, regardless of whether you place business or family first. Logic suggests that a business that is run to cater to family financial, employment and other demands will fail. Conversely, a business operated without any regard for the interests of its owners runs the risk of alienating family members. Even with appropriate balance, a culture or operating philosophy that is not accepted by the family or those in leadership positions is unlikely to last very long.

Furthermore, the experience of the founding family and, in particular, the founder affects how the business handles the succession process. A founder who dedicated his life to the hard work of building a company often can't envision giving up control or allowing someone other than a relative to run the business when he's gone. That perspective may change when second-generation owners reflect on their difficult succession experiences and pledge not to put their children through the same ordeal.

However, as the business grows and is handed down to the next generation and as new leaders add their influences, the culture of the founding family may become diluted. Preserving it becomes more difficult. Perhaps the founders felt any family member who wanted to come into the business should be allowed to do so. Compare that with a third-generation business run by successors with substantial credentials, job experience at other companies and little contact with one another growing up because they're cousins. These cousins may want only qualified family members to work in the business. They may question whether the business can survive for all family members or whether it should be sold, merged or taken public. They may want to take their equity out—and fast.

There are ways for business founders and leaders to perpetuate the linkage between family values and business culture, according to the *Family Business Advisor* newsletter. First, your children need to be brought into the business and groomed for possible successor roles while you're active. Your successors must observe you and pick up your values by seeing and listening. You should even go so far as to explain what you're doing, saying, "This is the way we do things," and explain why. Working alongside, you can also help instill a deeper feeling for the family and help the younger members understand what makes the business culture tick, from the leader's decisions all the way down to the custodial staff.

Here are some additional tactics suggested by the *Family Business Advisor* newsletter:

- Conduct new employee orientation sessions and management training programs.
- Visit all your business locations either on Founder's Day or some other significant day.
- Create a display or write a company history using old photos that document leadership, traditions and customers.
- Enable younger family members to tour or work summers at the company.
- Encourage family members to attend board meetings or strategy sessions as observers, which helps them understand the business and meet other family and nonfamily employees.
- Sponsor an award honoring employee excellence relating to the family's values.
- Ask the family to make an annual charitable gift in honor of employees demonstrating strong commitment to family values.
- Invite all extended family to attend ceremonies and important company events.
- Hold an annual meeting involving family and the board and/or executive management to share stories of family values that make a difference in the business' success.
- Communicate directly and openly and try to gain a consensus among younger family members, while building understanding and acceptance of members' differing philosophies.

Eliminating negative family values requires possibly even more work and sometimes the need to bring in outside experts, especially if there are signs of substance abuse or fraud. It's tough to change negative cultural values like members' beliefs that they are entitled to employment, unreasonable compensation and inappropriate perks. Education and frank discussion are required to change years of wrong signals sent by those who established the culture in the first place. You must explain the consequences of poor choices or exorbitantly costly decisions as well as the benefits of professional management, capital accumulation and a strong bottom line. Family members who don't understand the demands and needs of a business cannot be good owners and managers. Unfortunately, if negative cultures and values are too ingrained, it may take a crisis to alter mindsets and facilitate change.

Senior-generation family members need to understand that successive generations will add their own imprint and make changes to the company culture. That's crucial to helping a business evolve positively and change with the times. Keeping things totally static will hinder progress in a constantly changing business world.

Reality Check: A family business' culture is usually obvious in the fledgling stages, but the culture tends to get diluted as new family members and employees come on board. A healthy culture means one that encourages family members to do their best, while supporting them and being stewards of the business. You reinforce a healthy culture by introducing younger family members to the business, encouraging constructive involvement and constantly explaining the values that contributed to the business' success. An unhealthy culture can exhibit numerous traits—secrecy, fraud, dishonesty, and substance abuse. You can change these negative traits through education, communication and, perhaps, by bringing in outside experts. But it takes hard work and years to change.

91. How do you get management and employees to buy into your culture? How do you also market that culture to attract employees and customers plus impress others in the industry?

Just when you thought that all large companies were big impersonal monoliths with a performance-based mantra and a bottom-line culture, along comes SC Johnson, a true anomaly among large businesses. For 112 years, this giant company in Racine, Wi., has been owned and managed by the

Johnson family, which now includes fourth-generation member and chairman Sam Johnson and three of his four children: Curt Johnson, chairman of its institutional products business; Fisk Johnson, president of its consumer products business throughout Asia–Pacific and India; and Helen Johnson-Leipold, vice president overseeing marketing for the North American consumer products business.

Two prime reasons account for the company's longevity, determination to remain private and its financial success, reflected in its annual $5 billion in sales. It has adapted its innovative product line to suit changing times, and it has created a culture that may seem Jurassic compared to today's mega-merger mentality, but is one that cares deeply about its employees and the communities in which it operates.

Originally a firm that made parquet flooring, the company—which came to be known as SC Johnson & Son when founder Samuel Curtis Johnson and son, Herbert Fisk Johnson, Sr., entered the business—added a product to take care of floors when demand so warranted. Within 12 years of opening its doors, the consumers product side of the business led the company's sales. The change spurred company owners to change the name to SC Johnson Wax. In the 1950s, the company began to further diversify away from wood- and floor-care products and today is a leading global provider of household insecticides, air fresheners, home storage goods and bathroom, window and kitchen cleaning products as well. As a result of this shift, the fourth- and fifth-generation family members owning and running the 13,000-employee firm changed the name back to SC Johnson to reflect all its products rather than just wax.

But they also decided to add the tag line, "a family company." Part of the reason is to emphasize that the company is still owned and managed by family, says Cynthia Georgeson, director, corporate public affairs. "Family is the 'kind of glue' that brings everything together," according to chairman Johnson, who was quoted about the shift in a *Wall Street Journal* article. But another reason is the desire to communicate to consumers, employees and other stakeholders, such as neighbors in its various communities, that it remains committed to the core values that have represented its culture from its founding.

These core values are:

A COMMITMENT TO INNOVATION. Since 1935, the corporate headquarters has been a striking Frank Lloyd Wright-designed building, complete with interior Wright furnishings, which have been heralded by architects and management gurus as a "center of creativity." The company's recent track record in product innovation supports the designation. "Three of the top 10 most innovative consumer products named in 1997 came from the Johnson stable. That same year, three other SC Johnson products swept the American Marketing Association Edison Awards for innovation in the household products category," says Cynthia.

A COMMITMENT TO WORKPLACE EXCELLENCE. The company has pioneered important workplace concepts such as paid vacation since 1900, employee profit sharing since 1917, management pay cuts rather than staff downsizing back in the Depression, and healthcare benefits before they were commonplace. In recent years, the company has allowed telecommuting; brought in on-site banking and dry-cleaning services; established a company-subsidized concierge service to help employees meet personal commitments; and built a state-of-the-art childcare center which offers subsidized rates on a sliding scale so all staff can afford the center's services and programs. The company "pays fair," offers good benefits, and encourages employees to grow and learn new skills so they can keep improving their positions within the company.

A COMMITMENT TO COMMUNITIES AND THE ENVIRONMENT. The company strongly believes that a healthy community inside and outside the corporate structure goes hand-in-hand, and that the company has a responsibility to manage its operations soundly and to invest in strengthening the communities in which it operates. Since 1992, the company has eliminated over 420 million pounds of waste from its products and operations and saved over $125 million in the process. In the past 10 years, SC Johnson philanthropic investments have totaled over $66 million and focused on building the world's human, social and natural capital. The company champions sustainable community partnerships in half its host communities around the world.

Immediately after World War II, many servicemen returned from battle and started businesses as the economy refueled. As these firms grew and the entrepreneurs succeeded in accumulating wealth, many could afford to send their children to college and graduate school and eagerly encouraged them to pursue separate professional careers that bestowed prestige. Going into the family business was often considered an also-ran job for the inept, lazy or simply indecisive scion.

Fast-forward several decades, and with downsizing, global competition and small and large family businesses helping to propel the economy, many children are only too eager to join thriving concerns, particularly as parents retire or at least step back from full-time work. The firms that have moved successfully into second, third and sometimes even fourth generations offer another plus. They have come to connote stability, value and quality in the goods and services they offer.

Many owners have discovered the distinct advantage of using a family tie as a way to attract reluctant scions, as well as lure quality nonfamily employees and management. Sometimes, convincing nonfamily to join a family business requires good salesmanship, since rising to a top spot and earning equity are not always realistic possibilities. Even when those possibilities are available for the most talented and loyal nonfamily employees, smart family business owners know to develop a positive set of values over time that distinguishes their companies from more impersonal nonfamily conglomerates and even from other family businesses. These attributes help determine a company's "culture," and may be readily apparent to employees and their families and to customers, vendors and even industry observers.

A culture can reflect a positive or negative set of values and sometimes that's more a matter of perception than reality. For example, the idea of working in a company with a "collegial" or "paternalistic" culture may not appeal to a lone wolf looking to do business his way. For that person, a firm with an "entrepreneurial" or "competitive" culture may be more appealing. And for the employee looking for a place of employment where meritocracy rules rather than nepotism, a "professional" culture may be the smartest choice.

But exactly how do you develop and convey a culture? Quite often the business culture represents a continuum of the owner's family culture. Frequently, it's disseminated through a variety of tactics that reflect a way of relating to people, caring for family and nonfamily employees and clients, and conducting business.

To begin conveying your culture to the widest possible audience, compile the company's history to help explain the origins of its core beliefs and values. Your staff and others can view this history as the foundation of a deep-seated commitment to the company's values. Next, project these values and beliefs into the future in the form of a mission and values statement. Share these thoughts with everyone from your top nonfamily management down to your entry-level recruits. Put guiding principles in writing to demonstrate a seriousness of purpose. These principles can be distributed in a handbook, even enlarged, framed and posted in a lobby or "history corner."

PREPARING A COMPANY HISTORY

All the steps sound clear-cut and simple, but compiling a corporate history requires work, work and more work to unearth the nitty-gritty details. There is no canned approach, so basically you have carte blanche. But first things first. You must decide what you want, what approach to take, what purpose it will serve. Is the company history to be handed out to suppliers, clients and employees or is it to mark a special anniversary? What form do you want it in? What style of writing do you prefer (factual or narrative) and how do you want it presented?

To begin, you will need a strong sense of where you're going and how you're going to get there. Will the company history be organized chronologically? Most are. Will it be arranged in chapters profiling various personalities and aspects of the business over the years? Will the format be a typed manuscript to be put in a folder, a printed brochure, a softcover booklet or a hardcover book? What about art? Are there vintage company photos as well as current ones on file?

Once you've chosen the approach and format, you might compile a list of sources: where to gather information and whom to interview, such as retirees or current employees. Decide on the questions you'll need to ask. You might tape record these interviews or video tape them for posterity.

There are several good examples of company histories. *The International Directory of Company Histories* (St. James Press, 1988–1994) is recommended by the Boston Public Library Kirstein Business Branch. The 19-volume source includes two- to three-page histories on more than 2,000 public and private companies. The library also maintains a file of company histories clipped from newspapers and other periodicals. In addition, there are popular books in the business section of your local bookstore or library that profile companies such as *Barbarians at the Gate: The Fall of RJR Nabisco* (Harper & Row, 1990).

HOW DO YOU CONVEY YOUR COMPANY'S CULTURE?

When it comes to explaining the warm, fuzzy side of your culture, which every family business needs to do to give it a human dimension, you have an almost wide-open choice of strategies. The key is that the strategies should be consistent and reflect your interests and deepest beliefs, if they are to be maintained over time. For example, one owner proved his concern about his employees' well-being and financial success by buying houses for those unable to secure loans. He leased the houses with an option to buy at the prices he paid. Another owner eager to pat his employees on the back in a very public display took a full-page ad in a major daily newspaper to thank them for their contribution to the firm's success. He listed each employee, and he also went around the office, thanked them in person and organized a special dinner to recognize them.

Family-owned businesses can use similar approaches to show their vendors and suppliers, and to gain recognition within their industries. Don't hesitate to borrow ideas from nonfamily businesses. Zaca Mesa, a private wine company run by a nonfamily professional manager, holds a "Camp Zaca" weekend twice a year for its best-selling distributors. Those selected get to visit the gorgeous Santa Barbara, Ca., wine country, sleep in fancy tents on the grounds of the winery, eat gourmet food, mingle, discuss business and nonbusiness matters, participate in various recreational activities, explore other wineries and, of course, sip great wine. They also get to take home a Camp Zaca T-shirt and cap that help spread the word of a small winery, hoping to distinguish it from more than 100 California competitors.

Some companies promote their culture through their marketing materials, on TV or over the radio. Smucker's (known for its jams) stresses its more-than-100-year existence, as everyone knows who watches the "Today Show" or listens to National Public Radio. In addition to a company's longevity, marketing campaigns can play up how many generations have worked at the company; how many presently are employed; how many represent a second; third or fourth generation of nonfamily employees; what the key values are that have helped the company survive; and why it makes sense to do business with the firm, family members and employees.

The family firms that make the most convincing display of cultural values are those in which family owners roll up their sleeves and dig in on a daily basis. They come to work early, stay late, show up on weekends to boost morale, particularly if a special project is underway, don't take too much out of the company pot, hold fast to rules about job criteria, and become active in some way in their community, city or state.

Christopher G. Kennedy, executive vice president of The Merchandise Mart in Chicago, the largest building after the Pentagon and the center of the Midwestern furniture trade, is one of the most dedicated Chicagoans when it comes to raising funds for the Greater Chicago Food Depository, a charity that provides food for the homeless. Kennedy, son of the late Robert, actively recruits volunteers for the annual drive. Despite his Kennedy pedigree, he often can be seen filling boxes with canned goods in the Mart's gigantic lobby. And even after the Mart was sold to Vornado Realty, Kennedy continues to work at the Chicago Food Depository keeping alive his commitment.

While developing a culture requires time and commitment, changing it demands harder work: a desire on the part of owners to recognize and alter shortcomings. Values are not easy to change. It can require tough action to rout out people, including family members, who display inappropriate characteristics. Nonfamily leadership may be required. Clear communication and consensus building will be critical to success. But, it can be done. Many find that doing so can be their most significant legacy.

Reality Check: What distinguishes one family business from another? Size, location, success in its niche, products, and services are the easy-to-spot variables. But, there is a secret ingredient that acts as the glue to keep a company and its employees, whether family or nonfamily, chugging along and maintaining its special ways of doing business. These intangibles are the company's values. Values explain why the company is in business and how it operates. Values and beliefs come together to create the culture of a company. A culture can be a powerful marketing tool for attracting customers, employees and suppliers. Forging a culture typically takes years, but changing one takes longer. However, the intangible values nurtured by a family business and woven into an enduring culture can create the greatest legacy—one that can be passed proudly from generation to generation.

92. There are many publications and newsletters related to family business. Which are the best?

Family business owners are notorious for not having the time to sit down and read lengthy tomes, even when they most need them. There are times, however, when advice can be highly useful. A sampling of books, magazines and newsletters follows, but you may find others more useful for your own situation. Look under the headings "family business," "small business" and "entrepreneurship" at a library or on the Internet.

Also, read about individual family businesses in general business publications such as *BusinessWeek, Fortune, Forbes, Inc.,* and *Money* magazines or *The Wall Street Journal* and in the business sections of your daily newspapers. Family business has become a hot topic, particularly when it concerns the juicy sagas of warring dynasties.

Of course, titillation is not the primary reason for reading about family business issues. The coverage in the popular press tends to focus on problems, which helps you to identify issues that may develop in the future and actions you can take to prevent them.

There's yet a deeper reason. If you read about an issue that your family faces or may face in the future, you can use the information in an article or book to help educate family members and to trigger discussions about the subject. Find an article or chapter of a book that addresses an issue that does not currently exist in your family, but could arise in the future. Route it to family members and ask them to read it in anticipation of an upcoming family meeting. Then, at the family meeting say, "I think that this article addresses something that may be important to us in the future and I want to discuss it to see what we can do to prevent the problem." Some lively discussion should ensue. Perhaps the family members will agree on a solution. At least they'll be better educated about the issue and more attuned to the potential problem if it arises.

Here are some excellent resources for your consideration:

NEWSLETTERS:

The Family Business Advisor, published monthly by Craig E. Aronoff and John L. Ward with the Arthur Andersen Center for Family Business, P.O. Box 4356, Marietta, Ga. 30061, 800-551-0633; 770-425-6673.

Family Money, published by JGB Associates, 1515 Fourth St., Suite B, Napa, Ca. 94559, 707-255-6254.

Legacies, published by Baylor University, The Institute for Family Business, P.O. Box 98011, Waco, Tx. 76798.

BOOKS:

Beyond Survival: A Business Owner's Guide for Success by Léon A. Danco (University Press, Inc., 1975, 1977, 1980, 1982).

Corporate Bloodlines: The Future of the Family Firm by Barbara B. Buchholz and Margaret Crane (Carol Publications, 1989).

Creating Effective Boards for Private Enterprises by John L. Ward (Business Owner Resources, 1997).

Cultural Changes in Family Firms by W. Gibb Dyer (Jossey–Bass, 1986).

Entrepreneurial Couples: Making It Work at Work and at Home by Kathy Marshack (Davies–Black Publishing, 1998).

Family Business Leadership Series booklets by Craig E. Aronoff and John L. Ward (Business Owner Resources):

- *Family Business Succession: The Final Test of Greatness*
- *Family Meetings: How to Build a Stronger Family and a Stronger Business*
- *How Families Work Together*
- *Family Business Compensation*
- *How to Choose and Use Advisors: Getting the Best Professional Family Business Advice*
- *Making Sibling Teams Work: The Next Generation*
- *Preparing Your Family Business for Strategic Change*
- *Another Kind of Hero: Preparing Successors for Leadership*
- *Financing Transitions: Managing Capital and Liquidity in the Family Business*
- *Family Business Governance: Maximizing Family and Business Potential*
- *Developing Family Business Policies: Your Guide to the Future*

Family Business Sourcebook II: A Guide for Families Who Own Businesses and the Professionals Who Serve Them, edited by Craig E. Aronoff, Joseph H. Astrachan and John L. Ward (Business Owner Resources, 1996).

From the Other Side of the Bed: A Woman Looks at Life in the Family Business by Katy Danco (University Press Inc., 1981).

Generation to Generation: Life Cycles of the Family Business by Kelin E. Gersick, John A. Davis, Marion McCollom Hampton and Ivan Lansberg (Harvard Business School Press, 1997).

Getting Along in Family Business: The Relationship Intelligence Handbook by Edwin A. Hoover and Colette Lombard Hoover (Routledge, 1999).

In Love and In Business by Sharon Nelton (John Wiley & Sons, 1986).

Inside the Family Business by Léon A. Danco (University Press, Inc., 1980).

Keeping the Family Business Healthy by John L. Ward (Business Owner Resources, 1997).

Megatrends for Women by Patricia Aburdene and John Naisbett (Random House, 1992).

Outside Directors in the Family-Owned Business by Léon A. Danco (University Press, Inc., 1981).

Passing the Torch by Mike Cohn (McGraw-Hill, 1992).

Smart Growth: Critical Choices for Business Continuity and Prosperity by Ernesto Poza (Jossey-Bass, 1989).

Someday It'll All Be . . . Who's? The Lighter Side of the Family Business compiled by Léon A. Danco and Donald J. Jonovic (The University Press and Jamieson Press, 1990).

Success and Survival in the Family Owned Business by Pat Alcorn (McGraw, 1983).

The Successful Family Business by Scott E. Friedman (Upstart Publishing Co., 1998).

Sustaining the Family Business by Marshall B. Paisner (Perseus Books, 1999).

Transforming Business Families by Gerald LeVan (Biltmore Press, 1996).

Your Family Business by Arthur Pine with Julie Houston (Poseidon Press, 1990).

There is also a growing list of family business books in foreign languages, including:

A La Sombra del Roble: La Empresa Privada Familiar y su Continuidad by Ernesto Poza (Editorial Universitaria para la Empresa Familiar, 1995, [in Spanish]).

La Empresa Familiar—por Dentro by Ernesto Poza, Léon Danco and Ross W. Nager (Editorial Universitaria para la Empresa Familiar, 1998, [in Spanish]).

L'Enterprise Familiale by Léon A. Danco and Ross W. Nager (The Center for Family Business, FBN/ASMEP, 1998, [in French]).

MAGAZINES:

Family Business magazine, a quarterly publication of The Family Business Publishing Co., P.O. Box 41966, Philadelphia, Pa. 19101, 215-405-6072.

The Family Business Review, a quarterly publication of the Family Firm Institute (FFI), 221 N. Beacon St., Boston, Ma. 02135, 617-789-4200.

You might consider buying the video produced by MassMutual and broadcast over Public Broadcast System that profiles three family businesses and illustrates a range of ways to tackle important issues. The video can be ordered by calling 860-987-3120.

Many accounting and law firms also provide booklets and books on estate tax planning and assorted business issues.

93. Are there any good computer programs?

A check of several computer stores produced no software that relates specifically to family business. There are software programs relating to starting a business and drafting business plans. Examples include:

- Biz Plan Builder, $89.99;
- Business Plan Pro, $94.99;
- The Small Business Start-Up, $24.99.

MassMutual–The Blue Chip Company offers a CD-ROM entitled, "A Matter of Time." It is an interactive piece in which family business members express their perspectives of various issues and suggestions are made to address them.

Perhaps the dearth of family business-related software suggests a golden opportunity for a family business entrepreneur.

94. Are there any good resources on the Internet? Do any chat rooms focus on family business?

America Online has a chat room that can be accessed by using the keyword "chat," clicking on "find a chat," clicking on "life" in the categories column, and finally clicking on "careers and family" in the featured chats column.

Sharon Nelton, the former editor of *Nation's Business* magazine and a director of the Family Firm Institute, recommends the following websites:

- www.arthurandersen.com/cfb is the Arthur Andersen Center for Family Business website and it contains a large amount of useful information.
- www.fbop.com is Family Business Owner Resources, which publishes *The Family Business Advisor* newsletter.

- www.luc.edu/depts/fbc is Loyola University Chicago Family Business Center.
- www.kennesaw.edu/fec is Kennesaw State University's Family Enterprise Center.
- www.fccp provides information on Wharton University's Family-Controlled Corporation Program.
- www.slu.edu/eweb is eWeb, an entrepreneurship-education site at St. Louis University.
- www.fambiz.com, a site operated by NetMarquee Inc. in Needham, Ma., offers links to some university family-business sites as well as useful information.
- www.familybusiness.orst.edu is the Austin Family Business Program at Oregon State University.
- wwwfbrinc.com is put together by the Family Business Roundtable, a consulting group in Phoenix, Az.

Sites and chat rooms come and go, so a little web surfing is advisable. You might find just what you need.

95. What is the purpose of a family business retreat?

After five generations of hard work growing what started as a modest one-brand car showroom, a Midwest car dealership had made a leap into the big leagues with several franchises and $1 billion in revenues. Its leadership wanted to celebrate in style with the entire family. What about a family business retreat to which all family shareholders and their spouses would be invited? More than 100 family shareholders of the fourth and fifth generations would be treated to festivities and information about company goals.

There were 15 family members active in the business, some in marketing and finance, and some serving as managers of subsidiaries. One family member in the fifth generation, who was almost 40, had been named the successor CEO. Succession was a hot topic, an issue that caught everyone's attention. Family members wanted to know how it would affect their stock, so they eagerly attended.

To impart information to the large family group all at once and in an orderly fashion, a facilitator was brought in to organize and run the retreat, held on two consecutive weekends in July. The family was encouraged to bring children. There were family meetings in the morning with speakers and a state-of-the-business address by the business' leader to bring the family up-to-date on the company. A good chunk of each day was spent educating the family about business and family issues. Breakout sessions were held after large forums to discuss specifics in greater detail. After lunch, there was an afternoon of swimming, boating, fishing, golf and tennis. On Saturday evening a large informal buffet dinner was held under the stars. By the end of the retreat, family members all felt good about each other and the firm. The retreat was so successful that the family set a date to hold one again the following summer.

To see the softer side of family business, hold a family business retreat. Think of the family business retreat as a focus group for you, the head of the company, where you are able to track and solicit what your family thinks about the business and your vision for the company. Large companies in the public sector may spend hundreds of thousands of dollars to track shareholders and analyze feedback. Family firms can get feedback from family stockholders much more easily and personally. The retreat is an opportunity to gain support today and set policy down the road.

This is not to say that you should use the retreat to settle significant issues. For example, if you are ambivalent about whom to appoint as a successor or your family is squabbling over dividends or how to sell shares of stock back to the company, these are issues that are best addressed in a family council meeting, not a retreat. You could use the retreat, however, as a time to announce key decisions that have been made over the course of the year and how they will affect the business in the future.

While retreats provide family members a chance to admire the newest grandchild or recount the latest wedding, they also provide owners an opportunity to zero in on the family's special requests, complaints and any other issues that bear consideration.

Large companies have been holding retreats for years. Now, more small and mid-size family companies are enlisting family feedback in this type of relaxed retreat setting.

A family business retreat serves two purposes. It can be a forum for open communication among all family members who need to hear a consistent message. It offers time to discuss family issues and improve communication among family members to avoid the rumors, misconceptions, misstatements of facts and selective disclosure of information that is all too common in family firms. One of the best ways to build trust and communication among family members at a retreat is to use a facilitator who will monitor events and customize the family business sessions around the family's concerns.

Retreats also offer a chance to spend time together to bond, enjoy each other's company, and do something for fun. It doesn't need to exclude play or work, but can combine them, though it's best to try to separate the two at any one session. For example, business meetings can be scheduled for the morning, with the afternoon reserved for leisure activities. Overall, it's a prime time to fine-tune your communication and to cement family loyalty, values, continuity and linkage. Everyone will feel good afterward.

HOW RETREATS ARE HELPFUL

Experts strongly endorse regular family retreats. They see them as especially important during periods of change in the business, which might mean a transition of management or control, new family members entering the firm, rapid growth, acquisitions or financial disclosures that sales are hurting.

The need for a family retreat is dependent upon whether any other formal means of communication exist within the family. If you have regular family meetings, a retreat may not be necessary except as a fun way to gather members or as an annual tradition. Also, the success and attendance depend somewhat on how close the family is geographically and emotionally.

If many family members don't live in proximity, family retreats are crucial because the only other time the family may get together is for important holidays, birthdays, anniversaries or funerals, which generally are not conducive to meaningful business discussions and social gatherings.

Retreats are also good for families that aren't close emotionally. Some families are connected and talk to each other frequently. Others don't stay in touch on a day-to-day or even monthly basis. In these cases, family retreats are a terrific way to socialize, find out what is new, who is who and renew relationships.

SETTING THE RETREAT AGENDA

The initial step in organizing a retreat is to determine its agenda. What is your ultimate goal in holding it? What needs to be discussed? What outcomes are desired? Are there decisions that must be made at the retreat? Who will lead the discussions? Encourage family involvement.

Let the family help with the planning. Divide members into teams by family branches, one to set it up, one to oversee the program, one to handle the details of the weekend, and one to organize the speakers and room arrangements.

WHO SHOULD ATTEND?

Next, decide who should attend—just adults or children as well. Generally it's best to bring the children and grandchildren, or to alternate every other year—one occasion adults only and the next, children and adults. For older children and young teens, have activities planned: trips to museums, water parks, or boating or skiing if near a lake or mountain. The children may be a distraction, but a retreat gives them a chance at a young age to acclimate themselves to the business and to other family members with whom they may ultimately share ownership or work in the future.

In-laws should be invited. They can be responsible for fueling a lot of the conflict in family business unless they are made to feel part of the family. Excluding them may breed more resentment. Also, the retreat enables in-laws to get information firsthand from family and business leaders. So often they tend to receive information in such a filtered fashion that it may cause conflict.

What about nonfamily employees or key managers? Nonfamily should be excluded. A family retreat is not the place to discuss the management or detailed operations of the business. However, it might be a good idea to have management make presentations to the family. The nonfamily managers should come, talk and leave.

You cannot summon people to a retreat. You cannot make it a requirement. It's almost always voluntary and usually very well-attended if people are interested, especially if it's planned well in advance and business is mixed with pleasure.

HOW MUCH SHOULD YOU SPEND?

Retreats can be as elaborate or as simple as you want. Much of the cost will be determined by how long the retreat lasts and its format. There's no need to spend a fortune on retreats, however. If the company is struggling, a less elaborate retreat—such as a full day and evening at a local hotel—makes sense.

When estimating the cost, include travel, lodging, food, entertainment such as golf, tennis or boating, a facilitator, speakers, and some souvenirs such as T-shirts or mugs with a family or business logo.

On average, a retreat may run from less than $500 for a picnic at a local park to more than $1,000 a person for a more elaborate event. Whatever the cost, don't make family members pay their way. You are inviting extended family to an event of importance to the long-term future of the family and business. Perhaps portions of the retreat can be justified as a business expense. In some cases, people might pay for their own travel arrangements, but you should pick up the costs of the hotel, meals and entertainment.

WHERE SHOULD IT BE HELD?

A retreat should be exactly that, an escape. In other words, it should be held anywhere but the office. It can be some place that is within driving distance to cut down on travel expenses. A nearby park or nice hotel will suffice. But it's mandatory that it be outside the office and probably some place where the family can go and spend the night versus just a day-long event.

Why should it be held out of the office? The key to the success of a retreat is to eliminate as many day-to-day distractions as possible. Plus, the critical informal social aspects of a family retreat typically can't be handled at the company's offices. If held at the local country club, you might run into people you don't have time, or desire, to see. If held in town, you might be tracked down by people who need you for whatever reason or family members may be tempted to leave early to drive their children to soccer practice or ballet. If you move the retreat to an outside location and people spend the night, you cut down on these interruptions and make it more difficult for participants to leave early.

HOW LONG SHOULD A RETREAT LAST?

Typically, a retreat lasts a full weekend. It could be from Friday evening through Sunday noon or some portion of that time span. Generally speaking, it should be no longer than two full days of time together as a family, which could be three half days with afternoons open or one full day with the second day open. Typically, retreats last most of a Saturday and some of a Sunday. Most people like them to end by noon Sunday so they can travel back home.

A very successful large West Coast firm in the fifth generation decided to throw an extravagant retreat for its entire family of more than 150 members in Aspen, Co., one year. Many family members flew there in private aircraft. Another year the family went to Orlando and met at Walt Disney World with their children. Three years before, the family chose La Costa, a resort in San Diego, Ca., in the winter. An annual retreat has become a family tradition, to mix the social along with a business agenda. This has ensured good attendance. But this is the high-end retreat.

For less extravagant retreats, consider starting in the morning and concluding in the evening. It could be held at a local restaurant that starts with business and concludes with dinner.

Is a retreat deductible? The IRS has fairly detailed guidelines with respect to what's deductible and what isn't. The key is having substantive business discussions with agendas and meeting specific IRS requirements. Generally speaking, you need at least half the time dedicated to business meetings to meet IRS guidelines. Check with your tax advisor.

Several good resources for hosting retreats and reunions are available from Reunion Research: the *Family Reunion Handbook* by Tom Ninkovich (Reunion Research, $14.95), the *Fun & Games for Family Gatherings* book by Adrienne Anderson (Reunion Research, $12.99), and *The Directory of Reunion Sites* (Reunion Research, $3). Write to Reunion Research, 40609 Auberry Rd., Auberry, Ca. 93602 or call 209-855-2101 for more information.

One family owner said he never imagined that his retreat would be so successful. He remarks, "A facilitator kept things balanced and running smoothly. Now we meet with family members every year to talk over problems and focus on the direction of the company. Never in my wildest dreams did I think everything would go this well."

Reality Check: A family retreat should be a time to educate or work and a time to play. It's held in an informal setting where family members can bond and communicate. To handle the flood of information, questions, complaints and accolades, have a facilitator help plan the event and record comments and the actions you will take in response. You might find out a little more than you want, but at least family members won't feel discounted and can voice their concerns and feelings. Retreats offer a savvy family a chance to learn more about the business and debate the issues. They can be especially helpful in quelling family members' concerns and stopping rumors if the business is experiencing changes or problems.

The retreat should be broken into two components: 1) meetings where the working owners can address all family shareholders so they hear the same information at the same time and 2) play time. A retreat can cost less than $500 to more than $1,000 a person. Since the senior generation or the company should pick up the tab, it's best to have it reflect the company's economic profile. Regardless of how it's done, the bottom line should not be the money, but the advantage of bringing together family members in a collegial environment to learn and have fun. A retreat, regardless of the length of time, becomes a bonding event. If it's planned well, it can become a fun and even eagerly anticipated annual family tradition.

96. Where do you find a good facilitator to run the retreat? What criteria do you use to judge a facilitator and what kind of experience should that facilitator have?

Many CEOs of family firms go out of their way to make peace in the family. Bill Sweasy is no exception. The CEO of Red Wing Shoe Co. in Red Wing, Mn., a manufacturer of shoes for the occupational market, makes sure all family members, whether inactive or active shareholders, are on the same track. To zero in on a serious family issue after his father's death in 1991, Sweasy organized a weekend retreat in the country. The family hired a facilitator. "It was someone I met at a business conference," he said. He liked the person's demeanor. "We had some difficult and specific concerns we were trying to resolve within the immediate family revolving around ownership and succession of Dad's estate, which I had to work out with my five sisters," says Sweasy.

Because family members may have such different points of view, you may need an objective referee or facilitator to keep discussions focused. The person must be willing to take control of family meetings so that gatherings don't degenerate and digress. The facilitator keeps the meetings on track; helps define objectives; sees that they are met; takes questions; and sets follow-up sessions so issues can be resolved, actions taken and goals achieved.

It's important to select the right person for the facilitator role. Some are skilled in making the meeting run properly, but are not particularly knowledgeable about the family's or business' specific issues. Others have expertise that can actually guide the family in the issues that the family or business faces. Some, but not all, family business consultants have the combination of interpersonal, business and tax skills to address succession planning, estate, strategic and/or personal financial plans. An organizational development specialist might work to build teamwork, improve communication and find ways to recharge the family.

So how do you find a facilitator who suits the personality of all family members and their and the business' agenda? Ask your personal advisors for suggestions, talk to other business owners, call your trade group and search the Internet. Referrals are often the best sources. Spend time talking with the candidates to determine if their personalities, qualifications and methodologies suit the family. You want someone you can trust, who is objective, asks good questions and leads discussions in the right direction to control debate of difficult issues and avert family fighting. Look for someone who has a good track record of conducting meetings and has worked with family firms to develop concrete solutions.

Ask about the consultant's approach to dealing with your family's issues. Some conduct family meetings only, while others take the time to meet individually with family members and others first so that they can develop a fuller understanding of personalities, issues and possible solutions. Ask about follow-up six months or a year after you meet.

Don't neglect asking about the potential costs up front. Some facilitators may work per day; others over a weekend or several days, and still others over a period of several months or even a year. Their fees will vary widely. Daily fees can range from $1,500 to $7,500 or more. To obtain a realistic estimate of costs and time required, you need to provide as detailed a list of problems and issues as possible. Honesty in this case is absolutely crucial.

Reality Check: The qualities of a family business facilitator should be objectivity, leadership, focus, interest and experience working with family firms. Word of mouth is a great way to find a facilitator. Many consulting firms also have advisors skilled at facilitating business meetings. Always get references, ask about the person's style of working, estimated costs, credentials and experience, results and follow-up.

CHAPTER XII

CHANGE: TAKING THE BUSINESS PUBLIC OR SELLING IT

97. Business is booming. Should the family sell the company? What will life be like after the sale?

Sell from a position of strength. That's exactly what the venerable $45-million a year Sam's Wine and Spirits Warehouse in Chicago, one of the top-grossing liquor and wine stores in the country and certainly one of the most well known, intended to do when it almost sold out recently to a large California-based chain. The chain has 19 stores and wanted to add Sam's to its roster, says Fred Rosen, 63, head of Sam's which was founded by his father Sam in 1942. "It looked like a good deal for us to stay in the business and grow with them. This would have meant opening more stores in Chicago."

Fred considered selling when Sam's was number one. "During the 1998 holiday season alone, we piled up $8 million in sales for the four week-period, a record. Business was up eight percent for the first four months of 1999, considering January was the first slow month we've ever had because of a Chicago snow storm," says the athletic and energetic owner.

The plan to sell the business had nothing to do with a lack of succession, for Fred's two sons are in the business. Darryl, 31, CFO, is a CPA with a master's degree in finance, and Brian, 28, general manager, has a degree in business administration. Darryl's twin sister does not work in the company. The move was designed to take advantage of economies of scale, says Rosen. "Also, I was interested in a good sale, because it's a cashing in for my family. I come from humble roots. This was a chance to solidify some financial gain for my children."

What would it have felt like under new ownership? Fred admits that it would have seemed strange receiving a paycheck from someone else. "But they were willing to pay me lots of money and offer a good future to my sons and me in addition to a five-year management contract for all of us."

Both companies went through the paces of selling; however, the deal went south. "They ran out of money. Plain and simple, their financing fell through. Talk is cheap. We thought it was a done deal. When it came time to bring the money, they said they needed an extension. It ended up that they talked with what they didn't have. They still want to do the deal and are still trying to raise the money. We deal on our word when we buy wine all over the world. I don't have to put up deposits and I haven't reneged on any deal in 40 years," Fred adds.

Is he disappointed? "Not at all. Our growth rate in our one store is comparable to opening one store a year anyway. We'd only merge with someone if the deal involved quality people. Otherwise we're content to stay here. We have so much fun in our one location. I don't ever want to change that," he says.

Stories abound about family businesses that have been sold or merged. It can be a painful separation experience. Business founders and owners tend to get emotionally involved with their businesses and employees. You may miss the structure, culture, routine of getting up every morning and heading for the place you built with people you enjoy. You may find you have an excess of high energy you don't know how to channel after years of being busy around the clock and running the show. If you stay on and work, the way of conducting business is bound to change. If you leave the firm, you should have something productive and rewarding with which to fill your time or you'll experience the equivalent of a postpartum depression.

For that reason, some owners position a sale to occur slowly over months or years. You can sell just a portion of the business, perhaps a minority piece, with the expectation of selling the rest five or six years later. You can reach an agreement for the continuation of some family members' employment, at least for a set period of time. Understandings can be created about the future direction of your firm and how current employees will be treated and retained.

Of course, changes undoubtedly must be made because the new ownership will expect a reasonably high rate of return on its investment and have its own ideas of ways to achieve its goals. Furthermore, some operating procedures will be changed. One owner said that once he decided to sell, going back to work was painful until the final closing. You may have to let people go or some may quit. Chances are the culture will change, too, from one that might have been paternalistic to an "earn-your-keep" mentality. Work will be different after the sale, so set your expectations accordingly.

Yet some owners look back on selling as a blessing to gain more time for hobbies, spouses, children, grandchildren and charitable work. Others like the idea of going on salary for the first time with others responsible for results, though they may find it strange punching a time clock, waiting for their weekly or monthly paycheck and not controlling the purse strings. A major downside may be giving up choice perks. In the worst cases, owners sell a thriving business, only to stand by and watch someone else mess up results or alter the culture.

Owners sell for various reasons. Sometimes in consolidating industries such as insurance and banking, new technologies and alliances change the rules and way of doing business. An independent company can be left out in the cold. Some sell because they have no capable successor and want to travel or change careers. Others need shareholder liquidity and find a sale to be the best way for them to get it.

The issue of whether to sell isn't whether the business is booming. Rather, the first question should be: What is the future of my business given foreseeable external and internal conditions? Are we profitable and growing or stagnating? Is our timing right? Is this the optimal time to sell the company given its stage of development and the market it's in? Do we have the leadership and resources necessary to take the business into the future? Will our shareholders accept the financial risk of the future's inevitable challenges, or will they insist on extracting excessive capital for other needs? Is our industry changing and can we change with it?

Historical activity is not as relevant or important as the potential for growth. Historical performance is important from a credibility standpoint and you need to have a good story. The key attraction to making a sale appealing now is whether you are a leading-edge player in your industry or have some unique aspect to your business that makes it particularly attractive to a potential buyer at this time. Other considerations include:

THE CYCLE OF YOUR INDUSTRY. Are you selling in an up cycle or did you wait too long and are you facing a downward trend?

THE STAGE OF YOUR INDUSTRY. Is it consolidating? The recent "roll-up" trend, where small companies are combined into a large public company, can create the ideal time to sell and a threat to those who don't do so and must compete with the resulting larger player. If your industry is mature, your business may not be in demand. Things might get worse from the standpoint of maximizing the sales price.

THE COMPATIBILITY OF THE TWO FIRMS—THE SELLER AND BUYER. Many deals don't get done because the egos of the people who run the companies get in the way.

THE POSITIONING OF THE COMPANY. It's important to position yourself so that you can sell the company when the time is right. You might need professional assistance in strengthening your financial position in the short term in order to maximize sales proceeds. For example, a Midwestern restaurant group wanted to sell or go public. If it could boost its value through increasing sales and profits, it could make more on the sale, which would probably be based upon multiples of earnings. But it was looking at a two-year time frame to accomplish the improvements. It could accomplish its objectives, but the market might not be as good at the time it was ready to let go. Two key issues are at stake: The seller must be prepared when it makes sense personally and when it makes sense from a market standpoint.

Reality Check: Whether to sell is like a poker game. The cards need to be in place to deal. The reasons to sell may be many and, contrary to what most may think, it's best to sell when the business is doing well and you're in a position of strength rather than weakness. It's important for you to position your firm before the sale to make it as attractive as possible. The buyer is not just looking at your company's history or credibility, but its potential, which is more important. Preparing your business and family for a sale, and for life after the sale, takes time. Preparation must be complete when market and industry conditions are ripe for selling, and, of course, when there are suitors on the horizon.

98. At what point or under what circumstances should the company go public? If the company needs capital, are there ways to raise it other than by selling or going public?

After a much-needed vacation to Europe, Mary (not her real name) was back at work at the $30-million advertising business she started 30 years ago in California. However, she was burned out. She didn't have a successor. Her daughter, who was almost finished with medical school, wasn't an option. Her nephew wasn't interested in the advertising business at all and had gone back to school to learn computer programming. Mary's trip had restored some of her energy, but more important, her perspective. Overall, her company was doing well, but the business needed to grow to stay competitive in an industry that was rife with mergers and acquisitions. Mary also knew the firm could not assume any more debt. During her absence, a major advertising firm had called about the possibility of its buying a minority stake in the company as an effort to gain a foothold on the West Coast. While on vacation, Mary had read some good articles about the pros and cons of allowing a larger competitor to buy an equity stake in a smaller firm. She agreed to meet with the head of the other agency to find out what it had in mind. The competitor agreed to buy a minority stake in her firm now with the option of buying the entire company in six months. Mary was offered a five-year contract and liked the idea of starting another business with her newfound funds.

Between the business plan and the marketplace lies the reality. When an idea meets a customer, situations change. Fate intercedes; markets open, close and shift. All this may surprise you, the family business owner, who never thought you'd ever consider selling or going public. Timing is crucial. The best time to sell or go public is when your business has substantial growth potential and an impressive track record of sales and earnings. You have to be ahead of the curve. You need to put your business in a position of strength. You may need interim financing to take advantage of some opportunities and demonstrate your growth potential.

First things first. Consider estate planning before you get too far in selling or planning to go public. Your stock is probably worth less before the sale or public offering when discounts for lack of marketability are highest. That may be the best time to shift wealth to younger generations at a reduced gift tax cost.

SELLING THE ENTIRE BUSINESS

If you decide to sell your entire business, the shareholders can sell either their stock, or the company can sell the business and distribute the proceeds to the shareholders.

In an **asset sale**, the buyer purchases the assets of the company, which typically include accounts receivables, inventory, fixtures, leases, trucks and computers. Buyers prefer an asset transaction because they can write off the purchase price through future depreciation and amortization deductions, thereby saving substantial income taxes. Buyers also like an asset purchase because they don't have to worry about assuming contingent or unknown liabilities. The selling shareholders receive the cash when the company liquidates. Unfortunately, unless the company is an S corporation, the sellers also receive a whopping double tax bill: a corporate tax on the sale and an individual tax when the corporation distributes the proceeds to them. The total tax can run around 60 percent. An S corporation can sell its assets and distribute the sales proceeds with only a shareholder-level tax. But it must have been an S corporation since inception, or at least for 10 years, to avoid the double tax problem completely.

In a **stock sale**, the buyer purchases your corporation's stock and everything it owns, lock, stock and barrel. Taxwise, this is more advantageous for you because you pay tax only once and are entitled to the low capital gains rate. Unfortunately, a buyer of your company's stock is likely to offer a lower price because, unlike in an asset purchase, it won't get an increased basis to take depreciation or amortization deductions to reduce future income taxes.

SELLING PART OF THE COMPANY

Another option is to sell part of your company's stock to an unrelated investor or investors, or perhaps to an investment banking firm, through a private placement of stock. Some investment capital funds and other organizations specialize in buying a portion of a family business' stock. Typically, these deals provide capital to buy out selected family members and/or provide capital for inheritance taxes and other needs. Buyers will expect a higher rate of return on an investment than, say, a bank would expect on a loan to your company. They also often demand a pre-negotiated exit strategy that will give them either an option to sell their equity position back to the company, take the company public or force a complete sale of the business within five to seven years. A partial sale typically serves as an interim move for the family business to position itself better for a later sale. It can provide an infusion of capital to help the company grow and boost its value before a final sale is made or before the decision to go public and sell stock is transacted.

A partial sale poses several risks. First, the family must be willing to stick together long enough for the added capital to create the expected growth in value. Another danger is that the buyer may not prove as amicable a partner as you thought and may desire a greater role—a seat on your board and possible voting control. However, a partial sale can be a good alternative if the investor(s) chooses to remain a "silent" partner and contribute funds and some advice without dictating decisions.

An example of a typical private placement involved a thriving restaurant chain that initially had planned to go public within two years. To position itself, the business needed capital to open additional restaurants. The owner planned to sell a piece of the business and take in a partner. He knew how to run a restaurant, produce a great meal and turn his tables several times each day and night. The private placement raised capital to enable the chain to grow. Since businesses are valued based upon multiples of earnings, the increased revenue was used to ratchet up the overall business value before it went on the block a few years later.

GOING PUBLIC

An initial public offering (IPO) is a popular strategy that may solve succession problems and offer liquidity for business needs. Candidates for an IPO generally must have a favorable business outlook, fairly predictable earnings, an experienced management team that is expected to remain after the offering, and an auditable three-to-five year financial history. Typically, the family can sell between 20 percent and 50 percent of the stock in the initial offering. So, you can still control the company. In fact, by some counts, families control more than one third of all publicly traded companies in the U.S.

Consider an IPO primarily if there is a need for access to public markets, not just to raise money to build a new warehouse. Financial objectives should be predominant, not ego. If acquisitions are in your business plan, public listing creates a new form of currency, your company's stock, to use rather than cash and debt. An IPO can satisfy the need for large amounts of capital to enhance the business or to provide diversification for the shareholders. Perhaps you have internecine squabbles when some family members want to cash out for more than the business can afford. Access to the public markets can create a new exit strategy for the future because cashing out additional family-owned stock can be done by later registering and selling more shares to the public.

Preparing for an IPO can take its toll. Auditing, underwriting and legal fees can be very substantial. IPOs also require a large commitment of management time to explain the business to the marketplace. You also lose privacy. Once an IPO is in place, you must report results quarterly to your shareholders. However, some families find that the increased discipline required by public reporting is beneficial to the business. You'll also be subjected to Wall Street's demands for smooth earnings growth. Your ability to take long-term gambles may be curtailed or lost.

ROLL-UPS

Roll-ups are a more recent phenomenon. A roll-up involves the combination of a number of small companies in similar businesses, with the combined entity then taken public for additional cash. After the roll-up, the conglomerate may continue to acquire businesses by issuing more stock. Roll-ups typically occur in industries that are highly fragmented, but have a reasonably predictable future. They create economies of scale and enhance market coverage. In a typical roll-up, the deal promoters get as much as 15 percent ownership, the public receives about 30 percent, and the owners of the rolled-up businesses get about 55 percent.

All is not necessarily rosy with some roll-ups, however. Some fail because of poor management or direction. Others find that meshing varied management groups and operations is extremely difficult. Roll-up promoters often insist on your management's continued involvement. A *USA Today* article in 1998 pointed out, "It's important to have the entrepreneurs (heads of the family owned business) at the local level. He has the position in the community. He has the political contacts and the know-how to go after work in the community." Some seem to flourish in a bull market, but if earnings don't meet projections, the stock may fall. On the other hand, a roll-up may be a good way to partially cash out, diversify your business risk, continue your and your family's involvement, and position your family for later liquidity through subsequent sales of stock received in the roll-up transaction.

Reality Check: If you decide to sell or take your company public, do it for the right reasons and at the right time. Consider the many alternatives. To position your firm and have it appear more attractive to potential buyers, consider interim financing or selling a minority stake to pump in capital for growth. Seek advice and be sure that you understand the entire process, from preparing the firm for sale to operating it in the very bright, public spotlight.

99. How much does going public cost? Who should take the firm public?

The roaring stock market has meant change for many privately held firms. John F. Donahue, chairman and one of the founders of Federated Investors Inc., and his management team took advantage of the healthy market to take public the company that he and two high school friends had founded in 1955. Today the Pittsburgh, Pa.-based company ranks as one of the 10 largest mutual fund companies in the world.

This is not the first time the firm has gone public, however. It did so in 1960 and remained that way until 1982, when the firm was sold to Aetna Life and Casualty Company, then a multi-line insurance company. However, there was no synergy. So the management team bought the company back in 1989.

Just nine years later, in May 1998, the management group took the company public once again by making 17.6 million nonvoting shares available in an initial public offering. Right before the sale, John Donahue turned over the CEO post to his son, Christopher, 49, who had been president and chief operating officer since 1993. The timing seemed propitious to go from private to public, says Chris, the second of 13 children. Chris Donahue stresses that the money was not the deciding factor. "This has not been a capital-intensive business. There was a lot more concern about liquidity, valuation and estate planning. Going public was one way to deal with these issues," he says, ticking off four more solid reasons. "One, it gave us more financial flexibility. We now have currency to make more acquisitions and we are able to sell stock and put money on the balance sheet of the company. Two, we got our name out. Historically we were institutionally oriented and the investing public didn't know us well. Three, going public was good for keeping and attracting talented employees. It put a value on the stock. We enabled the population here to buy shares and this makes our options programs more valuable. Four, it was for the shareholders. Basically, the shareholders had this investment for almost a decade with no real return on it and no liquidity. The entire management group was in favor of going public, but it was a question of where (and when) the stars would line up. What was the marketplace situation? Did the market want a stock like Federated? Was it in our best interest at the time to go public at the price offered? It all came together," says Chris.

Federated filed its intent to go public with the SEC, and was underwritten by Merrill Lynch & Co., the lead underwriter, and co-managers PaineWebber Inc. and Salomon Smith Barney. After the IPO, all Class A common stock, the only shares with voting rights, were still owned by a trust run by the Donahue family. The employees of Federated and their families, which include only those Donahues who are active in the business, own 43 percent of the Class B nonvoting stock out of the 87 million shares outstanding.

In hindsight, says Chris, it was the right move and terrific timing. There was excellent distribution of the stock and the last six months have been wonderful, he adds. "It didn't cost us anything. We paid six percent of what we raised to the underwriters, who did a great job. What it cost us is giving up our status as a privately held firm. Now we are public where anything material has to be disclosed."

Like Classic Coke®, some things work better in their original form. On the other hand, if you know you don't want to continue as a privately held family business, it's time to hire a consultant to look at alternative business strategies.

The consensus might be that you should go public. If you do, you need to develop a strategy and find an investment banking firm (or two or three) to assist. Most often two firms get involved. One is the lead underwriter. The other may serve as part of the distribution network, getting analysts and industry experts to comment on and support your stock. Some brokerage houses have huge distribution networks and can sell large amounts of stock through thousands of brokers.

You also need to protect yourself as your investment bankers and their advisors watch out for themselves. Keep in mind that the investment banker effectively represents the public. You'll need to have your own advisory team that works specifically for you—legal counsel, accountant and other experts to put the deal together. Be smart and savvy with your advisors. It's up to you to negotiate with the investment banking firm to get the maximum value for your shares since it sets the offering price and determines the number of shares to offer. You need to gain a thorough understanding of the investment banking firm's thought process in determining the terms. With that knowledge, you often can help it to understand subtle, but important, points that can increase the value of your company. Your accountant should immediately start to let you know the steps involved and the costs.

What about costs? Investment banking firms often don't charge you unless the deal goes through. If it doesn't, the firm absorbs the costs and its own legal fees. If it's a done deal, costs range between seven percent and 10 percent or more of the total cash raised, depending on the deal's size. For instance, if the fee is seven percent (most deals sell in the seven percent range) and you raise $100 million, the investment banking firm will take $7 million of your proceeds. Other fees may total in the hundreds of thousands of dollars as lawyers and accountants perform their due diligence and prepare their portions of offering documents. It's not cheap by any means, especially compared with a private sale of a portion of the company's stock. However, it is one way to generate liquidity and diversify your family's investment portfolio.

Family firms go public for a variety of reasons. Those reasons dictate who takes the business public. A generational change within the family leadership may trigger the need to raise capital for estate taxes, buying out some inheritors or funding major strategic plans of incoming leaders. Some firms go public to provide investment diversification for the older generation to lessen the reluctance to pass control to the younger generation. Whatever the reasons, it ultimately is your business' growth potential and the vagaries of the financial markets that determine whether you can go public and what the proceeds will be.

Reality Check: If you and your family decide to take your firm public, start discussions with your attorneys and accountants. Then call in an investment banking firm. To protect your and your family's interests, don't rely on just the investment banker's advisors, but weigh all the evidence. This is not the time to skimp on advice. Typically, the process costs between seven and 10 percent of what you try to raise by going public.

100. How will family members' roles change after the business goes public or is sold?

Any way you slice it, when a family business is sold or goes public, family members' roles change. How they change boils down to planning or a lack of it. You have control of your career whether you're the founder or a successor. If you stay on, the most common change is that you will be held accountable to others for what you do. Gone is the autonomy and freedom to make your own decisions. You may become little more than a hired hand. Forget the perks.

Of course, not every family business member experiences this scenario. Ron Rubin was ahead of the game when he elected to sell his family's wholesale wine and liquor distribution business, Central Wholesale Liquor Co., in Mt. Vernon, Il. Selling the family company gave him the opportunity to become an entrepreneur.

Five years after the death of Rubin's father Hyman A. Rubin, who had started the business in 1950, the company was sold to a Chicago wine and spirits wholesaler as part of a big wave of consolidations and mergers in the liquor industry. Rubin opted to stay on one year as an advisor. However, he didn't decide to sell until he found another business venture. He positioned himself for a change, he says."The change was more of a transition. For 22 years of my career, I was a middleman and not a brand owner. The next 22 years of my career, I wanted to own a brand," he says."As a wholesaler, our business wasn't creative. Even if we saw opportunities in the marketplace, we had to sit back and wait for the supplier to bring us a new item or a new line."

His discovery of a company to buy was serendipitous."In November of 1992 I was reading, *The Republic of Tea* co-authored by Mel and Patricia Ziegler, founders of Banana Republic, and Bill Rosenzweig. I had an innovative idea for an upscale bottled tea to complement gourmet food. I faxed the Zieglers my idea and told them I'd like to become an equity partner in the tea company." So in May 1994, Rubin sold his family company and bought into the new venture. Shortly after, he bought the entire company, based in Novato, Ca. (in Marin County). Today, teas have gained cache for their flavors, blends and health benefits. The Republic of Tea flavors come with such catchy names as Mango Ceylon, Ginger Peach and Blackberry Sage.

Rubin says that he's now using his creative juices to build The Republic of Tea brand. He's also experiencing a total advance in technology that would not have been necessary or possible in the family business."I hire people in California by video conferencing. My national sales manager (Minister of Commerce) and I have videos hooked up to our computers so we can see each other when we talk," he adds.

Long term Rubin hopes to take The Republic of Tea global and to set up an e-commerce website. Another part of his dream is to pass on the business. "My father gave me the opportunity to come into the family business. I want to offer my son or daughter the same opportuniTEA," he chuckles while adding,"Be sure to end opportunity with TEA."

The trend in companies doing IPOs has been hotter than a steamy August day in Texas. Retailers, biological and medical concerns, publications firms, technology companies, food and wine-producing firms have been selling, merging, or going public. What does "going public" really mean for a family business owner? During the process of going public, the consultants helping you may say, "Let me explain and tell you what happens after you go public. It will be great." However, know that many things will change drastically.

Going from family firm to public company often means a changing of managerial ways. The biggest cultural change may be that you suddenly have "partners" who may be more outspoken than your family members. Or at least they will be outspoken in different ways. You will not be able to avoid public scrutiny of operations and plans. Your firm may go from a close-knit culture to a more impersonal corporation, accountable to independent directors and outside shareholders. Other potential changes:

- You'll have quarterly reporting of financial results and relationships to cultivate with analysts.
- Your firm might become a takeover target.
- Your and your family members' activities in, and dealings with, the business must become more arm's-length, and many of them must be disclosed to the public.
- Employee loyalty and team work might decline and weaken the firm. On the other hand, you may be better able to issue employee stock options to provide incentives to valued employees.
- You might lose the "family-owned" identity in the marketplace and be seen by customers and employees as a large impersonal conglomerate.
- There may be fewer perks and it may be harder to justify hiring family members who don't make contributions commensurate with their compensation and position.
- You'll need logical, well-documented approaches to solving problems. Shooting from the hip tends to be frowned on in public companies.
- You'll have fiduciary responsibility to the owners of the business. It isn't your business any more. You've become a shareholder in the firm and an employee like everybody else. You must look at transactions as a prudent business person would.
- There will be a capital infusion, which will strengthen the firm's finances in case of an economic downturn.
- The stock may become more valuable and certainly more liquid, which should make family shareholders happy.

There's a definite shifting and upheaval of roles. The following is the mindset of a man who took his company public but hadn't shifted gears: The family business head, who owned most of the stock in a company that he took public, couldn't understand why he had to have shareholders meetings. When others told him the reason was that the business was not his anymore, he responded, "The hell it isn't." He proceeded to tell everyone how he started the company and ran it for 25 years. He never understood that the day he took the business public, the process and the do's and don'ts had completely changed.

Taking a firm public is an exit strategy, albeit typically only a partial exit at first. In some cases, it's the only way the firm will survive. The firm might be owned by a dysfunctional family, it may need capital to grow, and it may need to professionalize its management. Going public is simply one way to get capital both for the owners and for the company. The family may retain voting control and leadership, but operations and the style of conducting business will change.

Reality Check: Going public means just that. Once privately held, now you and your company are accountable to the public. This means open communications and full disclosures, accountability and capital to grow. On the downside, going public can reduce the importance of, and need for, family members. The entire culture of your business may change from one of teamwork, collegiality and paternalism to a bureaucratic corporate structure. However, capable and willing family members often can retain key leadership roles and may appreciate the challenges and rewards of public ownership. With care, even public companies can be viewed by employees and customers with the same sense of attachment as a family-owned business. So a public offering can create the impetus and excuse to run the business and the family in a more professional manner. Despite the downsides, that can be the best solution to the issues that you face.

EPILOGUE

101. What will be the five major issues that family businesses will need to address in the coming Millennium?

For seven years, Albert Karoll, 35, worked in his family menswear retail clothing business in Chicago until the 300-member firm went bankrupt. Though he originally had not planned to enter the firm, Karoll's Red Hanger Shops, his grandfather convinced him to give up his writing career to get paid a decent wage by joining the family firm.

Albert eventually agreed. Over time, he found that he loved the clothing industry and was good at selling. When the family firm was shuttered, he continued in the industry, though in a different way, which he felt offered more promise in the changing men's fashion world. He started a custom menswear firm for harried professionals who didn't have time for or didn't like to shop but who wanted quality clothing with a good fit.

In 1991, he opened Karoll's Fine Custom Clothing in downtown Chicago, a company which manufactures custom shirts, suits, sport coats and trousers. He will take the measurements of a customer at the office, at home, or even in a car or parking lot. In addition to being a manufacturer rather than retailer, Karoll prefers working on his own. Due to his prior experience of working with family, sometimes as many as 10—his grandfather, father, uncles, cousins and in-laws—he also feels he understands the major issues that family business owners face in the coming years and Millennium.

"Like every other family business in America, we had relatives whom we were carrying, who weren't pulling their weight. Some knocked off at 4:15 p.m. but got paid more than I did when I was killing myself. To survive in the future globalization, tighter margins and increased competition, that's no longer going to be okay. It's going to be a challenge for family businesses that have a history of taking everyone in finally to say, 'No you can't join if you don't have the credentials or if there isn't a spot.' The other side of the coin is that as the market for highly skilled, technically qualified employees gets tighter due to the shrinking labor pool, family businesses are going to have to compensate better family members who are talented. The owners won't be able to pay them less than market rates or they'll risk losing them to huge companies that will reward them handsomely. Third, succession, which has always been an issue, will definitely continue to be, and will be brought into much sharper focus as more owners retire."

Does Karoll expect his own firm to be a family business some day? "Maybe," he says. His wife Sara may join him down the road. His own two sons are far too young to be considered or interested, he adds. "I'd encourage both to try something different. We can always talk in 25 years."

The following will be the five major issues:

INTERNATIONALIZATION. This will become a much more important issue. Family businesses will need to ask themselves what role they want to play in an increasingly global economy. There are both opportunities and threats. The biggest opportunity is that new profitable markets are opening rapidly for US firms. The threat is that many US family companies that do not do their homework will have a competitive disadvantage in international business. They will have to learn to stop thinking inwardly or only domestically, which they sometimes do because they don't have a lot of confidence or experience working with non-American cultures. But if they do their homework and get a good perspective on what globalization requires, they will be prepared and won't make mistakes. One thing they should do, particularly with the next generation coming into their firms, is to have those members travel, live and work abroad to gain a better global handle. An opportunity that all should take advantage of is to develop relationships with other family businesses in other parts of the world by attending international conferences, developing businesses together, and perhaps sending a family member to work in an overseas company.

CONSOLIDATION. There will be increasing incentives to sell the family business because more industries will be consolidating. As a result, a relatively small family business will feel threatened and pressed to decide whether to continue to exist or exit. That will lead to owners needing to search their souls and consider their financial as well as nonfinancial goals and visions. If they have a strong resolve to stay in the business as a family firm, they should do so, without rationalizing the financial incentives.

PUBLICITY VERSUS PRIVACY. In the new Millennium, private businesses will be challenged and expected to act more public by providing more information and to be more accountable. That runs in the face of many family companies that want to remain low-key, modest, private and even secretive. For them to change will be a real challenge. But if they do, it will protect and enhance the image of family businesses in our economy and potentially lead to happier customers and better federal estate laws. If the businesses rebel and recoil, however, public opinion may not be so favorable.

FAMILY FREEDOM. Family members increasingly are not feeling forced to meet parental expectations and take jobs in the family business. They instead pursue a dream and consider other opportunities. To entice them, families need to do a better job of presenting and promoting the advantages of working in a family business. One key: families need to present it as an opportunity rather than as an obligation or expectation. At the same time, corporate downsizing will remain, which will encourage some scions to join, but more on their own volition rather than from coercion.

BLENDED FAMILIES. The classic family of one mom, dad and two children from the same parents will continue to exist, but there will be more cases where the next generation won't have the same parents. That will create incredible complexities and potential rivalries. These questions will arise: How do you define a family? Who are the eligible shareholders? Who is entitled to come to family meetings? Who's eligible to work in the company? Who's best qualified to run the company?

Reality Check: One thing's for sure, competition won't get softer in the next Millennium. Declining prices, a shrinking talent pool, government regulation—all will continue to be significant challenges. Family businesses will be pressed more than ever before to capitalize on their unique strengths in order to excel in the increasingly global economy. With owners devoted to long-term success and family members who support each other, the opportunities surely will be boundless.

INDEX